Director's Guide to

MANAGEMENT TECHNIQUES

with glossary of management terms

*Editor*

DENNIS LOCK

*Advisory Editor*

GEORGE BULL

# DIRECTORS' GUIDE TO
# Management Techniques

## WITH GLOSSARY OF MANAGEMENT TERMS

Foreword by Sir Richard Powell, Bt, MC
Director-General, Institute of Directors

DIRECTORS BOOKSHELF

*First published in Great Britain by Directors Bookshelf*
*140 Great Portland Street, London W1N 5TA*
*1970*

*Second impression 1970*

*Second edition 1972*

*Reprinted 1974*

© Gower Press Limited 1970

ISBN 0 7161 0030 4

DIRECTORS BOOKSHELF is an imprint jointly sponsored by the Institute of Directors and Gower Press Limited. It is publishing a list of specially commissioned books which are designed for the senior manager with board room—or near board room—responsibilities and interests.

*Reproduced photolitho in Great Britain by*
*J. W. Arrowsmith Ltd, Bristol*

# CONTENTS

v

## Section Two:
## FINANCIAL MANAGEMENT

CONTENTS

CONTENTS

## Section Five:
## PRODUCTION AND DISTRIBUTION

CONTENTS

## Section Six:
## EDP AND MANAGEMENT SERVICES

# ILLUSTRATIONS

# FOREWORD

## by Sir Richard Powell, Bt, MC
### Director-General, Institute of Directors

After I said in the foreword to the first edition of this book that the publishers considered they were on to a winner, and that I believed they were right, I earned a modest reputation as a prophet. As the book quickly established itself as a best-seller, it became clear that a new edition was needed. This now makes its appearance, both to meet continuing demand and to extend and up-date its coverage of management techniques.

As every board room knows, a knowledge of techniques is no guarantee of business success. The qualities of inspiration and leadership are still paramount. But the days are gone when they were enough in themselves without a grasp of every facet of modern management. This book—which authoritatively and very readably discusses as many as thirty-two techniques—has established itself as an essential aid to businessmen seeking an up-to-date guide to sound management techniques. Its deserved success provides more evidence that British business is increasingly adding scientific management to entrepreneurial flair.

# ACKNOWLEDGEMENTS

The publishers wish to acknowledge their debt to the following for help in the preparation of this work:

The Institute of Directors, for granting access to articles first published in *The Director*, and for advice thereafter.

All individuals and organisations included in this work, for their goodwill in contributing to it.

# Part I

## GUIDE TO

## Management Techniques

*Section One*

# General Management
# and Organisation

—————— CHAPTER 1 ——————

# Resource Appraisal

*by* Denis Gamberoni

*Senior Consultant, P-E Consulting Group Limited*

Most directors would agree that it is their responsibility to know in depth the assets, the people and the systems they control, but many boards are taken by surprise by a bid and find it difficult to assess its worth or to marshal a defence. Too often, a declining trend in profits or liquidity is recognised so late that drastic surgery is required to put things right. Opportunities for acquisition or diversification pass unnoticed, and flagging production lines are propped up by uneconomic promotion programmes. In each case what the board needs is an early warning system—so that it can act while there is still time. Such a system—resource appraisal—has been develope: over the past few years.

# 1 : RESOURCE APPRAISAL

Resource appraisal gives a board the information that can be used as a basis for formulating strategies and deciding on future tactics, and as a first step towards drawing up an action programme to concentrate management effort on remedying operating weaknesses in the company's structure. Resource appraisal can also be used to:

1   Assess the vulnerability of the company to adverse conditions such as a credit squeeze, price war, or labour problems.
2   Indicate the degree of vulnerability to outside offer, to provide a basis for defence or to extract the best terms from a bidder.
3   Assess the viability and likely benefits of seeking a merger or making an acquisition.
4   Identify the need to investigate actively the feasibility of diversification.
5   Identify areas through which productivity may be increased, costs reduced, or overheads cut back.
6   Assess the completeness of the company's information systems.
7   Assess whether the management structure, planning, and operating procedures are adequate to meet future demands.

The first, and usually the most difficult step in resource appraisal is knowing what to look for, what questions should be asked and by whom? To provide the right answers RA must be objective, but directors and executives are frequently too close to the organisation. The use of a questionnaire is, therefore, crucial to the whole exercise.

## PREPARING THE QUESTIONNAIRE

The P-E Consulting Group has developed a series of checklists which can be used by chief executives as a basis for resource appraisal. Obviously the circumstances of each company are different, but the lists cover the basic points common to most. The complete set of checklists is included in Figure 1 : 1.

The object of these checklists is to identify the questions which should be answered when appraising a company's resources, and to indicate to the chief executive whether the answers are readily available. Accordingly, each checklist is provided with four columns, to be ticked as follows:

A     Readily ascertainable through formal information system (at not more than monthly intervals).

B     Not immediately ascertainable but regularly reviewed (at not more than annual intervals).

C     Considered irregularly and informally. Not readily ascertainable.

D     Not known. Not normally reviewed.

If the answers to the questions are to be truly objective, cutting across functional boundaries, the checklist should be completed by the chief executive. The questions are phrased in such a way that they call for objective answers, but it is up to the respondent to assess the quality of the information on which he bases his answers. The value of the questions is mainly the fact that they draw attention to specific areas of the company's activities, and together provide a useful picture of the company.

Every item on the list should be reviewed regularly, although in some cases only informally once a year. Questions such as: "Is there a member of the board who is sufficiently free from involvement in routine decisions to be able to apply himself to objective appraisal and original thinking?" or "What is the confidence limit acceptable for forward planning decisions?" are unlikely to be included in formal reporting systems but should be reviewed at least annually if account is to be taken of a changing economic environment and an evolving internal situation.

Although all questions should be answered A or B, the size of the company will affect the proportion of those answered A. Medium-sized and smaller companies will not have the resources, or the need, to operate reporting systems detailed enough to enable the answer A to be given as frequently as will be the case with larger organisations.

## EVALUATING THE ANSWERS

Once the questions are answered, the second and equally important task is evaluating the answers. A completed checklist can be interpreted as follows:

Where a few isolated items are checked C or D, these should be studied in detail. The indications are that this is a well-run company and that by allocating the responsibility for remedial action to the managers directly concerned the weaknesses that have been found can be overcome.

When a number of items are ticked C or D under any one heading, a survey of the relevant function or area of operating activity should be carried out to establish the cause and extent of the problem and to plan its solution. It is possible that an action committee should be established to carry out the study and make recommendations.

When a large number of items, spread over the checklist, are ticked C or D, then prompt action is necessary. A depth appraisal of the company should be carried out, by a multi-disciplinary team, to identify problem areas and to set priorities for their solution. A task force should be set up with an explicit programme to strengthen the weak areas identified.

A team approach is best when a survey of weak areas identified through appraisal is undertaken. Using a team means that a wider range of relevant knowledge and experience is brought to bear on the problem. One or more junior managers can be included in the team as this is an ideal form of management development. In fact, every team member carrying out a survey of a particular function, or of the business as a whole, will gain experience of new areas of company operations, as well as bringing a fresh viewpoint to the problem faced.

# UNDERSTANDING AND USING THE RESULTS

Care should be taken when assessing the results shown by the completed checklists, since the composite picture presented may be misleading. This is because the relative importance of individual questions is not highlighted, and will vary according to individual company situations. Contribution analysis and sales statistics, for example, are of less importance to a small engineering company manufacturing a single specialist component, than to a company producing a variety of consumer products. In the former case, value engineering and quality and reliability standards will be of greater importance.

Generally, the relative importance of the ten groups of questions will vary according to either company size or product market. Product analysis, sales/marketing, and research and development, will be of greater importance to the multi-product company, particularly those selling consumer products. Productivity, physical resources, manpower and finance, on the other hand, are likely to be of comparable importance to all companies regardless of size or variety.

Management, planning, and organisation increase in importance with size, being less critical in a private company employing less than 100 people, but taking on key significance in the larger more complex corporation. This is not to say that planning is unimportant in the small company, but merely that up to a certain scale of activity, formal planning or communication procedures are not crucial to success. What is frequently overlooked by the owner-manager—often with disastrous results—is the point in the growth of a company at which these procedures *do* become important. This point, known as the management barrier, is where the volume and variety of personnel and operating activity exceed the range which one man can control directly and informally.

It is therefore impossible to give a general rule about the overall balance which should be shown by a completed checklist. It is also impossible to pinpoint one or more critical questions, as these will vary between companies. The value of the checklist is in bringing to board-room attention virtually all the factors which may act as constraints on growth or profitability.

The questions on resource appraisal checklists illustrated here are directed towards a manufacturing company, but many of the questions are relevant to service and commercial organisations. Using these lists as a basis, it is a relatively simple matter to build a tailor-made model for an individual company.

It must be emphasised that resource appraisal will contribute only one part of the information requirements for planning. The other part, environmental data, must be collected and collated separately. Internally generated information should, whenever possible, be measured against national or industry statistics, such as those published by Dunn and Bradstreet, Centre for Interfirm Comparison Limited, industry trade and research associations, government departments, and subscription research companies, such as Nielsen and Attwood.

| | A | B | C | D |
|---|---|---|---|---|
| **PRODUCT ANALYSIS** | | | | |
| Are constraints on volume/mix of products clearly identified? (market, manufacturing capacity, raw material supply, technology, inter-dependence of products) | | | | |
| Are the contributions of each product/product group related to the constraints to establish the sales mix which will yield optimum profit? | | | | |
| Are the demands on management effort made by each production/product group evaluated? (in terms of quality and quantity) | | | | |
| How relevant are quality and reliability standards to marketing policies? | | | | |
| Is design oriented towards using the cheapest materials and components consistent with the express function of product/product groups? | | | | |
| What point in its life cycle has each product/product group reached? (vulnerability to technological/design obsolescence) | | | | |
| **SALES/MARKETING** | | | | |
| What is the trend in the ratio of sales to fixed assets? | | | | |
| What is the trend in the ratio of sales to employees/sales personnel? | | | | |
| How relevant is promotion expenditure and marketing effort to product priorities? (established through product analysis) | | | | |

FIGURE 1:1    RESOURCE APPRAISAL QUESTIONNAIRE

Checklists developed for resource appraisal by the P-E Consulting Group. Each question must be examined in turn (preferably by the chief executive) in order to determine the accessibility of the information demanded. This accessibility is graded from A (readily available) to D (not known), and a tick placed in the appropriate column.

| | A | B | C | D |
|---|---|---|---|---|

How flexible is the price structure? (vulnerability to competition)

To what extent is product pricing used as an active weapon in the marketing effort? (differentiating between product market value and cost plus)

Are selling and distribution methods right for the type of product/ customer? (distinguishing between customers as users and distributors as stockists)

What are the selling costs and distribution costs by area/type of customer/product group?

What are the sales trends by: Customer/outlet type? Area/region (home/export)? Product/product group?

What is the frequency and size of orders received by: Customer/ outlet type? Product/product group?

MANAGEMENT

Is the collective and individual ability and know-how of management assessed?

What is the future requirement for executives—can it be met?

What is the trend of turnover of middle and junior managers?

Is there a programme for management development (collective and individual)?

Are methods of remuneration and conditions of employment satisfactory to all management levels? Do they provide incentive/ motivation?

Does management have the ability to employ advanced management techniques for problem solving?

MANPOWER

How good are relations with labour/union(s)?

Are methods of training the workforce relevant to the needs of production/individual workers?

To what extent are methods of rewarding workers being developed with the object of raising morale and individual wealth?

What is the trend of labour turnover by skill/operating department?

PRODUCTIVITY

What are the trends for: sales as a multiple of capital employed? added value per employee/direct worker? added value as a multiple

Figure 1:1 *continued*

| | A | B | C | D |
|---|---|---|---|---|

of fixed assets? raw material utilisation (against target)? stock turnover?

PHYSICAL RESOURCES

What is the age, condition, life expectancy and current value of plant and vehicles (obsolescence risk?), and buildings?

Is the size/location of factories and offices suitable to requirements? (proximity to customers, suppliers, labour resources, administrative convenience, etc)

Are plant and vehicles used at their optimum capacity?

RESEARCH AND DEVELOPMENT

Is there a programme/budget against which performance can be measured?

How relevant is the R & D programme to marketing policies and programme?

What is the success ratio for R & D projects?

Is there any incentive towards innovation, or is the R & D programme solely oriented towards development and extension of existing product lines?

FINANCE

Is the trend of profits on capital employed improving?

Is liquidity satisfactory—what is the short-term cash flow?

Are capital projects effectively evaluated and are there clear-cut commitment approval regulations? Is progress reviewed against project appraisal?

Is full use made of available credit (from all sources including suppliers and capital investors)?

Are there any surplus assets which can be liquidated (obsolete/excess/slow-moving stocks, unused buildings, idle plant, etc)?

How reliable are the sources used for finance? (long- and short-term)

Is the capital structure (gearing) flexible, does it provide for the highest possible investment yield?

PLANNING

Are corporate objectives stated in writing and distributed to senior executives?

Figure 1:1 *continued*

| | A | B | C | D |
|---|---|---|---|---|

Are corporate and functional strategies prepared and published by top management, and distributed to key personnel? Is progress monitored?

Are short-range plans prepared by, and distributed to, relevant managers? (budgets). Are actual results compared against targets?

What is the confidence limit acceptable for forward planning decisions?

What is the degree of risk acceptable for investment projects—how is this quantified?

ORGANISATION

How relevant is the organisation structure to the achievement of corporate and functional strategies? Does the chart accurately reflect the existing structure?

Is the collective body of knowledge and experience contributed by the board adequate to meet the demands of future decisions?

Is the difference between directing and managing clearly understood by board members and senior managers, and successfully maintained?

Is there a member of the board who is sufficiently free from involvement in routine decisions to be able to apply himself to objective appraisal and original thinking?

Is there sufficient degree of, and response to delegation?

Do job descriptions and specifications for each major management position actively reflect existing authority and responsibilities?

Are all staff departments necessary—can their cost be justified in terms of quantifiable benefits?

Is the right information produced for the right manager at the right time? Is office equipment the most suitable obtainable within expenditure limits?

Figure 1:1 *continued*

For resource appraisal to be successful the initiative must come from the board, and the chief executive should maintain close contact throughout. RA can give a company a head-start over competitors who are less well informed. Its major aim is prevention, rather than cure.

———————— CHAPTER 2 ————————

# Organisational Structure

*by* H F T Wren

*Business Consultant*

British directors have never before had at their disposal so much information on management techniques aimed at the improvement of their
companies. Many businessmen are not able to exploit these techniques
because of basic problems concerned with the organisation of their firms.
There is, however, a logical organisation structure which can be adapted
to suit all sizes of company, based on the scientific division of functions.

# 2 : ORGANISATIONAL STRUCTURE

British directors have never before had at their disposal so much information on management techniques and on how to improve the performance of their companies. Many of them, however, and especially in the smaller firms, still find they are inhibited from applying new ideas and methods, simply because of weaknesses in the basic organisation of their businesses. The need for reorganisation may be seen and accepted; what is not always so clear to the chairman or managing director is how to start.

No director can function efficiently as one of the managerial team unless he understands exactly his own function and the responsibilities carried by his colleagues. Unless and until these responsibilities are clearly set down, there is confusion and lack of cohesion and collaboration. The first essential to putting things right is to create an organisational structure showing quite clearly the individual functions of each department or unit.

Whether it is a one-man business, or a vast undertaking, there are clearly specific areas—or units—into which an organisation should be divided. It is this dividing of the functions that presents the major problem to the board or chief executive. There are strong similarities between businesses in any one industry, yet substantial differences exist and textbook charts are very frequently difficult for the executive to adapt for himself.

Is there a basic organisational chart or structure that can be applied firmly and scientifically to the vast majority of undertakings—whatever their size and whatever their field of operation? There is indeed such a scientific basis, a very simple one, that can be followed easily and adapted to suit the requirements of almost any concern.

To illustrate this, consider a business of reasonable size, engaged in manufacturing and marketing its merchandise at home and abroad. With a little ingenuity the structure being set up can be applied to businesses operating on a narrower or wider basis, or even to very small concerns or those who are supplying services instead of merchandise, or dealing with the consumer direct rather than through the trade.

## IDENTIFYING THE MANAGEMENT CONTROL UNITS

All organisations can be split into two major areas:

1    The assets owned or used in the business
2    The movement of materials and merchandise

The balance sheet shows the assets owned by the organisation and employed in its operation. These are fixed and current. Included among these assets must be human beings, the greatest asset of all, which no accountant has yet found possible to assess in terms of balance sheet values. It is also assumed that whereas goodwill may not always appear in the balance sheet, nevertheless without good-will (of the trade and the consumer) a business quickly dies.

So the assets of the company can be listed as follows:

1    Personnel
2    Land and buildings
3    Plant, machinery and vehicles
4    Furniture and fittings
5    Goodwill
6    Cash
7    Investments
8    Debtors
9    Stocks

These assets need to be safeguarded in use, held to a minimum commensurate with efficiency, fully employed and maintained in proper condition, since they represent the shareholders' funds and investment. At the same time, the executives shown to be responsible for safeguarding these assets, must also provide "services" which are naturally related to these assets.

There is a natural and distinct sequence in the movement of

materials, from the day they are purchased from suppliers, to the time they are converted into finished merchandise and placed in the hands of the ulimate consumer. This is the sequence:

10   Materials purchased from suppliers
11   Materials storage
12   Production of materials into finished goods
13   Warehousing of finished goods (and ultimate dispatch
     to trade)

| Management control units (MCUs) | asset | manager | Buyer | Stores manager | Production manager | Warehouse manager | Sales manager | Promotion manager |
|---|---|---|---|---|---|---|---|---|
| 1 | Personnel | Personnel manager | ▲ | ▲ | ▲ | ▲ | ▲ | ▲ |
| 2 | Land and buildings | Engineer | ▲ | ▲ | ▲ | ▲ | ▲ | ▲ |
| 3 | Plant machinery and vehicles | Engineer | ▲ | ▲ | ▲ | ▲ | ▲ | ▲ |
| 4 | Furniture and fittings | Engineer | ▲ | ▲ | ▲ | ▲ | ▲ | ▲ |
| 5 | Goodwill | Product quality and development manager | ▲ | ▲ | ▲ | ▲ | ▲ | ▲ |
| 6 | Cash | Accountant | ▲ | ▲ | ▲ | ▲ | ▲ | ▲ |
| 7 | Investments | Accountant | | | | | | |
| 8 | Debtors | Accountant | | | | ▲ | | |
| 9 | Stocks | Planning manager | ▲ | ▲ | ▲ | ▲ | ▲ | |

| Manager ⟶ | Buyer | Stores manager | Production manager | Warehouse manager | Sales manager | Promotion manager |
|---|---|---|---|---|---|---|
| Movement of materials and merchandise ⟶ | Raw and anciliary materials purchases | Storage of materials | Fabrication and production of materials into finished merchandise | Warehousing (and dispatch) of finished merchandise | Sales to trade (home and export) | Purchases by consumers |
| Management control unit ⟶ | 10 | 11 | 12 | 13 | 14 | 15 |

FIGURE 2:1   INTERLOCKING ORGANISATION CHART
The placing of pyramids on this chart shows clearly how each manager can have responsibility for safeguarding an asset, and for providing the related services.

14   Sales of finished goods to the trade

15   Finished merchandise sold to consumer

## RELATING MANAGERS, CONTROL UNITS AND FUNCTIONS

Having established that these fifteen management control units blanket the entire business, an organisational chart can be set down. The assets can be shown vertically and the movement of materials and merchandise horizontally in sequence. The reason for setting out the chart in this way is to demonstrate that although the units of materials and merchandise movement are each self-contained and each the responsibility of the manager shown in control, yet the assets supplied to the movement units, at the same time as being "safeguarded" carry a range of services. These services will be listed below.

The layout of the organisational chart is shown in Figure 2:1. The pyramids on the bars of the chart indicate where the asset managers have responsibility not only for "safeguarding" the assets but for providing the related services which are detailed later.

On the surface it might appear that there is excessive criss-crossing of responsibilities, but this is more apparent than real. Properly controlled and co-ordinated by top management, overlapping of responsibilities is eliminated.

In studying the functions included under the fifteen headings or units below, a certain amount of thought (and imagination) is required.

## BASIC ORGANISATIONAL STRUCTURE

### Assets/management control units

PERSONNEL

*1   Personnel Manager*

**Functions and duties**

(*a*) Employee recruitment, standard personnel practice, job description and job evaluation

(*b*) Training programmes

(c) Salary administration, wage scales and incentives

(d) Life assurance, pension schemes and fringe benefits

(e) Welfare and health, canteens and other services and overall morale

(f) Staff magazine and internal propaganda

(g) Redundancies and dismissals

(h) Trade union contact and disputes

The personnel manager is *not* responsible for employees' efficiency and discipline when they are operating under functional management.

LAND AND BUILDINGS

2   *Engineer*

(a) Building maintenance (including gardens) and security

(b) Space allocation for staff and workers and machines, etc

(c) Lighting, heating, power, ventilation, lavatories, etc

(d) New building projects

PLANT, MACHINERY AND VEHICLES

3   *Engineer*

(a) Plant maintenance, registration and depreciation

(b) Plant layout

(c) Project engineering

(d) Research and development of plant, machinery, etc

(e) Patents and licensing

(f) Work and time study, job simplification and performance standards

(g) Maintenance and replacement of vehicles

FURNITURE AND FITTINGS AND EQUIPMENT

4   *Engineer*

(a) Maintenance and replacement, cleanliness, etc

(b) Telephones, telex, intercom, etc

(c) Maintenance and replacement of all office equipment (excluding data processing equipment)

The engineer is also responsible for surveying all proposed capital expenditure programmes and sale of capital items (obsolete plant, etc.) under units 2, 3 and 4.

GOODWILL

5 *Product Development Manager*

(*a*) Merchandise specification library
(*b*) Quality control (from raw materials to finished production, warehousing, etc.)
(*c*) Raw and ancillary materials research and development
(*d*) Development of new merchandise, designs, etc.
(*e*) Competitive merchandise testing and comparison
(*f*) Trade marks and licensing

The goodwill of the consumer and customer should be fostered by *all* employees but ultimately it is the quality of the merchandise and continued development of quality and new merchandise that is the true basis of a company's goodwill. The production manager is responsible for quality, the quality control department policing the standards laid down in the specifications.

Clearly merchandise and materials development—in most industries—allies very closely with machine and plant development and usage, so there must be close liaison between the engineer and the product development manager in this field.

CASH

6 *Accountant*

(*a*) Financial and management accounting, and taxation
(*b*) Cost and works accountancy, standard and marginal costings, etc.
(*c*) Budgetary control and (final) capital expenditure
(*d*) Banking facilities, cash flow, overdrafts, loans, etc.
(*e*) Cashier and general and factory offices
(*f*) Purchases, ledgers and payments
(*g*) Data processing and all statistics
(*h*) Organisation and methods, systems analysis and communications
(*i*) Operational research

Note: (*g*), (*h*) and (*i*) need not necessarily be included here but in larger organisations could be transferred to a separate unit under (say) the control of the secretary.

### INVESTMENTS

#### 7 Accountant

(*a*) Control of investments in subsidiary companies
(*b*) Control of external investments, etc.
(*c*) Handling of loans, mortgages, etc.

### DEBTORS

#### 8 Accountant

(*a*) Credit control
(*b*) Sales ledger, invoicing and debt collection

### STOCKS

#### 9 Planning Manager

(*a*) Stabilisation of stocks to meet sales demands, factory capacity, etc.
(*b*) Stock control records

The planning manager is the "bridge" between sales requirements and factory production. The planning manager is not responsible for physical stock (finished goods, raw materials or work-in-progress) yet by his actions he can maintain stocks at an economic level.

## Movement of materials and merchandise

### RAW AND ANCILLARY MATERIALS

#### 10 Buyer

(*a*) Buying of raw and ancillary materials for production
(*b*) Buying supplies for all departments of the organisation, including engineers' supplies
(*c*) Placing and following up all capital expenditure items

STORAGE OF MATERIALS

## 11   *Stores Manager*

(*a*) Acceptance and control of all materials ordered
(*b*) Issue of materials to other units—and control

PRODUCTION OF MATERIALS INTO FINISHED GOODS

## 12   *Production Manager*

(*a*) Production of raw materials into finished goods
(*b*) Maintaining close liaison (through scheduling officer) with planning manager
(*c*) Maintaining discipline among factory workers and all those who "service" the factory from other units
(*d*) Complete responsibility for quality maintenance
(*e*) Maintenance of all records of factory performance, idle time of plant and employees, "spare" capacity, etc.
(*f*) Responsibility for all direct costs and controllable overheads

WAREHOUSING AND DISPATCH OF FINISHED MERCHANDISE

## 13   *Warehouse Manager*

(*a*) Physical control of stocks and their condition
(*b*) Dispatch of goods to customers/consumers
(*c*) Acceptance (under authority) of returned goods

SALES TO TRADE (HOME AND EXPORT)

## 14   *Sales Manager*

(*a*) Sales to trade (home and overseas)
(*b*) Headquarters staff, sales administration, etc.
(*c*) Customers' correspondence
(*d*) Order handling (excluding credit control) for passing to warehouse
(*e*) Trade association contact

PURCHASES BY CONSUMERS

## 15   *Promotion Manager*

(*a*) Consumer and market research

(*b*) Presentation of products and packaging
(*c*) Consumer (and trade) advertising and promotion and point-of-sale display material
(*d*) Fixing wholesale and retail prices and trade terms
(*e*) Consumer quality complaints correspondence
(*f*) Preparation of catalogues, price lists, etc.
(*g*) Public relations (trade and consumer)
(*h*) Trade and consumer exhibitions

## Central functions

In addition to the asset and movement functions described here, there are two remaining functions to be covered.

*Company secretary.* His duties take care of the many statutory obligations of the company, dealings with shareholders, the handling of legal matters (including preparation, signing and recording of all agreements, leases, licences, trade marks, etc.), recording board minutes, etc.

*Internal auditor.* He is to be found usually in only the most sophisticated companies. His duties comprise the checking of all systems, methods, etc., in the organisation—financial and otherwise. He has the right to enquire into any matter affecting any department and all personnel at all authority levels. He usually reports direct to the managing director.

It has now been shown that fifteen management control units can be listed which, together with the internal auditor and company secretary, constitute the entire organisation. Against each function is the title of the appropriate manager, and a list of his specific responsibilities and duties.

All these managers must be regarded as standing at the same level of authority, since it is important to avoid the possibility of any one manager "pulling rank" over another in handling day-to-day problems.

How are these managers to be trained, led and controlled? In the larger companies one would probably find four directors responsible to the managing director for these units:

1    Finance director (and secretary) for MCUs 1, 6, 7, 8, 9 and 13

2    Production director, for MCUs 10, 11 and 12
3    Marketing director, for MCUs 5, 14 and 15
4    Engineering director, for MCUs 2, 3 and 4

In the smaller organisations these four directors might be called upon to take direct control of certain units, without any intervening middle management.

Obviously no small business could afford the organisational structure described above. Nevertheless, it tabulates the many facets of a business which must enter the thoughts of the small businessman, and indicates the functions he must consider if his business is to be controlled and expand in the right direction.

The owner, managing director or general manager of an organisation of any size must be both the dynamic of the business and a sound administrator. He should ensure that his managers are individually skilled in their jobs, collaborating as a team and leading their own departments with firmness and sense.

If he has a soundly constructed organisation and the right men are chosen to staff it, he should be able to command and lead without becoming too involved in the detail of the organisation. His top team of directors can be used as advisers not only in the day-to-day operation, but also in forward thinking and strategy.

## CHAPTER 3

# Long-Range Corporate Planning

*by* Hugh P Buckner

*Director, Industrial Market Research Limited*

In planning for growth directors should not think solely of developing their company's existing range of products or services. Rather, they should aim to exploit the company's skills and resources in the best market environment. The best plan is a flexible one which concentrates on markets with a record of innovation and the development of new business. In the process of long-range planning, there are five main steps for reaching objectives.

# 3 : LONG-RANGE CORPORATE PLANNING

All directors plan, but too often their plans stem solely from forecasts of the future performance of the company's present range of products and services. Such plans, however good the forecasts from which they are derived, ignore the fundamental basis for a company's existence and growth, and can only partly explore the future possibilities open to the company. More and more industrial organisations are recognising that in order to earn a full return on their investment, they must not only provide for present market requirements, but must also search for new areas of activity which will utilise their human skills, physical and financial resources to the full. These new areas of exploitation may, however, lie well outside the company's present area of operation.

The essence of a good plan is its flexibility. Plans are not primarily forecasts. Ideally, they are a course of action for today designed to place the company *in the best position to take advantage of whatever may happen tomorrow.* Many of the reasons given for not planning arise from misunderstandings of the basic concepts.

## CONCEPTS OF LONG-RANGE PLANNING

### 1 Setting the targets

*Targets should be set for the use and development of corporate skills and resources independently of the present products.* The assets of a company are the skills of its executives and employees and its physical, financial and marketing resources. It is these that should be utilised to best advantage, and added to, in the future. The present products, while obviously important today, can be incidental to the future of a dynamic company even in five years' time. For example, producers of vacuum cleaners or bowling equipment, who limit

31

their companies' potential to these largely saturated markets, will be earning profits in the future very much lower than those which could be produced by their present assets. Past examples of this are legion.

A company should decide on figures for minimum return on investment, minimum acceptable growth rate, stability and other standards. It is by now an old marketing saying that, "If you don't know where you are going—any road will do". Only after setting objectives can a company know what it is looking for in the future.

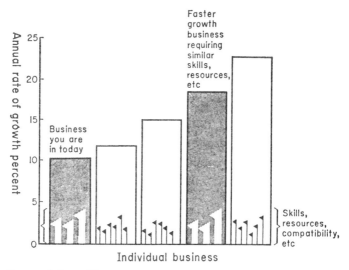

FIGURE 3:1    USING SKILLS AND RESOURCES TO BEST ADVANTAGE
*Concept 1* Set realistic targets for the use of your skills and resources, independently of present products.
*Concept 2* Use skills and resources in the best market environment.

## 2  Matching resources to the market

*Use the company's skills and resources in the best market environment.* Figure 3:1 illustrates both concepts 1 and 2. Many businesses require similar skills and a company should find, and use, its assets in areas which best fit corporate objectives. For example, J Stone of Deptford possessed basic skills in steam technology, mechanical equipment and controls. They were also successful manufacturers of railway equipment and steam boilers. After considerable analysis

32

this company entered the continuous laundry machine market with an advanced product of their own design which utilised most of their important skills.

## 3  Planning for flexibility

*Plan for flexibility by concentrating on areas having a record of innovation and development of new businesses.* Figure 3:2 illustrates two basic types of growth business, in both of which a company may be doing well. In the diagram, business (*a*) is growing but not originating new products, applications or markets which give rise to new business. It is, therefore, vulnerable to any change which alters the single product, market or application. Business (*b*) constantly gives rise to new areas and provides mobility to meet future change by presenting the businessman with new opportunities originating from his own industry.

To remain successful, businessmen will increasingly have to seek

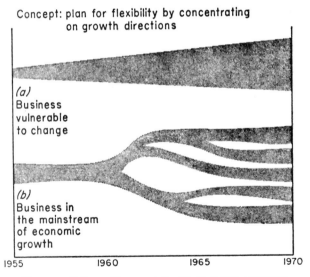

FIGURES 3:2    TWO TYPES OF GROWTH BUSINESS

(*a*) Some businesses grow but do not originate new products or applications which spawn new businesses. They are vulnerable to any change which alters their single market. (*b*) Other businesses spawn new ones and give mobility to meet future change by constantly presenting the businessman with a new opportunity originating from his own business—these are growth directions.

33

out this second type of growth business which provides the best assurance of an ever-recurring reserve opportunity. Reserve opportunities are of vital importance. Churchill wrote in his book, *The Second World War*, "... we should have something in hand for unknowable contingencies. Here would be, in fact, that mobile reserve, that mass manoeuvre, which alone could give superior options in the hour of need." Technologically based industries, in particular, provide recurring opportunities for manufacturers and services. For example, the science of communications in most of its ramifications from transport to data processing is changing and new products and business are appearing all the time.

## 4  Choice of business

*Select a business where it is possible to maintain a unique position.* Some form of unique position is essential to achieve an above-average growth or profit level. Totally imitative situations can be avoided by concentrating on areas where a competitive advantage can be maintained. This may be accomplished, for example, by leadership in research and development, patent protection, unique process knowledge or capture of leading distribution channels as well as creative marketing.

## TWO ESSENTIALS IN LONG-RANGE PLANNING

### Level of decision

It is obvious from the nature of the concepts that corporate planning can be conducted only at policy-making director level. Staff below this level cannot set objectives or take basic decisions on where skills and resources are best used. Planning below this level is an extension of departmental forecasts: it is *not* corporate planning.

### Step-by-step approach

A step-by-step approach to planning has become essential by the failure of other methods. Attempts to plan in one move or by considering possible opportunities singly and in isolation often fail. Difficulties often arise over knowing where to start to plan; sometimes whole development schemes are subsequently found to be unrelated to the company's needs. The step-by-step approach weighs all important aspects in turn and arrives at a balanced appraisal of where the best opportunity lies.

## THE FIVE STEPS IN DEVELOPING THE LONG-RANGE PLAN

### 1 Determining the size of the long-range problem

The long-range problem is the gap that may result at the end of the planning period between the objectives (defined as the realistic return on corporate skills and resources) and the forecasted return which may be expected if the business continues in its present form.

How far ahead the planning period should extend will depend on the company and should be geared to such factors as product development cycles, market development time, physical facilities development time and resources development time. Oil companies or electricity boards will plan further ahead than consumer goods manufacturers. Most companies should plan at least five years ahead.

Determining the long-range problem for a company falls into three stages, which are:

1    Set quantitative objectives
2    Set qualitative objectives
3    Project the present business

*Setting quantitative objectives.* Targets for profit level, growth and relative stability (that is, vulnerability to business depressions) should be set by comparison with other companies and industries. A company should attempt to be above average, while setting itself below the record of the fastest-growing companies. The latter are growing on the strength of some particular unique product or service and unless a company has one already in development it is wise not to expect to duplicate this kind of growth. For example the 700 per cent profit growth of Rank Xerox from 1963 to 1965 was exceptional and cannot be taken as a guide when setting objectives. It is more realistic to examine the profits of the industrial public companies analysed by the *Financial Times* which have grown by an average of 6 per cent a year over the last five years. Exactly where a company should aim between average and the best will depend on its abilities—and often this is the hardest part of planning. The important point is that for the next steps in a plan to be meaningful, figures need to be produced at this stage. *Business Ratios*, published by Dunn and Bradstreet, may help to some extent.

*Setting qualitative objectives.* A company also needs to consider what kind of future it wants in non-quantitative terms. It may feel it ought to add certain skills or technologies to strengthen its resources. This would enable it to maintain a unique product or service position as well as extending its range of abilities which will form the earning power of the future. Again some companies can handle fast-moving consumer goods while others are at their most profitable when producing capital goods. Put another way, directors should ask themselves what sort of company they want to be in the future, and establish broadly written objectives covering these aspects.

*Project the present business.* Forecasts of sales and profits of the present business are developed at this stage. These forecasts represent

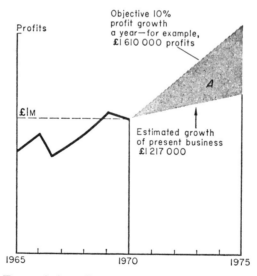

FIGURE 3:3    SIZE OF THE LONG-RANGE PROBLEM

The size of the long-range planning problem is defined by area *A*— the difference between the reasonable objective and the estimated growth of the present business.

the best estimate of future performance if the present business is continued in the existing fashion. The difference between these forecasts and the objectives, at the end of the five-year planning period, shows the size of the long-range problem.

For example, Figure 3:3 shows a company with 1965 profits of £1M which have been growing at 4 per cent a year for five years. up to 1970. The company decided that 10 per cent a year growth ought to be possible with its skills and resources without being over-ambitious. This would give them £1 610 000 profits by 1975. Their present business projected at 4 per cent a year would give them £1 217 000. Their long-range problem, therefore, was how to get an additional £400 000 profit by 1975.

Having established the problem, the next steps in planning consist of a systematic search to locate market opportunities which will enable the company to fulfil its objectives. The search covers four basic lines of corporate development:

1    Improve the performance of the existing products or services in the present markets
2    Find new markets for the present products or services
3    Develop or acquire new products or services for sale in the present markets
4    Develop or acquire new products or services for sale in new markets

## 2. Improving the performance of existing products or services in present markets

Logically, a company should look first into its present business to make a start on solving the planning problem. Divisional or operating management should be consulted about how the present profit position may be bettered.

Market studies to show if product and sales strategy can be brought further into line with user requirements may be coupled with a product-by-product profit analysis, to consolidate effort on the most profitable products and improve the existing performance in each market segment. Interfirm comparisons will indicate the necessity for more than the usual attention to functional efficiency.

37

Improved performance in the existing business will go some way to make up the difference between expected performance and the objectives.

| SECTION | COD-ING | FACTOR | WEIGHT-ING | RAT-ING | SCORE |
|---------|---------|--------|-----------|---------|-------|
| Profit objectives | a | Size* | 3 | +2 | +6 |
| | b | Growth* | 2 | +2 | +4 |
| | c | Level* | 2 | +3 | +6 |
| | d | Stability | 2 | 0 | 0 |
| Market | a | Durability | 3 | +2 | +6 |
| | b | Breadth | 2 | 0 | +2 |
| | c | Major business direction* | 3 | +3 | +9 |
| | d | Captive possibilities | 1 | +1 | +1 |
| | e | Difficulty in copying | 1 | −2 | −2 |
| | f | Unique character of product or process | 3 | −1 | −3 |
| | g | Demand supply ratio | 3 | 0 | 0 |
| | h | Rate of technological change | 2 | +1 | +2 |
| | i | Export potential | 2 | −2 | −4 |
| | j | Degree of competition | 2 | 0 | 0 |
| | k | Ease of market penetration* | 3 | +2 | +6 |
| Production | a | High value added | 2 | +1 | +2 |
| | b | Existence of waste products | 2 | +2 | +4 |
| | c | Utilisation of existing equipment | 3 | +2 | +6 |
| | d | Reliability of process of know-how | 2 | +1 | +2 |
| Contribution to company skills | a | New technology added | 3 | 0 | 0 |
| | b | New marketing skills | 3 | +1 | +3 |
| | c | New production skills | 2 | +2 | +4 |
| | d | New management skills improved position | 2 | 0 | 0 |
| Compatibility | a | Relationship to existing markets | 3 | +1 | +3 |
| | b | Company's image in allied fields | 1 | 0 | 0 |
| | c | Existing technology | 2 | +1 | +2 |
| | d | Existing manufacturing | 2 | +3 | +6 |
| | e | Existing management | 2 | +2 | +4 |
| | | Supersedes present products | 2 | −1 | −2 |
| | | Overall Weighted Score: | | | +67 |

* Bad performance disqualified whole product or business area

FIGURE 3:4   "NEW BUSINESS" SCREEN

An example of the screening process used to highlight business areas which are especially suitable for corporate development.

## 3   Finding new markets for present products—or new products for present markets

To fill the remaining profit "gap" and reach the objectives, new business areas need to be sought. This, again, will be more success-ful if the search starts with products and markets known to the company and proceeds outwards. To be comprehensive the indus-tries close to those already served by the company need to be identi-fied and studied. The products and services comprising these industries may be grouped into different user segments, showing types of distribution and major competitors. Information needs to be developed on the size and growth of each segment, the critical factors for success (marketing, production, R & D), competitive strengths and weaknesses of companies operating in the business, and an indication of the profit environment. Any significant trends which would affect the different industries and their interrelated businesses need to be studied and evaluated.

Possible new business areas for the company may then be found by screening each of the market segments against the objectives, limitations of the company, and feasibility of entry including such factors as capital requirements or number of available acquisition candidates.

Figure 3:4 shows a typical screen. The screening process would result in the identification of priority business areas suitable for corporate development. Combinations of these new businesses should fill the remaining profit gap. Because the industries studied at this stage are close to the original business of the company, many of the new products will have similar technological and marketing requirements to the existing products of the company. This, where it occurs, will increase the chances of success in the new areas while reducing the costs of market entry. It is possible in this way, and over several successive long-range plans, for a company to move steadily into areas quite removed from the present business.

## 4 Development or acquisition of new products or services for sale in new markets

This approach is the most difficult form of corporate development. It is normally considered only if the present skills and resources of the company cannot provide a reasonable return on investment in any areas related to the company's existing business. Completely new opportunities can be located by studying all businesses having an above-average return on investment and screening the businesses against the company's abilities. Business areas which fit the corporate objectives, and are compatible with the company's abilities, can then be investigated both to assess the future prospects in detail and determine the feasibility of successful market entry.

## 5 Implementing new product plans

A company is faced at this stage with a number of potential new product groups rated by priority according to how they would suit the company but all of which could supply the needed additional profits.

These product groups may be obtained by acquisition, licensing or research and development. In whatever way they are obtained detailed departmental plans can be drawn up within the long-range plan. These subsidiary plans will cover each functional aspect of the company's development including sales, finance, research, personnel, legal, manufacturing and administration requirements. The company will then be geared to a single set of objectives, decided upon by the board. These will place the company in a position to grow with the flexibility needed to capitalise on future opportunities as they occur.

# CHAPTER 4

# Management by Objectives

*by* J W Humble

*Director, Urwick, Orr and Partners Limited*

Planned objectives are obviously necessary if a company is to operate successfully. But this success is dependent upon the individual performance of managers and their staff. Management by Objectives provides a system which identifies the objectives and contribution of individuals with overall company objectives and performance.

# 4 : MANAGEMENT BY OBJECTIVES

Management by objectives (MBO) is: "a dynamic system which seeks to integrate the company's need to clarify and achieve its profit and growth goals with the manager's need to contribute and develop himself. It is a demanding and rewarding style of managing a business." The appeal of the approach to the board of directors is obvious, since the need to establish strategic plans for the total business lies at the heart of its responsibility. Without competent and committed managers, however, these plans will remain "pieces of paper". So the board must continuously be concerned with developing the business's human resource. One difficulty is that there are now so many management tools and techniques which can contribute to the board's work that it is essential to have a framework into which these methods can be fitted. Management by objectives provides this framework.

## MANAGEMENT BY OBJECTIVES AS A CONTINUOUS PROCESS

When MBO is operating successfully in a company there will be a continuous process of review and measurement, summarised in the key factors listed below:

1   Critical review and restatement of the company's strategic and tactical plans.
2   Definition with each manager of the key results and performance that he must achieve, in line with unit and company objectives. Managers will be expected to contribute and commit themselves to these objectives.
3   Agreement with each manager for a job improvement plan which makes a measurable and realistic contribu-

tion to the unit and company plans for better performance.

4    Provision of conditions which make possible the achievement of key result and improvement plans, notably:

(a) *An organisation structure* which allows a manager freedom and flexibility in operation.

(b) *Management control information* in a form and at a frequency which makes for more effective self-control and better and quicker decisions.

5    Use of systematic performance reviews to measure and discuss progress made towards results, and potential reviews which identify men with their potential for advancement.

6    The development of plans for management training, so that managers can be helped to overcome their weaknesses, build on their strengths and accept responsibility for self-development.

7    Improvement of motivation by the provision of effective plans for management payment, selection and succession.

MBO in essence is a practical approach to the fundamentals of good general management. It integrates activities often regarded as separate—for example, manager development and strategic business objectives; it provides a valuable and continuing stimulus for companies to challenge traditional assumptions. It bridges the results orientation of the "quantitative school" and the teamwork and personal motivation concepts of the behavioural scientists. And it helps to develop a forward-looking, vital spirit amongst managers.

Figure 4:1 shows MBO as part of the total business process. Figure 4:2 illustrates the link with management development.

## COMPANY OBJECTIVES

The central objective of a company must be to maximise the long-term return on resources which it employs. Planning for profit must be done in the context of a critical analysis of the company's strengths and weaknesses, of the threats and opportunities arising

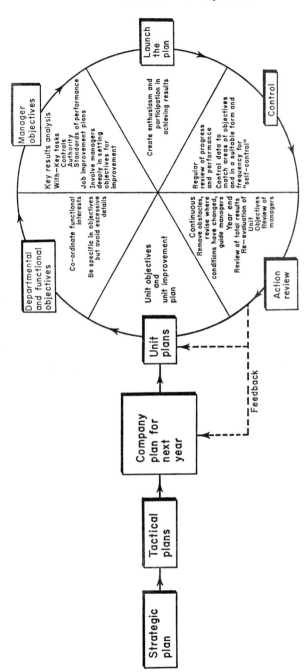

FIGURE 4:1    IMPROVING MANAGEMENT PERFORMANCE: A "BUSINESS VIEW"

This diagram presents an overall view of company objectives, showing how continuous appraisal of results is used to provide constructive feedback and control.

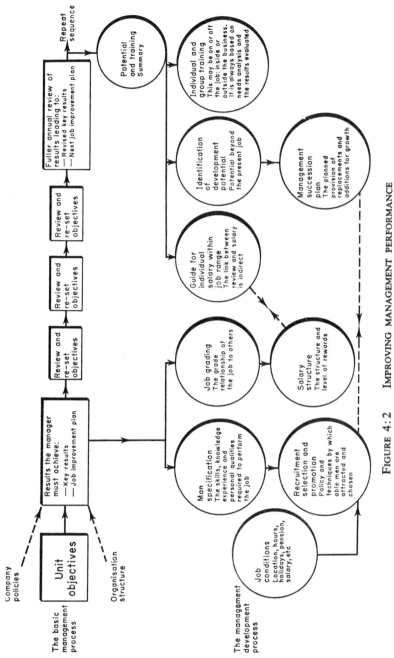

FIGURE 4:2   IMPROVING MANAGEMENT PERFORMANCE

No objectives can be achieved without competent managers. This diagram illustrates factors which are important to the improvement of individual managers' performance.

from the external environment in which it operates and of the expectations of the owners, employers, employees and customers. A critical analysis of this kind, projected several years ahead, invariably demonstrates action to secure immediate improvements. More important, it leads to the development of long-term strategic plans which deal with, for example, future markets; the planned return on investment from individual markets and products; the elimination of non-profit making and diversification.

The real value of making the first strategic plan is educational. It gives a discipline to the collection of important facts and—more important—stimulates directors to interpret the data and ask *fundamental* questions such as:

1    What *is* our real business?
2    What rate of return on assets are we determined to achieve?
3    Are we going to achieve this merely by making our present business more efficient? Should we not think of bolder moves such as divestment of low-growth products and divisions and acquiring high-growth companies that will fit the pattern of the business we are trying to create?
4    Is the quality, motivation and knowledge of our executives adequate to meet future demands which will be made on them?
5    Are we allowing high-quality resources to "drift" into low-opportunity areas?

Once the strategic plan is established, supporting tactical plans can be worked out in areas such as organisation changes, product/market development, allocation of financial and physical resources, operational tasks—see Figure 4:3.

One British company, for instance, prepares a detailed profit plan for the next twelve months which also incorporates a broad indication of forecasts for a further four years. Its profit plan is set out in four parts:

1    *Specific objectives* under such headings as:
     (a) *Profitability*—for example, return on net assets.

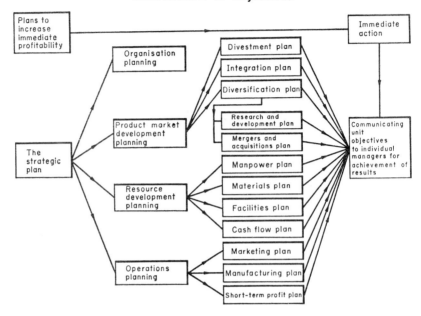

FIGURE 4:3    TYPICAL RANGE OF TACTICAL PLANS
The achievement of a strategic plan must depend upon the development of a practical plan of action. The above chart illustrates the
steps linking the strategic plan with objectives for individual
managers.

(b) *Market standing.* Share of market, volume of sales, product quality and leadership; pricing policies.

(c) *Productivity.* Improvements in ratio of input to output
such as number of units per worker or period of time;
output per measure of space or £ of investment; sales
per salesman, etc.

(d) *Finance.* Cash flow; capital structure.

(e) *Innovation.* Planned development of new and better
products, processes and services.

(f) *Management development.* Introduction of management
by objectives to a subsidiary company; critical review
of management training methods; improvement in the
appraisal scheme.

(g) *Worker performance and attitude.* Preliminary negotiation in a new productivity bargain; changes in the joint consultative machinery.

2  *Basic assumptions.* A succinct statement is made in support of the specific objectives giving basic assumptions on economic, political, competitive and technological trends. For example, it might be assumed that there will not be a Labour government in Britain in the next five years.

3  *Outstanding problems/opportunities: improvement plan.* This sets out a small number of high-priority objectives, and supporting action plans, which if they are implemented vigorously and are well co-ordinated will overcome persistent problems or rapidly exploit new opportunities.

4  *A financial summary.* The detailed plan is summarised in financial terms and a few key performance ratios and indicators, financial and non-financial, are identified.

What this type of profit plan achieves is a disciplined and self-critical approach to forward planning, a richer and broader set of objectives and a sharper basis for delegation, progress and control. Such a plan is never perfect. But it does reflect a company's determination to try to shape its own future and not merely react to events.

## MEASURING AND IMPROVING MANAGEMENT PERFORMANCE

Each manager must be clear about the results he is expected to secure, in line with company objectives, or he may direct his time and energy into unimportant tasks. Moreover, there will be no agreed base against which to review performance and on which to build his training. Although most companies assume that their managers already know what is expected of them, in fact many are uncertain. This is a significant reason for an apparent unwillingness to accept responsibility or to delegate. Traditional statements of duties and responsibilities are usually too generalised and lengthy and are concerned with activities rather than results.

The key results analysis (Figure 4:4) is a useful way to get each manager to analyse his key tasks, performance standards and control

49

information, and to suggest ways in which all these could be improved. A draft can be discussed with his immediate superior and finally approved at one management level higher. A skilled adviser should counsel managers on the best way to make this analysis, and be a catalyst to original thought.

| KEY TASK | PERFORMANCE STANDARD | CONTROL DATA | SUGGESTIONS OR COMMENTS |
|---|---|---|---|
| DELIVERY To ensure that manu-facturing orders are delivered on time | —When 90% of all orders are delivered within the standard cycle times —When no order is late by more than half its standard cycle time —When the standard cycle times do not exceed those specified | Weekly delivery performance returns  Weekly delivery performance returns Delivery programme and weekly delivery performance returns | I do not get this control infor-mation  I do not get this control information Capacity of machine shop by types needs recording |

FIGURE 4:4    SET OF PERSONAL PERFORMANCE OBJECTIVES
An example of a set of objectives which might be agreed for a manager responsible for production or production control. Notice that there is no ambiguity in the performance standards. Each objective is given a sound, quantified basis against which the eventual results can be measured.

The discipline of preparing such an analysis is an excellent on-the-job training method and creates a more constructive sense of purpose and understanding between each manager and his superior. A performance standard is "a statement of the conditions which exist when the result is being satisfactorily achieved". It is not a statement of the ideal results in ideal circumstances nor the minimum acceptable standard. Standards are of two main kinds:

1    *Measured or quantitative.* Those standards which can be expressed in terms such as goods produced per month; cost levels; market penetration per product; per cent delay time.

2    *Judged or qualitative.* Those standards not directly measurable in quantitative terms, but which can be verified by judgement and observation.

Many performance standards already exist in a business through budget allocation, technical specifications and so on; the new contribution is to integrate them with key results and controls. Clearly standards relate to the job, not the job holder.

Setting standards is not easy in human terms. Unless there is a constructive atmosphere, a manager will be defensive and see the exercise as a threat to his security. Planning and control problems also arise, since it is essential to integrate key tasks and standards horizontally as well as vertically.

The quality and volume of suggestions for improvement made by managers is always impressive. A typical example is a manufacturing unit where forty-seven managers made 240 worthwhile suggestions covering points such as cost information, materials handling, tool delivery service, incentive schemes. A manager who has been involved in preparing his key results analysis and then agreed with his superior a specific improvement plan has both developed himself and become committed to reaching higher goals.

Particularly since the Industrial Training Act, management training (Figure 4:5) has become a "growth business". Yet few companies as yet use a disciplined approach to need analysis, training plan, imaginative implementation and evaluation of results. MBO insists that a course is never run in a company until the need for it has been demonstrated and the managers attending it do so because it will help them to acquire specific knowledge and skills which will improve their performance.

Through setting clear performance standards and improvement plans, discussed between each manager and his senior and progressed through performance review, "on the job" training becomes a reality. The diagram also illustrates that training is concerned with developing tomorrow's knowledge, in line with the company's long-range plan.

## SUCCESSFUL IMPLEMENTATION OF MBO IN THE ORGANISATION

Management by objectives is not a perfected package-deal. On the contrary, every business must take the basic concepts and methods and tailor them to meet its own needs. Its introduction shows up problems and the sources of problems. It usually makes it clear that

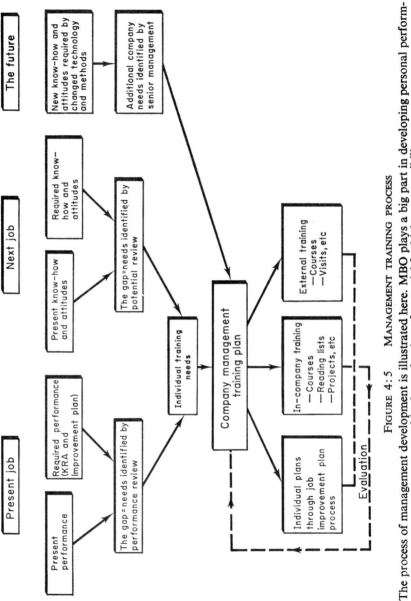

FIGURE 4:5    MANAGEMENT TRAINING PROCESS

The process of management development is illustrated here. MBO plays a big part in developing personal perform-ance and in the evaluation of potential for higher responsibility.

a company is rarely thought of as a total system. Functions, departments, regions and so on often operate as though they were an end in themselves. Whatever the cause—an inadequate control procedure or a badly designed organisation structure, for instance—management by objectives provides a discipline and opportunity to bring conflict areas into the open in a constructive and co-operative atmosphere.

It encourages unemotional, factual analysis of the wider implications for the business and its overriding purpose—a reassessment of its market orientation and a recognition and evaluation of the impact of its decisions on our industrial society.

Management by objectives is in conflict with autocracy and with parochial enthusiasm for individual department results. Moreover, MBO seeks to overcome the tendency for systems to become inflexible and bureaucratic.

The benefits can be significant as the management team concentrates on really important, profit-influencing tasks. Obstacles to securing improvement are identified and can then be overcome by the continuing MBO process. The whole pattern of control information is challenged to make sure that it is providing managers with timely, relevant, comprehensible data which will strengthen the speed and quality of decision-making.

The organisation structure is inevitably tested as every manager's job is analysed and related to the business objectives. Overlapping responsibilities, too many levels in the structure, ineffective groupings of tasks, failure to delegate—these are common weaknesses which are identified. Less tangible, but equally important, is the change in management development. Training needs are precisely defined and can be satisfied in a planned way, substantially on the job. A more objective basis for appraising a man's performance and potential means that the company's succession and career plans can make a better contribution. Clearly not all these benefits lend themselves to precise measurement, but at the operational level MBO can often be judged by quantified improvement. For example:

1    Delivery service in an engineering group improved from
      40 per cent on time to 85 per cent on time.
2    In a chemical plant maintenance man-hours per ton of
      product were reduced by 11.2 per cent.

3   Eighty-seven managers in one company made an average of twenty suggestions for improvement each. Those referring to savings totalled £120 000 a year, of which £60 000 was entirely attributable to MBO.

4   A 50 per cent improvement in wastage in a cigarette factory.

In recent years there has been a greater understanding that the manager is a member of a team, rather than an isolated individual with limited and selfish ends. Unfortunately, this has led some people to underestimate the unique contribution which the chief executive can and must make in terms of personal leadership.

No one suggests that personal leadership is the *only* requirement nor that the chief executive is an entirely free agent to do what he wishes. In fact his leadership is really educational in generating purposefulness, creativity and a commitment to company goals amongst his team. So often in practice we see that this man's courage and example can set the whole tone of the business. Certainly management by objectives, simply because it is a style of managing with built-in assumptions about human nature and response, cannot succeed unless it is understood, accepted and led by the chief executive. A business in real trouble either stimulates new effort from the top team or finally has to replace it: the challenge of survival is a powerful stimulus to action. The more common and difficult problem is the business where things are going along reasonably well and complacency has crept in—continuing success has grown to have an air of inevitability. As Selznick comments about such a "going concern":

> . . . with many forces working to keep it [the going concern] alive, the people who run it can readily escape the task of defining its purpose. This evasion stems partly from the hard intellectual labour involved, a labour that seems but to increase the burden of already onerous daily operations. In part, there is the wish to avoid conflicts with those in and out of the organisation who would be threatened by a sharp definition of purpose, with its attendant claims and responsibilities.

A chief executive with a powerful personal will to succeed and the courage to create a risk-taking, entrepreneurial spirit can transform this drift to bureaucracy into a vital and sustained effort to improve results.

Management by objectives seeks to integrate the company's objectives for profit and growth with the personal goals and satisfaction of its managers. We are gaining new insight into the interdependence of the techniques, viewed as a total business system in the context of a changing social and economic environment. Above all, it is clear that the real key to success in business is the more effective use of our human resources: the talent and drive are there if only we will release them.

## ACKNOWLEDGEMENTS

Diagrams are reproduced by permission of Urwick, Orr & Partners Limited.

## FURTHER READING

The author's views are developed further in:

1   *Improving Business Results*, 1968, McGraw-Hill for Management Centre/Europe. This is the basic text for MBO.
2   *Management by Objectives in Action*, McGraw-Hill, 1970. An edited collection of case material.
3   The AB-Pathé colour film series *Management by Objectives*. Details of the four films from AB-Pathé, 142 Wardour Street, London W1.

# CHAPTER 5

# Strategic Space Planning

*by* Peter Lebus

*Office Planning Consultant*

Office space costs have soared in recent years, to the extent that in some cities office accommodation has become as expensive to provide as the staff housed. Working environment is recognised to be a major factor in individual motivation and staff turnover. Application of a logical space planning approach can lead to a bigger return on capital invested in office buildings and savings in the sensitive area of overhead expenses.

# 5 : STRATEGIC SPACE PLANNING

The planning of office space used to be a simple and largely arbitrary activity. However, the decisions that now face senior management in this field involve considerable investment and have a significant effect on staff efficiency and profitability. Space planning is a convenient term that encompasses all the techniques, old and new, which can be brought to bear in order to pre-plan, design and implement a successful office project. Many factors have to be considered. Final decisions are more likely to produce an optimum solution if all the factors are considered in a logical sequence and the results presented on a matrix display to aid the decision-making process. This chapter examines the pre-planning process and identifies three separate phases.

## DEFINING COMPANY NEEDS

Before any possible solution to office space problems can be attempted it is obviously essential to define company objectives and policies in relation to the new or expanded facilities. Since these objectives are linked to future strategy, and involve investment of capital, planning during this stage must be undertaken by senior management and approved by the board. A typical analysis would examine the following factors.

1 *Economic period.* This is the period of time during which the new offices should satisfy the company's requirements. Ideally this should not be less than five years and is unlikely to exceed twenty years. If possible, plans should be based on a period of ten years from the date of occupation.

2 *Timing.* How soon must action be taken? If a major company

reorganisation is essential within the next six months, then accommodation must be made available at that time. However, any time constraints should be weighed carefully against the risk of solving a short-term problem at the expense of creating a long-term one. The true cost of delay must be assessed.

3 *Manpower planning.* It is assumed that staff forecasts will exist as a direct result of short-term budgeting and long-range planning. These figures must obviously dictate office requirements to a large extent, but it is important to realise that it is rare for such forecasts to prove excessive in retrospect. Past growth patterns in the company can be analysed to form a basis for comparison; provision of an office building that proves to be 10 per cent too small is likely to be a far more expensive mistake than the provision of 10 per cent spare capacity.

4 *Facilities.* Conference space, training rooms, computer, canteen, kitchen, library, print services, telephone exchange, reception area, post room, staff shop, storage space, toilets, surgery, and other facilities all make claims on space. The provision of many of these facilities are matters for the board to decide, as they are policy, rather than planning decisions. The outcome must affect capital outlay, and detailed layouts and building specifications cannot start until these questions have been resolved.

5 *Quality standards.* Once again, a policy decision will be involved in deciding the general standard of accommodation to be provided. Directors will probably want to visit other modern offices, to derive benefit from the experience of others. It is not necessarily true that the cheapest office exhibits the worst quality standards. The correct planning sequence here is to decide the requirements first, and then set out to achieve them for minimum cost.

6 *Communications.* Disposition of offices with respect to each other, to production or distribution facilities, and to senior management offices will be planned best if communication needs are first analysed. This can be done by establishing a grid (Figure 5:1) that displays the estimated number of trips made by staff each day. The example shown was actually used to decide the position of new engineering offices for a machine tool manufacturer. Although this grid refers to a single company site (occupying fifty acres in the example shown) the same principles would be extended to aid decisions

| Department | Estimated trips per day |
|---|---|
| Marketing/sales | 30 |
| Purchasing | 30 |
| Production engineering | 75 |
| Production control | 25 |
| Accounts | 10 |
| Print room | 180 |

(a) Design office communication chart

| | Marketing/sales | Purchasing | Production engineering | Production control | Accounts | Print room |
|---|---|---|---|---|---|---|
| Purchasing | 10 | | | | | |
| Production engineering | 5 | 25 | | | | |
| Production control | 2 | 125 | 150 | | | |
| Accounts | 25 | 140 | 15 | 10 | | |
| Print room | 20 | 45 | 50 | 120 | 1 | |
| Design office | 30 | 30 | 75 | 25 | 10 | 180 |

(b.) Interdepartment grid analysis

FIGURE 5:1     COMMUNICATION GRIDS

Location of a new office must depend to some extent on factors outside the direct control of management, but wherever possible communication requirements between departments should be satisfied. By estimating or measuring the daily number of trips between departments, grids can be constructed to aid the decision-making process. Two very simple cases are shown here. In (a) the chart demonstrates a checklist compiled to highlight communication, priorities between a proposed new design office and other existing offices. Chart (b) takes the process a stage further; it provides a grid analysis that would assist in the organisation of a total office complex.

| | OPEN SPACE | OPEN PLAN | CELLULAR | | HALF-HEIGHT PARTITION | CARREL |
| --- | --- | --- | --- | --- | --- | --- |
| | | | INDIVIDUAL | SHARED | | |
| PRIVACY | xx | | xxx | x | x | xx |
| FREEDOM FROM DISTRACTION | xx | x | xxx | | x | xx |
| COMMUNICATION | xxx | xxx | | x | xx | x |
| FLEXIBILITY | xxx | xx | | | x | x |
| SUPERVISION | xx | xxx | | x | x | |
| WORK FLOW | xxx | xxx | | x | x | |
| SPACE UTILIZATION | xxx | xxx | | x | x | xx |

FIGURE 5 : 2    CHARACTERISTICS OF LAYOUTS

This table illustrates the relative merits of six types of layout. The greater the number of x's, the better is the result.

on the choice of a geographical locality, where they would take their place alongside the social and economic factors on the grid.

**7** *Office layout.* Directors must decide the type of layout to be used for each department and function. Several alternatives should be considered and the choice will depend on the characteristics of the layout and the priorities of the user department. Figure 5:2 shows a method for making this comparison for six commonly used layouts.

An open-space office is one which has been planned using the principles popularly known as landscaping or panoramic office planning. The furniture is located giving an informal appearance which satisfies both the company's need for communications and the individual's need for identification. Departments and sections are placed for efficient work flow, and the working environment is designed to a high standard.

An open-plan office is the conventional "bull pen" with regular rows of desks and no screening for staff. Distraction is usually quite high.

A conventional cellular office, used either by one person or shared by several, is too familiar to need description.

A half-height partition layout is a compromise between the cellular and open-plan office. Fixed partitions from four to six feet high are installed, and staff work in the boxes which are created.

A carrel is a layout defined by the furniture. The individual is surrounded on three sides by his working furniture and storage, which are designed to provide screening up to about five feet in height.

**8** *Space allocation.* When the basic questions of number of staff, facilities needed and standard of quality have been decided, each of these decisions must be translated into actual space requirements. The space standards must be based on an assessment of individual working needs, storage, privacy and communications. The Offices, Shops and Railway Premises Act lays down minimum standards, but it is usual for space to be allocated more liberally. Again, a policy decision from the board will be expected. Directors must agree the number of square feet allowable for each staff function or facility. Addition of all these space figures, together with an allowance for access, will fix the usable office area to be provided and enable first estimates of cost to be made.

**9** *Budget.* Detailed cost estimates will not be possible until building specifications have been drafted and put out to tender. However, the board will require a budgetary estimate from which to organise the provision of capital. The level at which this estimate is set must depend on the outcome of all the policy decisions already outlined; it is not possible to be specific without analysis of quality and other standards. Some indication of current building costs can usually be gleaned from reports published in the *Architects' Journal*, but target costs and budgets are best established by consultation with professional advisers. Naturally, an external adviser should be acting independently of any possible contractor.

## ANALYSIS OF ALTERNATIVE SOLUTIONS

At this stage no decision should have been reached regarding the type of action to be taken. A new purpose-designed office could be built, existing offices which were designed for letting or for a previous tenant could be leased, or an industrial building could be converted. There are, of course, many possibilities and they must be analysed and compared on a common basis.

Such a comparison is illustrated in summary form by Figure 5:3. In this example a company is analysing the alternatives prior to deciding on a course of action. The company requirements have already been established showing that during the next five years a total of 250 staff will have to be accommodated. In order to provide adequate working areas, together with space for other office functions and circulation, 37 500 square feet of usable space is required. This has been calculated on the basis of 70 per cent of the area being used for open offices and 30 per cent for cellular offices. A number of service requirements and environmental standards have been fixed on the basis that any shortfall will tend to create inefficiencies within the company.

During the five-year period of occupation it is anticipated that 10 per cent of the staff and furniture will have to be moved each year due to internal reorganisation. It is also desirable to have an additional 20 per cent of space available for further expansion after the five-year period. This additional space may be in the form of floors that have been sub-let on a short-term lease, space for further

| | REQUIREMENTS OF COMPANY | NEW BUILDING A | LEASED BUILDING B | LEASED BUILDING C | LEASED BUILDING D | CONVERTED WAREHOUSE E |
|---|---|---|---|---|---|---|
| Number of staff | 250 | | | | | |
| Usable area (sq. ft.) | 37 500 | 38 000 | 41 000 | 37 000 | 39 000 | 47 000 |
| Net lettable area (sq. ft.) | | 38 000 | 45 000 | 39 000 | 42 000 | 54 000 |
| Gross built area (sq. ft.) | | 51 000 | | | | |
| Layout | 70 per cent open | x | x | — | — | x |
| | 30 per cent cellular | x | x | x | x | x |
| Service | Telephone | x | x | x | x | x |
| | Power grid | x | x | — | — | x |
| Facilities | Computer room | x | x | x | — | x |
| Timing—Available | Dec. 1973 | x | x | x | x | x |
| Environment | Air Conditioning | x | x | x | — | — |
| | 600 lux illumination | x | x | x | — | x |
| Flexibility | 20 per cent growth | x | — | x | — | x |
| | 10 per cent annual change | x | — | — | — | x |
| Construction cost £ | | 765 000 | 135 000 | 117 000 | 126 000 | 270 000 |
| Conversion cost £ | | | | | | 108 000 |
| Fitting-out cost £ | | 76 000 | 90 000 | 78 000 | 84 000 | |
| Total capital cost £ | | 841 000 | 225 000 | 195 000 | 210 000 | 378 000 |
| ANNUAL COSTS | | | | | | |
| Interest on capital at 8 per cent | | 67 280 | 18 000 | 15 600 | 16 800 | 30 240 |
| Rent | | — | 90 000 | 87 750 | 63 000 | 54 000 |
| Running costs | | 9 500 | 11 250 | 9 750 | 8 400 | 10 800 |
| Maintenance costs | | 3 800 | 4 500 | 3 900 | 4 200 | 5 400 |
| Staff cost differential | | — | 10 000 | 5 000 | 15 000 | 10 000 |
| Cost of building over 30 years £ | | 25 500 | — | — | — | — |
| Total annual cost £ | | 106 080 | 133 750 | 122 000 | 107 400 | 110 440 |

FIGURE 5:3   ANALYSIS OF ALTERNATIVE BUILDINGS

This table summarises the factors that must be considered when deciding the type of building solution to company needs.

development on the site of the new building or areas which have not been converted for the short term.

Five alternative solutions are considered in this example. Building *A* is purpose designed and consequently satisfies all the company requirements, including the ability to expand in the future. As the design will have been based on a detailed user specification the net lettable area and the usable area will be the same.

The net lettable area within a building is the total area inside the walls, but excluding the service areas and vertical circulation. This figure is used primarily for costing purposes. The usable area is equivalent to the net lettable area reduced by a factor based on the shape of the building, the partition modules and inactive space. In particular this reduction depends upon the minimum size of individual offices (controlled by column positions and window sizes) and the use of internal areas, which may be suitable only for storage or circulation. This factor is normally between 5 and 20 per cent, but it is not uncommon to find it as high as 30 per cent. The effect of this can be seen when a company calculates that it needs 10 000 square feet of office space, leases a building of 10 000 square feet net lettable area and finds that it cannot accommodate all its staff without a considerable reduction in standards.

Alternatives *B, C* and *D* are three leased buildings of approximately the right size that are all available within the time limit. The designs of these buildings result in a different usable space in each case. Buildings *C* and *D* have floor shapes which are long and narrow, and are not suitable for open office layout. The remaining company requirements are met to varying extents by each building.

Building *E* is a converted warehouse with large floor areas. Considerable alterations would have to be made in order to prepare it for use; however it has the potential to provide all the company requirements with the exception of air conditioning.

The estimated capital cost for each building has been calculated on the basis of £15 per gross square foot for building anew; £3 per net square foot for converting the leased buildings to provide lighting, power, telephones and other services and facilities; and £5 per net square foot for converting the warehouse. The fitting-out cost for internal fittings, furniture and equipment has been estimated to be £2 per net square foot for each building.

Annual costs are based on interest and amortisation charges, rent, power, heating, cleaning, maintenance and other running costs. In order to compare the buildings on a common basis, a staff cost differential should also be calculated. This is a reflection of the greater efficiency that can be expected by the provision of good working conditions for staff. If it is assumed that a new building has been designed to optimise working conditions and provide the most appropriate layout and staff space standards, then the other buildings will incur an additional cost as a result of the inferior working conditions. Information in this field is not yet conclusive, but there is evidence to suggest that this differential can be as high as 5 per cent of staff costs. For the purpose of this example, differences of 1 per cent, 2 per cent and 3 per cent have been used.

The totals for the annual costs allow a cost comparison of the five buildings. This, together with the comparison of facilities, services and other factors, forms the basis for choosing the most appropriate course of action. In practice, it is likely that cost calculations would be subjected to discounted cash flow or other investment appraisal techniques.

A useful example of an actual comparison has been published by the Whitehall Development Group (*Planned Open Offices—A Cost Benefit Analysis* Department of the Environment, Directorate of Home Estate Management, Elizabeth House, York Road, London SE1).

## PREPARING A SPECIFICATION OF REQUIREMENTS

Once the decision to build or move has been taken, professional help should be used to prepare a specification of requirements which sets out all the detailed information required by the architect or interior planner. This is a pre-design document and forms the basis for the planning and design work which will follow. For a purpose-designed building, this should be a comprehensive document dealing with all aspects of the building design. Many of these requirements will have been established during the definition of company needs. Additional guidance will also be necessary which reflects the decision to build. The specification for a new building should include information under the following headings:

1    Company profile
2    Project timing

3    Company policy
4    Staff numbers
5    Company organisation
6    Layout needs
7    Space standards
8    Departmental space needs
9    General and facility areas
10   Circulation considerations
11   Total space needs
12   Relationship patterns
13   Design implications of the layout needs
14   Environmental needs
15   Service needs

The specification must be agreed by the board or by a project committee before it is formally presented to the architect for the design stage. The final success of the new offices will depend on this interpretation of the specification of requirements.

It is probable that the ideal answer to any particular requirement will not necessarily be wholly compatible with all other requirements. Therefore the process of selection and compromise, which is inevitably required, should be closely monitored to ensure that the right priorities are given. The suitability and cost effectiveness of the design should be checked as it develops. Ratios and functional details should be compared with the company specification of requirements and good space planning standards. It is advisable to use trained staff during this process to ensure that the best solution is achieved. Particular note should be made of:

1    Ratio of gross space to net space
2    Ratio of net space to usable space
3    The type and quantity of services that are provided
4    Partition and building modules, and their effect on layout and flexibility
5    Running and maintenance costs, which are influenced by design decisions taken at this stage
6    Shape of the building, and its effect on space utilisation and layout
7    Size of floors, and the effect on company communications and work flow

8    Column positions, which can control the position of corridors or partition walls

9    Detailed designs and specifications of internal finishes, which will influence the visual and acoustic environment

10   Block layouts, showing the allocation of space to departments and main facilities

11   Furniture and equipment, and the suitability for work performance and storage

12   Detailed layouts of individual work stations, which should reflect staff and company needs

13   Plans of telephone and power requirements, which should provide flexibility for the future

These design features will be developed progressively through the preliminary and detailed design stages. At intervals, the architect will present his design recommendations which must be agreed by the board or project committee before he can progress to the next stage of details. Final agreement of the design completes the planning phase of the project. This is followed by the preparation of a bill of quantities by the quantity surveyors, which will be used as the basis for tendering by contractors.

This chapter has described the application of space planning techniques to one of the major accommodation problems that face management from time to time. However, constant changes which take place in company organisation, staff numbers, office equipment, work methods and social expectations are reflected in the demands made on the total office environment. It is therefore important that management, and in particular the office manager, should apply the principles of analytical space planning on a continuing basis. By this means a company will ensure that flexibility planned into the building is used to provide an efficient, cost-effective office.

———— CHAPTER 6 ————

# Panoramic Office Planning

by J R Passey

*Chief Consultant, Bürolandschaft Limited*

In recent years there has been an increasing swing from conventional office layouts towards POP or "landscaped" arrangements. This innovation has led to improved flexibility for change and expansion, whilst working environment and communications have been improved at the same time. Despite these advantages, POP techniques are not an automatic solution to every company's office problems. Careful consideration must always be given to the nature and size of departments, as well as the size and shape of the building to be occupied.

# 6 : PANORAMIC OFFICE PLANNING

POP is nothing to do with "pruning office plants" or, as some people mistakenly believe, with "popular office planning". Panoramic Office Planning is the name frequently used in this country to describe the Bürolandschaft (office landscaping) method of office layout. Bürolandschaft originated in Germany during the post-war redevelopment programme when a new style of architecture gave rise to new shapes of buildings and the opportunity to experiment with office layout planning.

The extent to which different shapes of buildings influenced the growth of office landscaping is arguable. It is understandable that there should be a move to break away from the conventional method of laying out lines of desks in straight formation. Certainly, the visual aspect of varied formations of desks is more pleasing to the eye—hence the visual description of "office landscaping" or "panoramic office planning".

As a gardener will know, landscaping takes a considerable amount of planning in order to achieve the required effect. In this country, the phrase "panoramic office planning" satisfied the emphasis on the visual aspect, as well as the importance of locating the groups of desks with good communications and efficient work flow.

While all these factors were having an impact on the development of office planning, there was a general recognition of the fact that the office environment had been sadly neglected in the past. The 1963 Offices, Shops and Railway Premises Act laid down minimum standards for working conditions.

For some organisations there was little hesitation in spending money on acoustic ceilings, carpeted floors, screens and plants etc. The costs of implementing POP techniques were justified on the grounds that improved morale and good communications produce a contented staff, and such staff are more likely to stay with an efficient organisation. Other organisations are more cynical when considering the importance of working environment and its effect on efficiency. In the final analysis, the success of POP as a technique depends on the type of work being carried out by the employees, the size and shape of the office areas, and the degree of thought which goes into the planning and design of the overall scheme. A visit to several different installations will soon reveal the different interpretations of the technique and the varying degrees of success achieved.

Office work, normally concerned with processing information quickly and accurately, needs good facilities and communications. As the volume increases and work flow becomes more complex, communications between office blocks, different floors and partitioned offices can cause delays and frustration. There has in consequence been a tendency to occupy larger floor areas and to reduce the number of partitions.

In order to keep pace with the demands of a rapidly expanding business, the modern office must satisfy three basic requirements:

1    Working conditions must be of a high standard in order
     to promote a stimulating environment conducive to a
     high level of productivity.

2    The layout of departments must follow the work flow
     as closely as possible to avoid bottlenecks in com-
     munications.

3    The detailed layout of departments must be sufficiently
     flexible to allow for the regrouping of staff to meet the
     needs of expansion and contraction without having to
     face the problem of reconstruction.

It is immediately apparent that "panoramic office planning" satisfies all these requirements for the modern office. At first sight it could be argued that these requirements are met by the conventional "open-plan" offices with modular furniture arranged in long rows. Whilst the "bull-pen" method of layout is economical in space utilisation and is reasonably flexible in large open offices, it certainly does not produce the right working environment. The noise and visual distractions are too high for concentrated clerical effort, and the outlook of employees sitting in long rows is more akin to a factory production line than an office. Nevertheless, there are firms in which space economy is more important than working environment. Usually these would be organisations employing large staffs to carry out routine clerical functions.

It should be pointed out that where a concept has arisen from design, functional, and cost considerations, there are bound to be different interpretations and preferences expressed in its application. On the one hand there are the firms who think that it is only necessary to knock down the walls in a conventional office block, disarrange the furniture a little and stick a few potted plants here and there. On the other hand, there are the firms which favour carels (boxed-off working units forming cubicles). Neither of these approaches does justice to the visual and functional considerations inherent in the landscaped office.

The basic ingredients of POP can be assessed against the main objectives by drawing an analysis table. The objectives are:

1    Good working conditions (environment)
2    Efficient work flow and communications
3    Flexibility, allowing change or expansion

An analysis table is shown in Figure 6:1 from which it is apparent that although many factors are common to the satisfaction of all three objectives, most are concerned with improving the working environment.

## ENVIRONMENTAL FACTORS IN POP OFFICES

### External factors

Psychologically, people do not like being shut in, and windows enable them to relate to the outside world. Whilst windows are mainly functional in allowing natural daylight to penetrate the office, they should be double glazed to reduce the effect of outside traffic noise, and to minimise heat loss in winter. In the summer, curtains or blinds are necessary to prevent the penetration of solar heat. Curtains have the added advantage of sound absorption. Ideally, in air-conditioned offices, windows should remain shut to avoid draughts, noise and smells.

| | Working conditions (environment) | | | | | | | Work flow (communications) | | | | Flexibility | | |
|---|---|---|---|---|---|---|---|---|---|---|---|---|---|---|
| | (a) External | (b) Thermal | (c) Subjective | (d) Spatial | (e) Social | (f) Visual | (g) Aural | (a) Between individuals | (b) Between sections | (c) Between departments | (d) Between internal and external sources | (a) Locations of individuals | (b) Location and size of sections | (c) Location and size of departments |
| Visual aspect | | | • | • | | • | | | | | | • | • | • |
| Housekeeping | | | • | • | | • | | • | • | • | | | | |
| Tea breaks | | | | | • | | | • | • | • | | | | |
| Status symbols | | | • | | • | • | | | | | | • | | |
| Building shape and size | | • | • | • | • | • | • | • | • | • | | • | • | • |
| Gangways | | | • | • | • | • | • | • | • | • | | • | • | • |
| Desk groupings | | | • | • | • | • | • | • | • | • | | • | • | • |
| Distraction | | | | | • | • | • | | | | | • | | |
| Colour schemes | | | • | | • | • | | | | | | • | | |
| Smells | • | | • | | | | | | | | | • | | |
| Noise | • | | • | | | • | | | | | | • | | |
| Artificial light | | • | • | | | • | | | | | | • | | |
| Daylight | • | | • | | | • | | | | | | • | | |
| Draughts | • | • | | | | | | | | | | • | | |
| Cold | • | • | | | | | | | | | | • | | |
| Heat | • | • | | | | | | | | | | • | | |
| Chair fabrics | | | • | | | • | | | | | | | | |
| Design of furniture | | | • | • | | • | | • | | | | • | • | • |
| Photo-copying equipment | | | • | | | | | • | • | • | | | | |
| Duplicating equipment | | | | | | | • | • | • | • | | | | |
| Typewriters | | | | | | | • | • | • | • | | | | |
| Muted telephones | | | | | | | • | • | • | • | • | | | |
| Engaged signs | | | | | • | • | • | • | • | • | | | | |
| Acoustic ceilings | | | • | | • | • | | | | | | | | |
| Plants | | | • | • | • | • | • | • | • | • | | • | • | • |
| Screens | | | • | • | • | • | • | • | • | • | | • | • | • |
| Underfloor ducting | | | | • | | | • | • | • | • | • | • | • | • |
| Carpeting | | | • | • | | • | • | | | | | | | |
| Lighting | | | • | • | | • | | | | | | • | • | • |
| Air conditioning | | | • | | | | • | | | | | • | | |
| Heating and ventilation | | | • | | | | | | | | | • | | |
| Curtains, blinds etc | • | | | | | • | | | | | | • | | |
| Double glazing | • | • | | | | • | | | | | | • | • | |
| Windows | • | • | | | | • | • | | | | | • | • | • |

FIGURE 6:1    ANALYSIS TABLE OF PLANNING INGREDIENTS

The table illustrates the various factors affecting the successful application of POP techniques, and highlights the multi-purpose use of the various ingredients. Thus, screens have acoustic properties as well as providing a decorative visual barrier which can be used to define departmental areas and access routes.

## Thermal factors

Temperature control is an important factor in any size of office, though more difficult to achieve in larger offices. Localised regulation of central heating and air conditioning is more expensive, but well worth the additional cost. Heat emission from extensive runs of fluorescent lights should not be overlooked in larger offices. Carpeting, acoustic ceilings, double glazing and curtains all have some insulating as well as acoustic properties. Larger buildings with a high percentage of glass and plastered walls will obviously suffer from greater heat loss. It should be remembered that women are more susceptible to temperature fluctuations than men, and working in a hot humid atmosphere is just as detrimental to productivity as working in a cold draughty office.

## Subjective factors

The effect of the various environmental factors on the individual is the most difficult to assess since different individuals at each level react in different ways. In general, it can be said that individuals react favourably to high standards of working conditions (carpets, curtains, plants, well-designed furniture, comfortable chairs, attractive colours, good lighting, comfortable working temperatures. A more varied response would be obtained from individuals asked to sit on their own, in separate offices, in a group, in a corner, facing a window, facing a wall, screen, filing cabinet or plant trough, opposite a door, opposite the boss etc. The size, shape and appearance of the office are obviously factors affecting the attitude of the individual. The loss of privacy is resented more strongly by staff with a low work load, who fear the possibility of being exposed in an open office area.

But perhaps the most important factor of all is status. There can be no doubt that the echelons of the office hierarchy are riddled with status symbols. This is where POP has the greatest contribution to make. By generally raising office standards at all levels, it is possible to smooth over the transition between clerks, typists, supervisors and managers. Needless to say, the progressive democratic companies find the loss of partitioned offices more palatable than the conservative status-conscious companies. No doubt new status symbols will spring up in some of the existing POP offices, for old habits die hard and status aggrandisement is an all-too-common fact of modern life.

## Spatial factors

As a reaction to the line of boxes down a corridor and the regimentation of long rows of desks in over-crowded open offices, a set of basic principles has been formulated which applies to office landscaping layouts. The layout of desks should be such that staff are not visually distracted by passers-by. At the same time staff must have ease of access to clearly defined departments via gangways which should be marked by the position of screens, plant troughs and furniture. Main passage-ways should not be less than five feet wide, whilst branch routes should be at least three feet. Desks should not be placed facing windows, but rather side on to allow side light without casting shadows on the working surface.

The desks of senior staff should be arranged so that visitors approach from the front rather than from behind. It is therefore important that no changes to the layout should be made by individual departments without authorisation.

The correct selection of office furniture and colour schemes is an integral part of any successful landscape layout. The shape of the office building also plays an important part in the effective use of space. Many conflicting views have been expressed about the ideal shape of building for the application of POP techniques. Some would prefer a round shape, others a rectangular or square building with a minimum open area of $80 \times 40$ ft ($24 \times 12$ m). In advocating large open rectangular areas, the costs of construction, heating, lighting and air conditioning are often played down. All are agreed that pillars are a nuisance to layout, though sometimes necessary for construction.

The location of lifts and other services can be a problem, though one or two firms have successfully shown that a central services core running up through the centre of the office block is not necessarily a bar to the adoption of POP techniques. In fact, it could be argued that such arrangements make for easier access to the central services, whilst at the same time breaking up the non-related departments. In the final analysis, the suitability of a particular shape or size of building will depend on the nature and size of departments which are going to occupy it. Whilst the office planners and building architects are still arguing about this point, many firms have proved, with varying degrees of success, that POP techniques can be applied to new or existing buildings of most shapes and sizes.

## Social factors

The general decor (more resembling the house than the factory), informal grouping of desks, and the playing down of status symbols, all help to make the office a more sociable place to work in. However, it is a fact that whereas people are less inclined to knock on doors and enter private offices, they are more likely to wander over to chat to someone in an adjacent office area. There is no excuse for this situation getting out of hand in landscaped offices where each group is under the surveillance of the supervisor. The fact that senior staff are more approachable can be controlled by the use of "engaged" signs on prominent positions outside their office areas.

Some companies argue that social mixing is inevitable in an office community, and that it can take place during tea-breaks in areas set apart on an informal basis away from the working areas. This practice is further justified on the grounds that the perambulating tea ladies with their trollies are a major source of disruption to the working routine, whilst the spillage of tea and eating of biscuits at desks are hardly conducive to efficient and tidy offices. Vending machines are often provided in the tea areas, so that breaks can be taken at any time of the day without interruption of the working routine.

Ultimately, the success of such practices depends on the good sense of the staff and effective supervision. Otherwise, as with any social benefit, the abuse of them can cause a serious setback to the level of productivity in the office.

## Visual factors

The most important factor for the individual is good lighting, yet until recently, it was often sadly neglected. It is not uncommon to find light intensities as low as 300 lux in some offices during the winter months at desk-top height. In this country, 500 lux is an acceptable standard (forthcoming legislation may make this the minimum standard), whilst on the Continent, a more realistic standard of 800 lux for clerical work is in use. Non-reflective work surfaces and low glare colours for fabrics and carpets help to achieve the required effect.

The visual aspect of the office as a whole is, as the name suggests, an important feature of panoramic office planning. Although opinions vary as to the maximum height for office furniture, a height of 5 feet for screens and lateral filing cabinets would appear to be the most practical solution. New wooden furniture is warmer and more pleasing than steel, whilst the careful arrangement of desks in informal groupings creates an effect which no photograph can capture.

## Acoustics

Much attention has been given to the subject of aural distraction. Acoustic ceilings (preferably designed to prevent sound deflection) are essential in most modern low-ceilinged buildings, whilst carpeted floors, acoustic screens, double glazing and curtained wall surfaces are desirable if noise disturbance is to be reduced. Whilst the use of flashing lights or muted telephones has been successfully carried out, electric typewriters are still a source of noise which has to be carefully controlled. The shape and size of the building, the height of the ceiling, and the location of groups of desks are key factors affecting the acoustics.

It is generally recognised that a certain level of background noise is desirable to prevent any one noise emerging above the general noise, which ideally should be between 50 and 55 decibels. Thus in small office areas the noise of a typewriter would be noticeable, whereas in a larger busy office it would be less so. Those with special claims for privacy should remember that in offices where ideal acoustic conditions prevail, it is claimed that the limit of intelligibility lies about 13 ft (4 m) away from the speaker, and the limit of audibility about 23 ft (7 m) away. It should be added that there is a natural tendency for people to lower their voices when speaking in a landscaped office, and alleged cases of eavesdropping are more imaginary than real.

## Work flow

A study of the systems work flow and internal communications is an essential part of any layout exercise. It is, however, even more relevant when the restrictions of narrow partitioned offices are removed, and replaced by large open areas which give the layout planner a greater freedom of choice. Having defined the communications network, it is possible to allocate zones for each department within the context of the space available in a given shape and size of building. In this respect, a minimum area of 80 × 40 ft is desirable for medium-sized organisations, but bearing in mind the construction costs of the larger-sized building, it is often possible for organisations to apply landscaping techniques in smaller buildings.

## FLEXIBILITY

In POP offices the flexibility which is necessary for any expanding business can be achieved by the use of self-standing screens, plant troughs, uniform office furniture design, good overall lighting and an underfloor grid system of ducting for power and telephone cables.

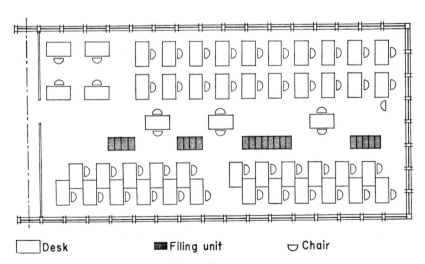

☐Desk          ▣Filing unit          ▽Chair

FIGURE 6:2     OPEN-PLAN OFFICE

Open-plan offices use space efficiently in the sense of floor area usage, but the overall working environment does not encourage or allow individuals to operate most effectively.

81

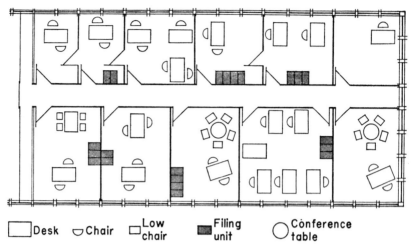

Desk ▽ Chair □ Low chair ■ Filing unit ○ Conference table

FIGURE 6: 3     PARTITIONED OFFICES

In the partitioned office layout, space is used wastefully and status problems can be aggravated or introduced.

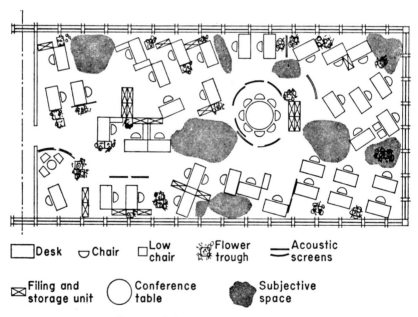

Desk ▽ Chair □ Low chair Flower trough — Acoustic screens

Filing and storage unit ○ Conference table Subjective space

FIGURE 6:4     LANDSCAPED OFFICE

Example of the kind of arrangement which could result from a study of all environmental factors in a specific case.

82

Rows of underfloor ducting placed 8 feet apart enable 4-feet long telephone or electric leads to be led out in any direction from risers, which can be positioned anywhere along the rows of ducting. Without taking down partitions, altering electrical wiring and redecorating, it is possible to move whole sections of departments from one area to another, or to expand some sections and contract others as necessary.

The results of a POP study are shown in the example of Figure 6:4. This can be compared to the more conventional layouts shown in Figures 6:2 and 6:3. In terms of area used for each employee, the open-plan arrangement is economical. Fifty desks are accommodated in the example, against only half this number in the partitioned arrangement and about thirty-six desks (plus additional workplaces) in the POP scheme. Space usage must be measured, however, in terms of total efficiency, expressed in work throughput and staff satisfaction (employee turnover rate).

It may be argued that a well-designed POP office could cost more than a conventional office if construction, heating and air-conditioning costs are included. It must be emphasised, however, that panoramic office planning is a total concept in which all the items discussed have an important function affecting the success of the installation. It should be apparent that most of the ingredients of POP offices have a dual function. They not only improve the various aspects of environment, they also improve communications and provide a flexibility which companies require in the course of expansion. The intangible costs of improved productivity and increased flexibility should therefore be borne in mind when attempting any cost justification of POP ingredients.

There are several facets of office landscaping which the Anglo-Saxon mentality is reluctant to accept. Many of these are more psychological than real, based on lack of experience and insufficient knowledge of the facts. Unfortunately some of the POP layouts installed in this country have only had a limited success. The total effect can only be achieved by the correct application of the basic principles of layout and design, geared to the requirements of each specific installation. However, there seems to be little doubt that the technique of POP, Bürolandschaft or office landscaping will become the standard layout of the seventies.

# Section Two

# Financial Management

# CHAPTER 7

# Achieving Real Growth From Acquisitions

*by* C St J O'Herlihy

*Urwick, Orr and Partners Limited*

According to recent surveys about half the companies in the US and UK engaged in making acquisitions do not feel them to be successful. One major factor for failure to achieve real growth from acquisitions is that too much is paid for the acquisition. In many companies, the sophisticated control of credit or capital expenditure simply does not extend to acquisitions. This chapter outlines a method of financial planning for acquisitions, taking into account all the complex features of both the acquirer and potential acquired.

# 7 : ACHIEVING REAL GROWTH FROM ACQUISITIONS

The primary function of a business must be to increase the wealth of its shareholders. Under present tax laws, where income is taxed more severely than capital gains, it is more attractive to shareholders to receive £1000 in the form of capital gains than as dividends. Consequently, there is an increasing tendency for companies to set as their ultimate objective an increasing share price over the long term only, ignoring short-term and cyclical movements. But growth in the share price needs to be sustained by a growth in the business.

## DEFINITION OF GROWTH

Growth is not, for this purpose, assessed as growth in turnover, assets employed, or even profit for its own sake. Real growth is measured in earnings per share—that is the profit after tax attributable to shareholders, divided by the number of shares. A company that doubles its sales and profits by acquisition but trebles the number of its shares (excluding scrip issues of course) does not have real growth. Indeed those shareholders who have held shares while the company expanded will be worse off. If the market price remains a fixed multiple of the earnings, then they will have lost one-third of their capital as a result of the "expansion".

## CONTROL OF BORROWING, LIQUIDITY AND ASSETS

As a general rule the stock market will give a share a good rating, and its share price will move upwards in line with growth in earnings per share if the latter can be attained regularly in conjunction with growth in "assets per share", control of borrowings and liquidity. "Assets per share" or "net worth" is found by dividing the sum of capital and reserves by the number of shares. In the normal well-run business it tends to grow at the same rate as earnings per share. Borrowings are important to gear up profits for shareholders. A good management will borrow up to a reasonable level to exploit those benefits for their shareholders.

However, if there is too much borrowing, shareholders can be put at risk; indeed the stock market views with suspicion companies that are "highly geared". Liquidity is important on the one hand simply to protect the company's trading position in the event of unforeseen circumstances (such as a postal strike), and on the other to enable acquisitions to be made without dependence on the issue of equity. Borrowings, liquidity and the underlying assets position are important for the stability of a business and when a company ceases to control these, investment analysts are quick to note the fact and a company's share price can be re-rated downwards before any crisis results.

One other important factor that companies need to watch is the growth of shares issued. A too rapid growth can make the market in the shares unstable, subject to substantial fluctuations and thus unattractive to investors.

An ambitious management seeking growth through acquisitions must preserve the balance between earnings per share, assets per share, borrowings, liquidity and the issue of new shares if it is not to court disaster. But if while acquiring they achieve the right balance, the rewards to the company can be great. The more cautious management not making acquisitions runs less risk of losing control but its rewards will be smaller.

Take this example. A service-based company became over-geared. It made one major acquisition using a too high proportion of debt and found it had difficulties in borrowing for purely trading purposes. It then became completely dependent on its share price for its next acquisition. At this stage a major shareholder became disgruntled and unloaded his shares as a result of which the share price collapsed. The "next" acquisition, therefore, could not take place. The company did not go broke but as its share price plummeted it lost the growth rating it held in the stock market. It has not as yet recovered its rating nor is it likely to do so.

Some companies have grown so fast that they have issued large amounts of new shares. This was a major factor in the collapse of the conglomerate glamour shares over the past few years. By increasing the market for their shares so rapidly they became very sensitive to speculation—and once the share price goes down it becomes very difficult to surface again.

Another example relates to liquidity. A profitable retail company took over another making losses in the expectation of turning it around quickly. The acquiring company had to borrow substantially to make the acquisition. The management problem proved more difficult than anticipated, the losses of the acquired company were not stemmed and a liquidity crisis resulted. The margin of risk was not covered by the company. In this particular case shareholders were lucky as they were taken over on generous terms. Although this chapter places the emphasis on the financial aspects of acquisition, clearly a great many management aspects are also involved. Where one management might easily turn a loss-making company into a profit-making one, another might find it too difficult.

A company intending to grow by acquisition needs considerable financial control to ensure a real growth. The assets and earnings being acquired, the price paid and how it is financed, the borrowings and liquidity of both acquiring and acquired all have a vital and irreversible effect on the future of the acquiring company. Once the price is paid it is generally too late to try to renegotiate the terms.

## PLANNING AND EVALUATION OF OBJECTIVES

Let us now consider a problem that many top executives will have experienced. Company *A* looks attractive on a variety of criteria and for a proposed bid price 25 per cent up on the current market price, the sums suggest that earnings per share will benefit and that the balance of borrowing, assets per share and liquidity will be retained. The bid is announced. However, the other company resists, producing (typically) splendid profit forecasts and surplus properties. Expectations are raised in the market place; advisers recommend an increased bid.

The chief executive has to make his decision in an excited atmosphere. Typically before he knows where he is, the final bid price (now recommended by the contesting board of directors) is 75 per cent above the pre-bid price. But is it attractive at this price? Will he get real growth? If he knew before making the bid that the maximum price he should offer—the point beyond which it was no longer attractive—was perhaps 40 per cent up on the pre-bid price, his strategy and decision would be different. This maximum or cut-off price can come best from the type of planning process outlined below.

The first stage in the process is the setting of overall corporate goals for earnings per share, assets per share, the scale of borrowing and liquidity and the amount of shares that can be issued. The goals for earnings and assets per share evolve from the planning process and would be essentially attainable and not "pie in the sky" figures. The liquidity and borrowing ratios would be those that the stock market would feel reasonable (and even slightly conservative) for this kind of business. The amount of shares to be issued would be such that the market for shares would not be destabilised.

The second stage is to indicate what is the gap between growth from internal sources and the overall objectives. This is the gap to be filled from acquisitions. This gap is in earnings per share and not simply earnings.

The third stage is to set financial criteria for acquisitions. These criteria arise on the one hand from the amount of resources available for acquisitions—mainly the amount of equity that can be issued—and on the other from the earnings required to fill the gap. This can be shown in the following example.

1    The objective is to increase EPS by 10 per cent per annum
2    The limit on the growth of shares issued is 10 per cent per annum
3    Therefore the growth in total equity earnings must be 21 per cent per annum
4    Internal growth provides (say) 3 per cent per annum
5    Acquisitions are required to provide 18 per cent per annum
6    Thus 10 per cent of the equity must earn 18 per cent of the earnings or the earnings per share of each new share issued must be 1.8 times the existing earnings per share.

As long as acquisitions are made that satisfy this last condition then the earnings per share gap will be filled and the overall corporate objective of 10 per cent per annum attained.

Similar criteria are evolved for assets per share and the borrowing and liquidity limits satisfied. Once these criteria are evolved a maximum or cut-off price (with a specific equity/debt mix) can be established for each potential acquisition. It is important to recognise that this maximum price depends on a thorough analysis of each potential acquisition including the making of reasonable estimates of movements in earnings, cash and assets in the future after the acquisition—and of course including the effects of any integration measures proposed.

Using this type of approach the chief executive of the growth-oriented company will now be faced with a list of companies that are attractive for acquisition on marketing (i.e. non-financial) grounds (Figure 7:1).

| COMPANY | MAXIMUM PRICE AS PERCENTAGE OF CURRENT PRICE |
|---------|------------------------------------|
| A | 125 |
| B | 220 |
| C | 180 |
| D | 150 |
| E | 140 |

FIGURE 7:1    MAXIMUM PRICE TABLE
Clearly the chief executive will give top priority to acquiring company B.

Broadly speaking, companies making acquisitions either shake up the acquired company or leave it more or less alone. The former leads to an aggressive strategy while the latter leads to a negotiated settlement. In the case of quoted companies, prices in contested bids tend to average 75 per cent above the pre-bid price. For the agreed bids, the price premium is typically 25 per cent. Clearly then, the "maximum price" estimated for a potential acquisition which is attractive because of major changes to be made needs to be at least 75 per cent above the current price to reduce the risk of failure. Such a high margin is not needed in the case of potential acquisitions where agreed bids are desired. While the discussion has been in terms of the acquisition of quoted companies, it is also important to calculate maximum prices for potential unquoted companies.

Sometimes companies overprice their acquisitions because they get trapped in a contested bid (and counter bids); sometimes it is because of miscalculation. Sometimes one wonders how it occurred at all. A major retail company acquired another, not so profitable, in the same line of business. A very high price was paid—several times the underlying assets—and although profits were raised substantially, and although considerable management effort was put into the acquisition, the company did not get real growth. The effort and expense left shareholders no better off than they would have been without the acquisition. At least they did not lose but how much would they have benefited if this effort had been directed usefully?

A one-product company in its diversification policy acquired an efficient and profitable retailing operation. It acquired for cash at a price seventeen times earnings and almost three times the assets used. At one stroke, it had reduced its own assets per share by 7 per cent, reduced its borrowing power and not benefited its earnings per share compared to such alternatives as using preference shares—the favourite of finance-oriented companies— where after-tax rates of return of 10 per cent are currently available.

The game of growth through acquisition is dangerous and requires a system of financial planning which can reduce the risks of over-gearing, paying too high a price, and so forth, and generally enable the opportunities of real and balanced growth to be attained. A crucial element of such a system is the calculation of maximum cut-off prices based on the company's overall objectives.

# CHAPTER 8

# *Financial Ratio Analysis*

*by* Adrian Buckley

*Management Consultant, 10 The Drive, Esher, Surrey*

In competitive markets it is desirable for any company to find some way in which performance can be compared to other firms operating in the same industry. Besides providing the framework for effective inter-company comparisons, management ratios can be used as the basis for a system of financial control through management by exception.

# 8 : FINANCIAL RATIO ANALYSIS

The measure of company performance which has gained most ground in British industry over the past few years is growth in earnings per share. This criterion forms the performance objective of some of the most successful UK companies. For example, the Beecham Group (the outstanding company in the *Financial Times* Ordinary Share Index over recent years) seeks a growth rate of 15 per cent compound in earnings per share. Mr J D Slater, chairman and managing director of Slater Walker Securities is on record as stating that his company's objective is "a smooth and regular growth in earnings per share". The use of management techniques, improvements in efficiency and the method selected to finance expansion all have the same ultimate objective of maximising the return achieved on shareholders' funds and earnings per share. For this reason, the growth in earnings per share is one of the prime determinants of a company's stock market rating.

## GROWTH IN EARNINGS PER SHARE

The earnings per share ratio focuses upon the return that a company has achieved relative to the funds invested by the equity shareholders. It is measured by dividing the profit available for distribution to the equity shareholders by the company's total number of such ordinary shares. For this purpose, "profit" is taken to mean the amount left after deduction of debenture interest, taxation and preference shareholders' dividend.

In the numerical example shown in Figures 8:1 and 8:2 earnings per share for the year 1967 amounted to £0.1011. This is found by taking the profit before charging the ordinary dividend (£16 175) and dividing the result by 160 000, the number of ordinary shares in issue.

## HYPOTHETICAL COMPANY LIMITED
### Balance sheet as at 31 December 1967 and 31 December 1968

| | 1967 | | 1968 | |
|---|---|---|---|---|
| FIXED ASSETS | | | | |
| Land and buildings at cost | | £80 000 | | £80 000 |
| Plant and machinery— | | | | |
| cost | £78 000 | | £108 000 | |
| depreciation | 42 000 | 36 000 | 58 200 | 49 800 |
| Fixtures and fittings— | | | | |
| cost | £6 500 | | £7 000 | |
| depreciation | 4 000 | 2 500 | 4 700 | 2 300 |
| | | 118 500 | | 132 100 |
| CURRENT ASSETS | | | | |
| Stock | 48 000 | | 51 250 | |
| Debtors | 30 500 | | 35 500 | |
| Bank balance and cash | 854 | | — | |
| | 79 354 | | 86 750 | |
| CURRENT LIABILITIES | | | | |
| Creditors | 38 500 | | 39 000 | |
| Dividends | 4 400 | | 5 400 | |
| Taxation | 12 503 | | 17 130 | |
| Debenture interest | 176 | | 176 | |
| Bank overdraft | — | | 1 019 | |
| | 55 579 | | 62 725 | |
| NET CURRENT ASSETS | | 23 775 | | 24 025 |
| | | 142 275 | | 156 125 |
| FINANCED BY: | | | | |
| Issued capital | | | | |
| 4% preference shares | | 10 000 | | 10 000 |
| Ordinary shares of | | | | |
| £0.25 (5s) each[1] | | 40 000 | | 60 000 |
| | | 50 000 | | 70 000 |
| General reserve | | 50 000 | | 32 000 |
| Profit and loss account | | 32 275 | | 44 125 |
| | | 132 275 | | 146 125 |
| Debenture loan 6% stock | | 10 000 | | 10 000 |
| | | 142 275 | | 156 125 |

FIGURE 8:1     NUMERICAL EXAMPLE: BALANCE SHEET
Example balance sheet, providing data from which several ratios can be calculated.

[1]In this particular case an issue of bonus shares has apparently complicated measurement of the rate of growth in earnings per share. The bonus issue must be ignored for this purpose, with the total number of ordinary shares for 1968 being taken as unchanged from 1967.

## HYPOTHETICAL COMPANY LIMITED

Profit and loss account for the year ended
31 December 1967 and 31 December 1968

|  | | | 1967 | | 1968 |
|---|---|---|---|---|---|
| Turnover | | | £350 000 | | £395 000 |
| Profit before interest and | | | | | |
| taxation | | | £29 600 | | £35 600 |
| Debenture interest | | | 600 | | 600 |
| | | | 29 000 | | 35 000 |
| Corporation tax | | | 12 425 | | 15 750 |
| Profit after tax | | | 16 575 | | 19 250 |
| Dividends | | | | | |
| Preference (net) | 230 | | | | |
| Income tax | 170 | 400 | | 400 | |
| Ordinary·dividend (net) | 2 350 | | | | |
| Income tax | 1 650 | 4 000 | 4 400 | 5 000 | 5 400 |
| Profit after tax and dividend | | | 12 175 | | 13 850 |
| Transfer to general reserve | | | 2 000 | | 2 000 |
| | | | 10 175 | | 11 850 |
| Add opening balance on profit and loss account | | | 22 100 | | 32 275 |
| Balance carried forward | | | 32 275 | | 44 125 |

FIGURE 8:2    NUMERICAL EXAMPLE: PROFIT AND LOSS ACCOUNT
The data included in this profit and loss account is directly associated with the specimen balance sheet in Figure 8:1.

In terms of measuring growth of earnings per share over a period of time it is, of course, necessary to recognise the effect of capitalisation issues of shares, by the way of bonus issues, for example. Thus in the numerical example of Figure 8:1 the impact of the bonus issue of shares made during 1968 should be ignored. The relevant earnings figures per share are, therefore, £0.1011 for 1967 and £0.1178 for 1968, a growth rate of 16.5 per cent.

## Return on equity

Closely allied to the concept of earnings per share is return on equity. This ratio compares profit available for ordinary shareholders (as already defined) with the total funds which, on the balance sheet,

|  | 1967 | 1968 |
|---|---|---|
| Earnings for ordinary shareholders | £16 175 | £18 850 |
| Equity assets |  |  |
|   Ordinary capital | £40 000 | £60 000 |
|   General reserve | £50 000 | £32 000 |
|   Profit and loss account | £32 275 | £44 125 |
|  | £122 275 | £136 125 |
| Return on equity | 13.23% | 13.85% |

FIGURE 8:3    CALCULATION OF RETURN ON EQUITY

The figures used here are derived from the balance sheet of Figure 8:1. Profit available for ordinary shareholders is compared to the total shareholders' funds.

represent shareholders' funds. These are calculated by taking all assets at book value and deducting fixed interest loans, creditors and preference capital. Return on shareholders' equity for 1967 and 1968 can be calculated as the example in Figure 8:3 shows. It can be seen that the growth in return on equity is not as great as that of earnings per share. This is because the base of comparison in the case of return on equity is bolstered by ploughed back profits, whilst in the example given the base in the earnings per share calculation remains constant.

In assessing overall company performance, it is necessary to distinguish clearly between the role of return on equity and return on capital employed. Return on equity takes into account how assets have been financed; in the example above debenture interest was deducted as a charge before calculating profit. Similarly, in setting the base for comparison only ordinary shareholders' funds were taken into account—gearing was excluded. Specifically this means that the percentage which best reflects the company's total management effort, including its financial strategy, is return on equity.

## Return on capital employed

The definition of return on capital varies from one analyst to another, and there appears to be no universally accepted interpretation of the ratio. Because of this, it is necessary when using this criterion to be precise in defining terms. Here the denominator of the ratio is made up of *net assets*, that is, fixed assets plus net current

|  | 1967 | 1968 |
|---|---|---|
| Profit before interest and taxation | £29 600 | £35 600 |
| Capital employed | | |
| Fixed assets | £118 500 | £132 100 |
| Net current assets | £23 775 | £24 025 |
| | £142 275 | £156 125 |
| Return on capital employed | 20.80% | 22.80% |

FIGURE 8:4    CALCULATION OF RETURN ON CAPITAL EMPLOYED
One basis for the calculation of the return on capital employed. There are other variations, according to the preference of the individual analyst involved. When using this ratio, therefore, it is important to ensure that comparative results have been derived on a common basis.

assets (net current assets are current assets less current liabilities). The numerator is given by the profit before deducting loan interest and taxation.

Figure 8:4 sets out an example of a return on capital employed calculation based on the 1967 and 1968 accounts and balance sheet. This ratio provides a means of judging how efficiently operational management has utilised the total stock of assets under its control. How these assets are financed is not material. The criterion of return on capital employed makes no distinction between funds raised by equity capital, preference shares or fixed interest stock. Therefore, in terms of using ratios to compare the relative performance of operational management in an industry, it is this ratio, rather than return on equity, which should be used.

## PROFIT ON SALES, AND SALES ON CAPITAL EMPLOYED

The first of these two ratios focuses upon profit margins achieved by a company. It acts as a guide, in conjunction with the "sales on capital employed" ratio, in explaining variations in return on capital. This percentage, as its name implies, compares (pre-interest, pre-tax) profit with turnover. Broadly, a high ratio indicates the extent to which costs have been kept down by efficient production and administration, and the ability of a company, through its marketing effort, to achieve profitable pricing.

The ratio of sales to capital employed, sometimes referred to as the rate of turnover of capital, shows how fully a company is employing its capital. As a measure of the use of resources, generally speaking, the higher this ratio, the more intense is the utilisation of capital. Rate of turnover of capital is calculated by the comparison of sales to capital employed.

It should be apparent from the definitions of the above two ratios that their interaction helps to explain variations in return on capital employed. This is clear from the equation:

$$\frac{\text{Profit}}{\text{Capital employed}} = \frac{\text{Profit}}{\text{Sales}} \times \frac{\text{Sales}}{\text{Capital employed}}$$

The numerical example referred to throughout (Figures 8:1 and 8:2) shows that during 1967 the above ratios amounted to:

Profit on sales: $\dfrac{29\,600}{350\,000} \times 100 = 8.46\%$

Sales on capital employed: $\dfrac{350\,000}{142\,275} = 2.46$

## OTHER PERFORMANCE RATIOS

By breaking down the above ratios still further, additional information can be obtained. For example, factors accounting for variations in the ratio of sales to capital employed may be highlighted by looking at the ratios:

1 Sales to fixed assets
2 Sales to net current assets

because capital employed is made up of fixed assets and net current assets. Similarly by studying the components that make up net current assets the analysis can be taken further, for example to "sales to stocks", "sales to debtors", and so on. During the course of this brief introduction to business ratios, it is impossible to comment upon every ratio. For more detail on this topic, see *Managing Money and Finance* by G P E Clarkson and B J Elliott, Gower Press, 1969. However, Figure 8:5 shows how the process can be extended to focus upon other relationships.

## CREDIT RATIOS

So far in this review of ratio analysis, the concern has been with performance ratios. From the standpoint of the creditor, information about the strength of a firm's financial capacity can be gleaned from a study of certain ratios, of which the most frequently used are:

1 Current assets to current liabilities
2 Liquid assets to current liabilities

The former ratio, often called the current ratio, is a guide to the strength of a firm's working capital. Too low a ratio in comparison with other firms in a similar line of business may be a sign of strains on liquidity. But an element of bias may be inherent because this ratio includes "stock" in the item "current assets" and accounting practice values stock at the lower of cost or market value—whilst in fact subsequent selling price might be greatly in excess of this figure, although of course such stock may not be turned into cash for some time.

Because of this, the more frequently used short-term debt-paying ratio compares current assets excluding stock with current liabilities. This ratio, often called the "liquid ratio", thereby concentrates upon those assets that can readily be turned into cash. Short-term creditors are therefore interested in this ratio as a guideline in assessing a firm's liquidity.

# LIMITATIONS OF RATIO ANALYSIS

One of the most important claims made in favour of using ratio analysis is that it enables the firm to highlight deficiencies in its management performance through comparisons with other firms in the same industry. But taking figures from published balance sheets without any further refinement is undoubtedly the best way to obtain misleading results in this respect! This is, in part, because of the multiplicity of accounting methods adopted by UK companies. For example, fixed assets might be shown in the balance sheet of one company at cost less depreciation. Cost could be the price paid fifty or more years ago; and in the case of freehold land this would give rise to a material undervaluation. Another firm in the same industry may show its assets at, say, current revaluation.

Similarly methods for calculating depreciation vary from firm to firm even within the same industry. Moreover depreciation will probably be based on the cost or written down value of an asset. With assets bought at varying times in different companies' histories the movement in the purchasing power of money will mean that even if two companies are applying the same method of providing for depreciation they will (because of the different capital base values) write off different sums for depreciation.

How assets are financed produces another bias against easy inter-firm comparisons. For example two retail chains might be identical except that one has purchased the freeholds of its shops and shows them in its balance sheet as fixed assets whilst the other firm rents its premises. Then the return on capital ratios of the two groups will be widely divergent.

In practical terms, operating ratios are a useful monitoring tool. Their use, like all management techniques, demands judgement. Given this judgement there are various sources of data on company operating ratios analysed by industry that can be harnessed to improve management results. Interfirm Comparison Limited, sponsored by the BIM, offers a service which produces a series of operating percentages for various industrial activities. This organisation specifically aims to iron out the limitations mentioned above. This it does by asking participating companies to provide data about operations on a comparable basis. Each participant receives a report

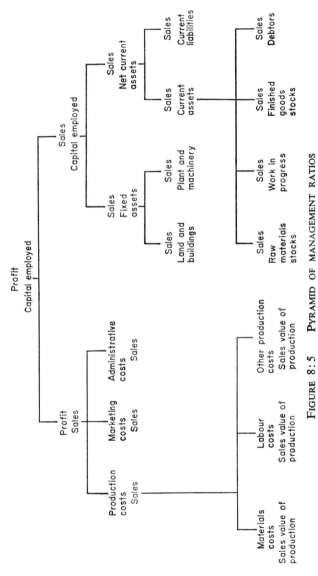

FIGURE 8:5    PYRAMID OF MANAGEMENT RATIOS

This chart shows some of the ratios which can be calculated at various levels in an organisation and demonstrates their interrelationship.

interpreting the ratios and detailing the comparative ratios of each other participant in its industrial sector. The other responding companies are not mentioned by name but are identified merely by an anonymous number. The pyramid of ratios shown in Figure 8:5 gives some idea of the kinds of ratios highlighted in the course of an inter-firm comparison.

Similarly the publication *Business Ratios*, produced by Dunn and Bradstreet and Moodies Services sets out numerous ratios based on the analysis of accounts of a wide range of companies broken down by industry.

## MANAGEMENT USE OF OPERATING RATIOS

Following analysis of comparable companies' operating ratios, preferably through an inter-firm comparison, strengths and weaknesses of a company may be highlighted. In the light of identified deficiencies, targets designed to improve efficiency can be set for divisional management.

Setting clearly defined—and agreed—targets provides a strong motivation to divisional management. From the standpoint of the manager, he is aware that success in achieving standards is being recognised by head office; and from the viewpoint of the head office, those managers who regularly meet agreed performance are brought to notice as are other managers who constantly fail to achieve targets and whose operations demand further scrutiny. What is more, in a company with a philosophy of decentralised management, regular comparison of achieved ratios against target standards acts as part of the system of control through management by exception.

This system of financial control is, in fact, part of the mechanism adopted by Mr Arnold Weinstock of GEC as a monitor of management achievement. The ratios pinpointed in the GEC system of evaluation and control are:

1    Profit to capital employed
2    Profit to sales
3    Sales to capital employed
4    Sales to fixed assets
5    Sales to stocks

6     Sales per employee
7     Profits per employee

As part of the control system, which may vary from one company to another, operating ratio analysis is an effective facet of the mix of management information by which a head office can monitor divisional performance. But it must be emphasised that such analysis is not in itself a substitute for management judgement; judgement is integral to the establishment of a control system by management ratios, and above all in their interpretation; they can only tell the head office where things go wrong and cannot indicate how they should be put right.

# CHAPTER 9

# Risk, Return and Discounted Cash Flow

*by* Balint Bodroghy

*Director, Peter Ward Associates (Interplan) Limited*

Discounted cash flow techniques can help to clarify decision-making since they take account of time. Payments to be made next year do in fact cost less than equal payments made today. Simple computing aids are available to take the tedium out of discount calculations. DCF is being applied increasingly in industry and risk analysis is a logical extension.

# 9 : / RISK, RETURN AND DISCOUNTED CASH FLOW

Financial analysts have for years used the concept of discounted cash flow to assess the value of securities. The technique is also being adopted by industry because investing in plant and productive facilities is seen to differ little in principle from investing in stocks and bonds.

Financial analysts are beginning to migrate to industrial and commercial firms in increasing numbers, and their cash flow techniques have now become accepted practice. The principles and application of DCF to industrial problems are not difficult to understand.

## ECONOMIC EFFECT

The object of financial analysis is to measure the economic sense of a proposal. The term "economic sense" is used instead of "profitability" as a better translation of *rentabilité*, the preferred concept. The obvious measure of economic sense is the relationship of cost to economic effect, which is often, though not always, the profitability.

Cost must include all costs—that is, all money spent in connection with a proposed project, throughout its economic life. Thus, by definition, costs must include taxes, because taxes represent money spent, but take no account of depreciation since no payment of cash is involved. The expenses incurred over the years may be called the negative component of cash flow.

In past assessments of industrial projects, a distinction was drawn between capital expenditure on plant and equipment, which was amortised over a number of years, and expense connected with operations. This practice can be misleading and is undesirable in financial analysis.

The artificiality of the distinction is exemplified by the common

111

practice in coalmining of considering the cost of sinking a mine shaft as capital, but the cost of tunnels as expense, although coal may be produced by both (or neither). The distinction is also ingrained in our whole tax structure. In fact, capital expenditure and expense differ only with respect to time. Otherwise they are identical —it's all money of the same colour.

The economic effect must be similarly accounted over the life of the project. To permit a comparison with cost, the economic effect must be expressed in the same units as cost, even if the proposal is not intended to be profit making. A new bridge, for instance, may not be built to make a profit, but must have a measurable economic effect if financial analysis is to be applied. The economic effect over the years represents the positive component of cash flow.

The important point is that a distinction between capital expenditure and expense is artificial and should be eliminated in financial analysis. Unfortunately the distinction may be perpetuated in accounting until the tax allowance system is modernised in keeping with modern management practice.

Having estimated the negative and positive components of cash flow, we have in fact reduced the problem of a complex industrial project to that of a simple financial exercise: money is spent to achieve a desired effect. The only remaining task is to find a relationship between cost and effect.

## Example 1    Rent or buy decision

Consider the problem of choosing a heating system for a house. It will be assumed that the house is to be demolished after five years, and that the heating system can be salvaged. Assume also that it takes a year to install the equipment.

One enterprise, which we shall call Cashco, suggests an installation costing £300; offers to buy back the installation after five years for £100; and estimates the annual fuel bill at £200. A guarantee covers all service costs for the first five years.

Another company, Hireco, offers to lease the equipment for five years, with an annual billing of £250, including fuel and service. Which is the better offer? Obviously, the one that costs less.

Traditional thinking would suggest that the cash offer, counting £40 a year depreciation, plus £200 a year fuel and service, is £10 a year cheaper than the leasing offer at £250 a year. More accurate analysis starts by establishing cash flows. The result for this example is shown in Figure 9 : 1.

Comparing the cash flows for Cashco and Hireco, which proposition offers the better bargain? In the cash offer the total outlay over five years is £1200, in the other case £1250, but the manner of payment is totally different. Obviously, money paid out at a future date hurts less than money paid out today (which is why moneylenders flourish in the world). But how much less?

| | YEAR | 0 | 1 | 2 | 3 | 4 | 5 |
|---|---|---|---|---|---|---|---|
| CASHCO | | | | | | | |
| | Negative | (300) | (200) | (200) | (200) | (200) | (200) |
| | Positive | | | | | | 100 |
| | Net | (300) | (200) | (200) | (200) | (200) | (100) |
| HIRECO | | | | | | | |
| | Negative | — | (250) | (250) | (250) | (250) | (250) |
| | Positive | — | — | — | — | — | — |
| | Net | — | (250) | (250) | (250) | (250) | (250) |

FIGURE 9:1    CASH FLOW COMPARISONS BETWEEN THE HIRECO AND CASHCO ALTERNATIVES.

Tabulation of cash flows in this way is the first step towards setting up a DCF calculation.

The answer to the dilemma is some form of discounting. One must reduce (or discount) the effect of the pain felt at present as a result of money spent in the future. The mathematics of the operation is

$$DCF = CF \ (1 + x)^{-n}$$

where *DCF* is discounted cash flow; *CF* is cash flow; *x* is the discount rate; and *n* the year. The values of $(1 + x)^{-n}$ for the usual range of discount rates are given in Figure 9 : 2. In Figure 9 : 3 several discount factors have been tested in order to demonstrate the effect of discounting on the two proposals. At a discount rate of 5 per cent the two alternatives have equal present costs. Below that rate the

9—GTMT • •

| YEAR/RATE | 2.5% | 3% | 5% | 7% | 7.5% | 10% | 15% | 20% | 25% | 30% | 35% | 40% | 50% |
|---|---|---|---|---|---|---|---|---|---|---|---|---|---|
| −3 | 107.7 | 109.3 | 115.8 | 122.5 | 124.2 | 133.1 | 152.1 | 172.8 | 195.3 | 219.7 | 246 | 274.4 | 337.5 |
| −2 | 105.1 | 106.1 | 110.2 | 114.5 | 115.6 | 121 | 132.2 | 144 | 156.2 | 169 | 182.2 | 196 | 225 |
| −1 | 102.5 | 103 | 105 | 107 | 107.5 | 110 | 115 | 120 | 125 | 130 | 135 | 140 | 150 |
| 0 | 100 | 100 | 100 | 100 | 100 | 100 | 100 | 100 | 100 | 100 | 100 | 100 | 100 |
| 1 | 97.6 | 97.1 | 95.2 | 93.5 | 93 | 90.9 | 87 | 83.3 | 80 | 76.9 | 74.1 | 71.4 | 66.7 |
| 2 | 95.2 | 94.3 | 90.7 | 87.3 | 86.5 | 82.6 | 75.6 | 69.4 | 64 | 59.2 | 54.9 | 51 | 44.4 |
| 3 | 92.9 | 91.5 | 86.4 | 81.6 | 80.5 | 75.1 | 65.8 | 57.9 | 51 | 45.5 | 40.6 | 36.4 | 29.6 |
| 4 | 90.6 | 88.8 | 82.3 | 76.3 | 74.9 | 68.3 | 57.2 | 48.2 | 41 | 35 | 30.1 | 26 | 19.8 |
| 5 | 88.4 | 86.3 | 78.4 | 71.3 | 69.7 | 62.1 | 49.7 | 40.2 | 32.8 | 26.9 | 22.3 | 18.6 | 13.2 |
| 6 | 86.2 | 83.7 | 74.6 | 66.6 | 64.8 | 56.4 | 43.2 | 33.5 | 26.2 | 20.7 | 16.5 | 13.3 | 8.8 |
| 7 | 84.1 | 81.3 | 71.1 | 62.3 | 60.3 | 51.3 | 37.6 | 27.9 | 21 | 15.9 | 12.2 | 9.5 | 5.9 |
| 8 | 82.1 | 78.9 | 67.7 | 58.2 | 56.1 | 46.7 | 32.7 | 23.3 | 16.8 | 12.3 | 9.1 | 6.8 | 3.9 |
| 9 | 80.1 | 76.6 | 64.5 | 54.4 | 52.2 | 42.4 | 28.4 | 19.4 | 13.4 | 9.4 | 6.7 | 4.8 | 2.6 |
| 10 | 78.1 | 74.4 | 61.4 | 50.8 | 48.5 | 38.6 | 24.7 | 16.2 | 10.7 | 7.3 | 5 | 3.5 | 1.7 |
| 11 | 76.2 | 72.2 | 58.5 | 47.5 | 45.1 | 35 | 21.5 | 13.5 | 8.6 | 5.6 | 3.7 | 2.5 | 1.2 |
| 12 | 74.4 | 70.1 | 55.7 | 44.4 | 42 | 31.9 | 18.7 | 11.2 | 6.9 | 4.3 | 2.7 | 1.8 | 0.8 |
| 13 | 72.6 | 68.1 | 53 | 41.5 | 39.1 | 29 | 16.3 | 9.3 | 5.5 | 3.3 | 2 | 1.3 | 0.5 |
| 14 | 70.8 | 66.1 | 50.5 | 38.8 | 36.3 | 26.3 | 14.1 | 7.8 | 4.4 | 2.5 | 1.5 | 0.9 | 0.3 |
| 15 | 69 | 64.2 | 48.1 | 36.2 | 33.8 | 23.9 | 12.3 | 6.5 | 3.5 | 2 | 1.1 | 0.6 | 0.2 |
| 16 | 67.4 | 62.3 | 45.8 | 33.9 | 31.4 | 21.8 | 10.7 | 5.4 | 2.8 | 1.5 | 0.8 | 0.5 | 0.2 |
| 17 | 65.7 | 60.5 | 43.6 | 31.7 | 29.2 | 19.8 | 9.3 | 4.5 | 2.3 | 1.2 | 0.6 | 0.3 | 0.1 |
| 18 | 64.1 | 58.7 | 41.6 | 29.6 | 27.2 | 18 | 8.1 | 3.8 | 1.8 | 0.9 | 0.4 | 0.2 | |
| 19 | 62.6 | 57 | 39.6 | 27.6 | 25.3 | 16.4 | 7 | 3.1 | 1.4 | 0.7 | 0.3 | 0.2 | |
| 20 | 61 | 55.4 | 37.7 | 25.8 | 23.5 | 14.9 | 6.1 | 2.6 | 1.2 | 0.5 | 0.2 | 0.1 | |

FIGURE 9:2   TABLE OF DISCOUNT FACTORS

Useful range of discount factors. The discounted cash flow (DCF) is found by using the appropriate values of cash flow (CF) and discount factor (f) in the formula:

$$DCF = \frac{CF \times f}{100}$$

Cashco option is cheaper. Above 5 per cent the Hireco offer becomes the better proposition.

At this point the financial analyst stops and judgement takes over. The owner is now in a position to make a subjective decision on the basis of objective information: the time cost of the two proposals.

The discount rate in this context can be properly thought of as the pain killing effect of time—future rather than past. Pain being subjective, its effects will vary from person to person. Similarly, the acceptable discount rate is also subject to the effects of personal (or corporate) environment, physiology, and preference. More will be said of this later.

| | YEAR | 0 | 1 | 2 | 3 | 4 | 5 | TOTAL |
|---|---|---|---|---|---|---|---|---|
| Discount Factor = 0 | CASHCO | (300) | (200) | (200) | (200) | (200) | (100) | (1200) |
| | HIRECO | — | (250) | (250) | (250) | (250) | (250) | (1250) |
| Discount Factor = 5% | CASHCO | (300) | (190) | (181) | (171) | (165) | (78) | (1085) |
| | HIRECO | — | (238) | (227) | (216) | (206) | (196) | (1083) |
| Discount Factor = 10% | CASHCO | (300) | (182) | (165) | (150) | (137) | (62) | (996) |
| | HIRECO | — | (227) | (207) | (188) | (171) | (155) | (948) |

FIGURE 9:3     DISCOUNT TABLES FOR CASHCO AND HIRECO

Effects of different rates of discounting. The choice between renting or buying depends on the percentage rate to be applied.

The dilemma of the central heating installation was resolved by comparing the "present cost" of the two proposals under various assumptions about discount rate. The same reasoning may be applied to other investment opportunities by calculating their "present value".

## Example 2    Company acquisition

In cold financial terms the value of an investment is a function of its ability to produce cash in future years, and has no relationship to original cost or past performance. For instance, the value of a steel plant built for £50M a year ago becomes equal to its scrap value unless it promises to produce steel economically (and thus generate cash) in the foreseeable future.

Consider, for example, the problem of acquiring a business as a going concern. A manufacturer claims to have assets worth £750 000, based on first cost less straight-line depreciation over ten years. An examination of the books by a prospective purchaser shows that after a gradual decline in turnover, sales have held steady at £800 000 during the last five years. Market explorations forecast no further decline in business. On past record the company's cash flow (the sum of profit after tax and depreciation) is £80 000 a year and future increases in labour costs will just about match improvements in productivity.

The question is: how much to offer against the asking price of £750 000? The buying company is unwilling to trust the sales forecasts beyond seven years, but feels that land and other assets may realise £250 000 if forced to sell at that time. The buying company's criterion for investments of this type is a discount of 15 per cent, giving the cash flow forecast shown in Figure 9:4 (a).

| (a) YEAR | 0 | 1 | 2 | 3 | 4 | 5 | 6 | 7 | 8 | PRESENT VALUE |
|---|---|---|---|---|---|---|---|---|---|---|
| Cash flow | — | 80 | 80 | 80 | 80 | 80 | 80 | 80 | 250 | |
| DCF (at 15%) | — | 70 | 60 | 52 | 46 | 40 | 34 | 30 | 82 | 414 |
| (b) YEAR | 0 | 1 | 2 | 3 | 4 | 5 | 6 | 7 | 8 | PRESENT VALUE |
| Cash flow | — | 80 | 90 | 110 | 120 | 120 | 120 | 120 | 250 | |
| DCF (at 15%) | — | 70 | 68 | 72 | 68 | 60 | 52 | 46 | 82 | 518 |

FIGURE 9:4     CASH FLOW TABLES FOR COMPANY EVALUATION
In (a) a steady profit of £80 000 a year is assumed, whilst in (b) a gradual improvement in profitability has been forecast. These tables provide the basis for evaluating the company discussed in Example 2.

The company as a going concern, does not appear to be worth much more than about £414 000 in the view of this particular buyer. However, there are two considerations which could modify the buyer's view. One of his problems is that although funds are not available for investment, there are not many opportunities in fields

116

that fit in with the company's long-term policy. Hence he may have to compromise.

In addition, the buyer feels that the selling company has been ineffectively managed. There is a possibility, therefore, of improving performance. Although a careful study of the market shows that sales are not expected to increase, an improvement in net cash flow might gradually be achieved, under careful tutelage. Figure 9:4 (b) reflects this more optimistic view.

Reconsideration of the prospects for future cash flow has thus raised the buyer's assessment of the company's present value to £518 000. Hence, in negotiating this sale, either the asking and offering prices converge to a point somewhere between £400 000 and £500 000, or the transaction falls through.

Two observations in connection with the above examples are worth making. It is generally easier to forecast operating data (sales, prices and costs) than to forecast "scrap value" or "residual value" of fixed assets. An advantage of discounting is that, having stretched the time period of the study to the limits of the forecaster's confidence, the estimate of residual value becomes of relatively minor importance. An error of 50 per cent in valuation in the example makes a difference of only 8 per cent in the estimate of present value. A similar error in valuation would be completely unacceptable in other forms of assessment.

The other observation is that in discounting, the importance of cash earned (or spent) in the near future far outweighs that of long-term expectations or commitments. In the above example the buying company expects to achieve a 55 per cent improvement in total cash generation over eight years, nevertheless their estimate of present value increases by only 24 per cent (from £414 000 to £518 000) because the improvement occurs at a late date.

The emphasis of DCF is thus on the performance in the immediate future where forecasting is more reliable. As a corollary, DCF analysis tends to favour projects with rapid cash generation, that is projects that produce a dynamic economy.

## Example 3 Capital investment decision

Company acquisition is a particular case of financial analysis in which future cash flows and a selected discount rate are used to evaluate a price. In the more general case of capital investment, the price of the capital goods needed for the project is fixed in advance: a new plant will cost the same whether it will make a profit or not.

Thus, the task of the analyst is to determine whether the proposed project's cash flow is sufficient to satisfy the sponsor's criteria in relation to the magnitude of the investment. The problem is: given a known investment and a forecast of cash flow, what is the discount rate? (This is the inverse of present value calculations where the forecast cash flow and a chosen discount rate are used to determine the value of the investment.)

The process of finding the appropriate discount rate is one of trial and error: various rates are tried until the sum of the future cash flows equals the (known) present investment. The following arbitrary example illustrates the process.

An investment of £300 in plant generates a net cash flow of £100 a year for five years. Sale of the equipment in the sixth year realises £10. What is the appropriate discount rate?

By constructing the discount table shown in Figure 9:5, it is possible to find a rate of discount which equalises the "present value" and "present cost" of the investment. In this case, the result is about 20 per cent.

A further modification of the technique is needed to make it generally applicable. When large projects are undertaken, investment is usually spread over several years. Under these conditions discounting of some form must be applied to money invested as well as to money earned.

The practice of some companies is to charge interest (to discount) at bank rate during the construction period, regardless of later

| YEAR | 0 | 1 | 2 | 3 | 4 | 5 | 6 | TOTAL |
|---|---|---|---|---|---|---|---|---|
| Cash flow | (300) | 100 | 100 | 100 | 100 | 100 | 10 | 510 |
| Discounted at 10% | (300) | 90 | 83 | 75 | 68 | 62 | 6 | 384 |
| Discounted at 20% | (300) | 83 | 69 | 58 | 48 | 40 | 3 | 301 |
| Discounted at 30% | (300) | 77 | 59 | 45 | 35 | 27 | 2 | 245 |

FIGURE 9:5    TRIAL AND ERROR DISCOUNT TABLE
This table illustrates methods of calculating the effective discount rate by trial and error.

results. Other companies argue that there is no generic difference between money earned and money spent and, therefore, the same discount rate should apply in both cases. The latter view is more popular in North America, although it is by no means universally accepted.

The above example can be repeated to show what the effect would be if investment were to be spread over two years before production begins. The resulting table is shown in Figure 9 : 6.

By interpolation, the appropriate discount rate that equalises the last two columns of Figure 9 : 6 (or reduces the algebraic sum of the net cash flows to zero) is about 16 per cent, versus 20 per cent in the previous case. The effect of having to spend part of the money a year earlier is to make the project relatively less attractive (or "profitable") even though the absolute amounts of money spent and earned remain unchanged.

| [* *Derived from Figure 9:5*] | | | TOTAL | TOTAL* |
|---|---|---|---|---|
| YEAR | 1 | 0 | 1 & 0 | 1 to 6 |
| Cash flow | (150) | (150) | (300) | 510 |
| Discounted at 10% | (165) | (150) | (315) | 384 |
| Discounted at 20% | (180) | (150) | (330) | 301 |
| Discounted at 30% | (195) | (150) | (345) | 245 |

FIGURE 9:6     EFFECT OF ADVANCING THE INVESTMENT DATE

The tables of investment and return are the same as those used in Figure 9:5. In this case, however, the investment has to start earlier, being spread over the two years before the start of production.

The same general procedure is followed to establish discounted cash flow rates if periodic plant replacement is foreseen for later years, or for any other combination of positive and negative cash flows: by trial and error the discount rate is found that reduces the algebraic sum of the cash flow to zero.

## CHOICE OF INVESTMENT CRITERIA

It is time to take stock of the foregoing. A method has been demonstrated that permits the expression of the economic sense of a project by means of a number, the discount rate, that reflects the interplay of cost, effect and time. The discount rate is more relevant to the assessment of projects than other methods used at present because it takes the effect of time into logical consideration. Time-consciousness is DCF's only claim to fame, but that is sufficient to justify its use whenever more than a few pounds are at stake.

DCF in no way replaces judgement, since the technique itself makes no contribution to the choice of what is an acceptable discount rate. To use DCF effectively criteria for choosing the acceptable discount rate must first be established.

An impromptu survey of companies showed that a major manufacturer of industrial inorganic chemicals used 12 to 14 per cent DCF rate (after tax) as the border-zone of acceptability. Projects falling below 12 per cent were automatically rejected, projects above 14 per cent received favourable recommendation and those in between were restudied.

In contrast, a public utility company supplying natural gas to a major North American city used 8 per cent DCF rate as a preliminary screening criterion, while a company engaged in mass entertainment expected a minimum rate of 20 per cent.

Companies arrive at investment criteria on the basis of experience. The chosen rate reflects a combination of the average (or best) performance realised in existing installations, and the current availability of investment opportunities. In booming times the expectations rise, in slack times they fall until a level is reached (generally the level of past average performance) when investment in that particular industry becomes unattractive. Any cash on hand will then end up in Government bonds or similar securities until conditions improve, or the company will look around for opportunities to diversify in other industries.

The use of experience, or feel, to arrive at investment criteria is widely practised. It will be a reasonable guide as long as conditions remain unchanged, but the automatic application of "feel" may lead to disaster or missed opportunities if the underlying conditions are in a process of change, or if criteria derived from one industry are blindly applied in another during diversification.

The reason that the chemical company, the utility company, and the entertainment group use such widely varying investment criteria is that the inherent risks of these industries vary considerably.

A public utility operates as a guaranteed monopoly, with prices fixed by the Government in relation to changes in costs. The chemical company sells its products on five- to ten-year contracts with carefully defined renewal and renegotiation clauses, and the chief threat to profit is technical obsolescence. The entertainment group operates in the quicksands of fashion and taste.

The choice of investment criteria is an unconscious expression of the risks accepted by the investor. The relation between risk and expected return is obvious. It is codified in the rules of roulette, and it is recognised by everyone from widows to gun-runners throughout the world. But only rarely is a conscious attempt made by businessmen to analyse risk and relate to it their expectations of return.

## RISK ANALYSIS

Future efforts at financial analysis will be directed at evaluating in some numerical form a proposal's expected return (discount rate) and its associated risks (probability of achievement). Within a few years such analysis is likely to become standard practice in progressive companies since its adoption is becoming increasingly widespread and computer programs for handling the tedious calculations are available.

The adoption of risk analysis by a few companies in a given industry will tighten the belt of competition another notch, leaving a little less breathing space for others. Companies practising risk analysis will make fewer mistakes, and will move (often profitably) into situations rejected by others on the basis of feel.

The technique of DCF can be readily adapted to the assessment of risk by introducing the concept of probability into the estimate of future cash flow. For example, the choice between the two heating systems can be restated in the following probabilistic terms.

The offer by Hireco is subjected to very few uncertainties. A contract would be signed covering the obligations of both parties regardless of changes in weather, accidental breakdowns, or changes in costs. Only bankruptcy of Hireco could upset the contract, and since the company is in a strong financial position and has been operating at a profit for the last fifty years, the risk is considered negligible.

The Cashco offer in contrast is subjected to two important uncertainties: the annual fuel bill depends on the severity of the winter and the future price of fuel.

121

The fuel requirements were estimated on the basis of reliable weather records and represents the requirements in an average year plus a small factor of safety. It is a simple matter to convert the estimate into a statement of probability: there are 5 chances in 10 that the fuel requirement will be $\pm 5$ per cent of the estimate, 3 chances in 10 that it will be $\pm 10$ per cent, 1 chance in 10 that it will be $\pm 20$ per cent (the distribution need not be symmetrical).

Conversion of the price of fuel into a statement of probability is somewhat more difficult but quite manageable. The householder could interview a number of fuel marketing experts on their opinions of future price movements, or he could analyse the forces of supply and demand. He would consider the changes in Government policy towards the protection of the coal industry, the chances of finding gas in the North Sea, and the chances of war in the Middle East. Such considerations would lead to a set of probabilities that describe the reasoned expectations of future price movements of fuel.

The estimate of fuel requirement and the associated probabilities are based on meteorological records going back half a century. These are objective probabilities. The chances of falling or rising prices on the contrary are based on probability beliefs.

Although the two forms of probability, objective and belief, are totally different in kind, their mathematical shape and treatment is identical. The two can be mixed in a single problem provided that liberal quantities of intelligence are used as emulsifier.

By suitable manipulation of the cash flows and probabilities the previous judgement that a discount rate of 5 per cent will equalise the present cost of the two proposals can be expressed as a set of probabilities: there are 3 chances in 10 that the equalising rate will be 5 per cent, 2 chances in 10 that it will be 4 or 6 per cent, and so on.

For convenience in computation, it is usually assumed that the distribution follows one or another standard curve that has a simple mathematical expression.

Since presentation by means of a regular curve implies an order of accuracy that is not generally justified by the data available, it is preferable to express the end results in some variant of "$x$ chances in 10".

For more complicated examples the computation becomes quite

time-consuming and a computer has to be used. Suitable programs have been developed and these can be adopted to most problems without difficulty.

The introduction of risk analysis does not make DCF foolproof, nor does it reduce the element of judgement. All it does is to heighten the relevance of the analysis by forcing a more detailed and careful examination of future influences that have a bearing on the project, and relate these to cost and anticipated effect.

The history of decision-making shows a continuous increase of analytical relevance. Julius Caesar's concentration on the contents of birds' entrails was totally irrelevant to the problem at hand. Return on capital or payout periods are much more relevant techniques but still leave the effects of timing (and tax) out of consideration. Discounted cash flow and risk analysis are simply further important steps in the direction of heightened relevance.

It may be recalled that Caesar, although lacking sophistication in his analytical methods, was nevertheless a very successful man. His shrewdness no doubt helped him outmanoeuvre his rivals. They all used augury in their decision-making, but Caesar had better judgement.

# CHAPTER 10

# Responsibility Accounting

by E A Lowe

*Professor of Accounting and Financial Management,*
*University of Sheffield*

Responsibility accounting is a system of control accounting that depends upon costs and revenues being budgeted, accumulated and reported to correspond with the organisation of authority and responsibility within a company. This arrangement makes it possible for each manager, whatever his level, to be made accountable for the particular area of activity over which he has control, or for which he has responsibility.

# 10 : RESPONSIBILITY
# ACCOUNTING

Essentially, a responsibility accounting system may be said to be an attempt to solve the bureaucratic problem arising from complex operations which prevent an individual entrepreneur or manager from managing the whole economic task of an enterprise. In terms of managerial control, this procedure provides a solution to the organisational problem on the one hand, although it can create its own new problems in the area of behavioural aspects on the other.

## SETTING GOALS AND SUB-GOALS

Responsibility accounting depends upon the assumption that it is possible to analyse logically some overall objective into its constituent parts. In Figure 10:1 these parts are referred to as sub-goals. As indicated in Figure 10:1, the sub-goals can be further divided into sub-sub-goals, and so on. In this manner a general goal, such as a profit objective, can be analysed into its constituent parts within a decision-making context. Moreover, as each goal and sub-goal is further divided it takes on the nature of a task that is more clearly specified in operational terms. Standards of performance can therefore be measured more tangibly and definitely. Thus a basis for both responsibility accounting and budgeting systems is created which can be related to all levels of responsibility from board room to shop floor. Moreover, this is achieved in decision-making terms.

In Figure 10:1 there is an assumption that responsibility accounting systems possess properties of aggregation from sub-sub-goals, through to sub-goals and thence to an overall objective whilst being capable also of decomposition in the opposite sequence. This is indicated in the diagram by the use of two-directional arrows. Clearly, this assumption is strictly limited. In formal accounting terms, this problem can logically be overcome by attributing only controllable costs, as distinct from an arbitrary allocation of total costs. In the organisational sense, however, it is almost impossible to define closely the co-ordination that is required between sub-goal activities in order to achieve the higher-level objectives. But this is, perhaps, saying no more than there is a need to provide methods for co-ordination and delegation beyond those available from accounting and budgeting systems.

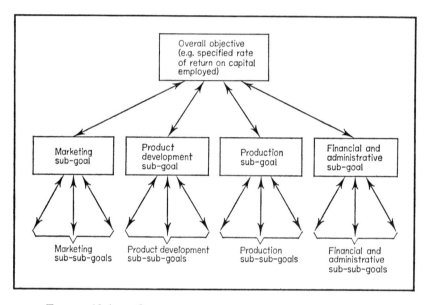

FIGURE 10:1    OVERALL PATTERN OF ENTERPRISE OBJECTIVES
Decomposition and aggregation of enterprise objectives are seen as a basis for constructing responsibility accounting systems in financial terms.

Organisation charts can clearly be seen to bear a close relationship with this aspect of the construction of responsibility accounting systems. It is suggested here, however, that the considerations of responsibility accounting should determine the authority structure, and not vice versa.

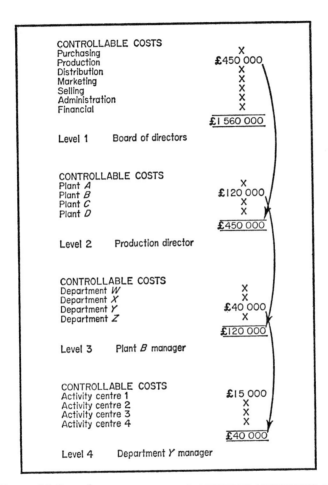

CONTROLLABLE COSTS
Purchasing       X
Production      £450 000
Distribution      X
Marketing       X
Selling         X
Administration   X
Financial        X
           £1 560 000

Level 1     Board of directors

CONTROLLABLE COSTS
Plant *A*         X
Plant *B*     £120 000
Plant *C*         X
Plant *D*         X
         £450 000

Level 2     Production director

CONTROLLABLE COSTS
Department *W*     X
Department *X*     X
Department *Y*   £40 000
Department *Z*     X
        £120 000

Level 3     Plant *B* manager

CONTROLLABLE COSTS
Activity centre 1   £15 000
Activity centre 2      X
Activity centre 3      X
Activity centre 4      X
        £40 000

Level 4     Department *Y* manager

FIGURE 10:2    ILLUSTRATION OF RESPONSIBILITY ACCOUNTING AS
A BOOK-KEEPING PROCESS

The objectives of each manager are related as a series of sub-goals
at lower levels, whilst contributing to the objectives of managers
at higher levels.

10—GTMT   *   *

## Illustration as a book-keeping process

In Figure 10:2, tables of controllable costs are shown for different levels of responsibility throughout an organisation. These tables show how the book-keeping process is organised to fit all objectives into a framework that gives each manager goals that align with the company's total objective. Thus, in this case, the board of directors is seen to be responsible for a production budget of £450 000 as part of their total budget of £1 560 000. At production director level, the production budget is divided into plant budgets, for which each plant manager is held responsible. At each level, the manager is only held responsible for costs within his control.

## Definition of the process

1     The objectives or goals of each separable activity within an enterprise are defined. Each such part of the enterprise may be called an *activity centre*. Note that activity centres can exist at all levels in the organisation, so that the first activity centre to be considered will be the company itself, as personified by the board of directors.

2     Each set of goals for an activity centre is sub-divided into sub-goals and sub-sub-goals of the overall enterprise objective.

3     A clearly specified standard of performance is established for every activity that forms part of each activity centre's task. These standards should preferably be based upon expectations rather than on past performance.

4     Standards of performance can then be related to individual managers. The expected performance is adjusted so as to motivate each individual to achieve his activity centre goal. This process may result in differences between the *expected performance* and the *performance standards communicated* for control purposes.

5     Actual results of each activity centre for each accounting period will be recorded as performed and compared with the equivalent standard set for that period.

6     The resulting performance report and comparison will be discussed and analysed.

7    Some action or other may then be taken, if necessary, constituting the managerial control of performance.

## RELEVANT COST AND REVENUE CONCEPTS

The concepts of controllable costs and revenues are basic to the design of a responsibility accounting system. In order for a cost or revenue to be controllable it may be argued that it must be directly associated with an activity or a responsibility centre in the sense that a particular cost or revenue will fall or rise according to particular decision variables within that centre. It will, however, no doubt be recognised that such a concept requires a degree of sophistication which is certainly beyond the scope of accounting methodology and probably also statistical method (even if the cost of doing such analysis matched the benefits of the added control information, which is unlikely).

There is however a more subtle point that requires to be made in terms of the control of complex organisations such as most business organisations represent. Most managers are required by the very nature of the task of managing to be associated with, or agree to make themselves responsible for, matters which they cannot be said to have control over in any direct financial sense. Consequently there are aspects of all responsibility accounting systems which defy the logic of the economist's principles of cost analysis and this is only to be expected bearing in mind the nature of all managing activities. Attitude and philosophy of approach to the use of the output of responsibility accounting systems are more important than their logic. They are *points of departure* for financial control processes and are by no means to be regarded as settling issues about the responsibility for observed deviations between standard expected performance and actual performance.

Thus with respect to the construction of responsibility accounting systems it is often accepted that in defining accountability at the higher levels of management it may well be self-defeating in terms of the overall aims of the enterprise to apply strict interpretations of non-controllability. Managers at that level are required to relate effectively to aspects of the business environment which are fundamental to the enterprise's financial welfare but which are not strictly controllable by them. They are required to predict and measure the behaviour of that part of the environment and to act appropriately. Such problems must clearly also be the subject matter of responsibility accounting systems.

## BEHAVIOURAL CONSIDERATIONS

It is perhaps not unreasonable to state that the traditional approach to budgeting and responsibility accounting by the accountant is to make similar assumptions to those made by the classical economist: namely that people can be treated as machine-like beings with simple reactions. Principally it has been assumed that if a human factor of production is paid a certain rate of reward, then he will perform his work in an entirely obvious and predictable manner—almost as if he were an inanimate object. Clearly this is an unrealistic assumption and is, of course, generally accepted as such.

Nevertheless many practices in control accounting still do not show sufficient awareness of the idea that accounting control standards are *messages intended to influence the behaviour of managers*, and that such standards should be analysed in those terms. In other words, it is not sufficient to predict simply how any given individual is likely to react to standards imposed. It is also necessary to recognise the inevitable conflicts existing between the objectives of the individual manager as a person and those relating to his role and task within the total business enterprise. The system of standard setting must attempt a reconciliation of these conflicts.

Thus it is necessary to seek answers to several important questions before finally deciding upon the structure of a responsibility accounting system.

1    Can the "controller" predict the manager's reaction to specific standards of responsibility?
2    At what level of standard will a manager curtail his rate of productivity? At what level will he give up completely?
3    Does the manager regard the responsibility accounting process as a helpful guide or as a means for manipulating his behaviour? If the latter, then why?

Current thinking has been directed towards solving such problems in a number of ways. These include, for example, developing an understanding of behavioural principles in relation to acceptance of the standards set by management, and by involving managers in the standard setting process. Other trends have revealed a different attitude to the analysis of control reports, emphasising them as collections of interesting data rather than as clear implications of success or failure on the part of particular managers.

# CHAPTER 11

# Overhead Accounting

by E A Lowe

*Professor of Accounting and Financial Management,*
*The University of Sheffield*

Some of the practices relating to overhead accounting are rather arbitrary for two main reasons: a certain vagueness in the definition of overheads and in the use of dichotomous categories of costs (such as direct and indirect, prime and overhead), both resulting in imprecise measurement; and secondly, the attempt often made to use a particular overhead allocation for all business purposes.

The two main purposes of overhead accounting are for control and decision-making. An analysis in terms of purpose will help to clarify the principles of overhead accounting.

# 11 : OVERHEAD ACCOUNTING

The problems of overhead costing may be partly clarified by a more careful consideration of what is exactly meant by the term overheads. The traditional definition of overheads is heavily dependent upon what may be regarded as a rather primitive approach to the function of cost accounting. In this conventional approach the total costs of a firm or production unit are divided into dichotomous categories. These are typically identified as:
—direct and indirect costs
—prime and overhead costs
—variable and fixed costs

## DEFINITIONS

Often, these three pairs of categories are discussed as if they were equivalent to each other. However, in view of the vagueness with which the first two pairs of costs are defined, this can only be described as imprecise analysis. It can be suggested that only fixed and variable costs are capable of being defined with precision.

The variable costs for any given production activity are those costs which change with the volume of output. Fixed costs, on the other hand, are costs that do not vary with changes in the volume of output for the time period under consideration. Somewhat in contrast, in terms of precision, direct costs are often defined as those costs traceable to the product itself, either as a physical part of the product (e.g. materials) or as costs incurred as part of the production process which act directly upon the materials (e.g. labour). Even the variable portion of plant depreciation attributable to the production process is sometimes included in the direct costs.

The term prime costs is usually restricted to the cost of raw materials and labour used in production. Often, however, the defini-

137

tions of materials and labour for this purpose are conventional and convenient. They may not include all categories of materials and labour used in production.

Consequently, both the terms indirect and overhead costs become correspondingly imprecise. Clearly the term overhead costs is not synonymous with fixed costs or with indirect costs.

A more precise definition of the term, overhead costs, in the context of the total cost of particular activities may be found in the idea that overhead costs are *not specific* to a particular activity. Instead, they arise from the execution of *a set of activities*, within which each individual activity is seen as an integral part of the

|  | £ | £ |
|---|---|---|
| DIRECT (PRIME) COSTS |  |  |
| Raw materials | 150 000 |  |
| Direct wages | 200 000 |  |
|  |  | 350 000 |
| OTHER DIRECT COSTS |  |  |
| Power for machines | 25 000 |  |
| User depreciation of machines | 40 000 |  |
|  |  | 65 000 |
| TOTAL DIRECT COSTS |  | 415 000 |
| INDIRECT COSTS |  |  |
| Indirect wages | 35 000 |  |
| Occupancy and space costs | 15 000 |  |
| Miscellaneous departmental costs |  |  |
| (allocated proportion) | 10 000 |  |
|  |  | 60 000 |
| *GENERAL WORKS OVERHEADS ALLOCATED* |  | 50 000 |
| Total product cost for period's output |  | 525 000 |
| Total output in units |  | 105 000 |
| Total average cost per unit |  | 5 000 |

FIGURE 11:1     TABLE OF TOTAL PRODUCT COST

This table shows the cost of product *X* over a given period. Whilst such a statement is typical, it is clear that the terms relating to the analysis of costs are by no means internally consistent; that is to say, the terms direct, prime, indirect and overhead are not easily reconciled with one another.

whole set. For this purpose, a set of activities can be taken as those activities required for the output of a particular product.

The relationship between some of these cost definitions is illustrated in Figure 11 : 1.

## SOME FUNDAMENTAL PRINCIPLES

Important general criteria in overhead cost analysis can be stated in terms of the following propositions.

1   No particular overhead cost analysis can be relevant for all decisions and control purposes.

2   For each analysis, the particular accounting unit in the organisation or separable activity must be clearly specified.

3   A particular analysis of overheads can only be related to a particular time period.

4   In general terms, the purposes of overhead cost analysis can be split into two categories. These are, analysis for *cost control* and analysis for making particular *economic decisions.*

5   In this context, analysis for cost control relates to the monitoring of the existing production system. Such monitoring is carried out in order to ensure that costs are minimised for any given level of output.

6   Analysis for particular economic decisions generally refers to decisions that govern alterations to the existing production system.

Further consideration of overhead cost analysis may, therefore, be related to the purposes of control and decision-making.

## ANALYSIS FOR MANAGEMENT ACCOUNTING CONTROL

From the viewpoint of cost control, the fundamental basis for analysis must be seen in terms of controllability. A cost may only be considered controllable by a particular person when he is able to influence the level of that cost incurred. But clearly the degree of control over a particular cost will be severely restricted by the extent and manner in which a person can influence the use of a particular resource. For instance, a departmental head may have no control over the skill level of his employees, or he may be denied direct control over the quality of his raw material ingredients. Thus the department head may have only very limited control over his prime cost inputs. In this sense it may be more appropriate to refer to particular "dimensions" of cost variability in relation to a given input cost.

Bearing these considerations in mind, it is often preferable to construct a responsibility accounting system, as a basis for cost control, with particular reference to the decision-making structure that influences the incurrence of particular costs. An analysis in these terms will give a rather different structure of cost controllability or responsibility from one by which heads of departmental or other activity centres are allocated a "share" of total overhead costs. Such allocations are often made in a very arbitrary manner, with departmental heads being given responsibility for "chunks" of costs over which they can exert very little decision-making authority.

Thus in the analysis of overheads for control purposes the primary task is concerned with classification of overhead costs according to cost centres or departments consistent with the firm's responsibility or decision-making structure. The control process within each of such cost or activity centres is mainly carried out by reference to a comparison of the actual total costs allocated or attributed to it on a responsibility basis. The standards should be set for varying levels of activity, measured in terms of the particular output of the cost centre.

The kind of output measured must clearly depend upon the function of the department or centre. Generally it will differ from the product of the whole organisation. For cost control purposes little is served by the proportional allocation of such departmental costs to other, directly productive departments.

In this manner most overhead costs are reclassified as the "direct" costs of particular activities or departments. This is done even though the total costs of each centre will be analysed in terms of a flexible budget related to that unit's particular kind of output. The use of such budgets and cost analyses are important as measures of relative efficiency for each department's activities. For accounting control of routine activities there is often little purpose served by reallocating departmental costs at higher levels in the organisation. From a decision-making viewpoint, however, there may well be a need to aggregate costs, provided the appropriate concepts of economic cost analysis are used.

## OVERHEAD COSTING AND ANALYSIS FOR DECISION-MAKING

From a decision-making viewpoint, overhead cost analysis is complicated by the number of significant attributes which the various categories of overhead costs possess. These include incremental, sunk, opportunity, common, historical and other costs.

Two statements can be made about the relationship of overhead costs and decision-making.

**1** Historical overhead costs, in common with other categories of historical costs, can have no direct relevance to decision-making. Decisions can only involve expectations as to future costs. Nevertheless, historical costs may be of relevance as points of departure.

**2** In general, all decisions should be based on the use of incremental costing. In other words, only those costs that will change with the decision should be considered relevant. In so far as overheads are related to such concepts as sunk costs and non-incremental costs they are not relevant. (A sunk cost can usually be described as one whose total is unaffected by the particular choice of decision alternatives.)

It is important to understand, however, that analysis in terms of cost variability is analysis in terms of the decision. Cost analysis related simply to output variability may not be appropriate because the decision may involve dimensions other than the volume of output. Consider, for instance, changes in the methods of production, as distinct from the volume of production. Even in the latter case some overhead costs may be incremental to the decision; this is illustrated by the table given in Figure 11 : 2.

Clearly, in terms of longer-run considerations this kind of cost analysis should not be related to decision-making in too simple minded a manner. For example, it could be suggested that so long

|  | (1) Previous Volume (105 units) | (2) New Volume (110 units) | (3) Incremental Costs (2) minus (1) of 5 units |
|---|---|---|---|
| DIRECT (PRIME) COSTS | £ | £ | £ |
| Raw materials | 150 000 | 162 000 | 12 000 |
| Direct wages | 200 000 | 215 000 | 15 000 |
| OTHER DIRECT COSTS |  |  |  |
| Power | 25 000 | 27 000 | 2 000 |
| User depreciation | 40 000 | 41 000 | 1 000 |
| TOTAL DIRECT COSTS | 415 000 | 445 000 | 30 000 |
| INDIRECT COSTS AND ALLOCATED OVERHEADS |  |  |  |
| Wages | 35 000 | 37 000 | 2 000 |
| Occupancy and space charges | 15 000 | 16 000 | 1 000 |
| Miscellaneous | 10 000 | 10 500 | 500 |
| General works overheads | 50 000 | 50 500 | 500 |
|  | 525 000 | 559 000 | 34 000 |

FIGURE 11:2    INCREMENTAL COST STATEMENT
This table indicates an estimate of the incremental (or marginal) cost for an additional volume of output per period of time, by reference to the difference between the total incurred costs per period of time for the new volume and the previous volume.

as the contract price for the extra five units exceeds £34 000, then it should be accepted. This reasoning might be wrong, however, from two economic viewpoints.

—It ignores the opportunity cost of using the extra resources in some other employment

—The contract price may have repercussions for the general price structure of outputs, and therefore involve the loss of revenues from future sales of other outputs

The expected costs from each of these possibilities must also be included in the cost analysis shown in Figure 11:2.

Thus it is important to emphasise that the relevant principles of overhead accounting vary considerably with the purpose in mind: principally whether the analyst has a control (monitoring the performance of the present production system) or a decision (deciding whether to change that system) purpose in view.

# CHAPTER 12

# The Value Concept

*by* Peter Fatharly

*Chairman and Chief Executive of Allied Polymer Group*

Recent years have seen the continuous evolution and development of management techniques which can help companies to exploit their resources more profitably. One of these, the value assessment concept, has gained rapid acceptance in companies anxious to minimise costs. The financial investment required can be recovered many times over—often in a comparatively short time.

# 12 : THE VALUE CONCEPT

It is progressively difficult for most companies to show stable or upward trends in net profit on capital employed and to improve the net profit yield per pound sterling of sales revenue. The applied value concept greatly assists in minimising prime costs, reduces the cost of work-in-progress, and raw material and finished goods stocks, and so leads to more economic use of working capital.

## OBJECTIVES AND EXPLANATION OF THE VALUE CONCEPT

The objectives of the value concept can be explained simply and appreciated readily at all management levels, yet its underlying detail needs to be understood only by those directly associated with its regular use. Thus top management can assess the effect that the value concept can have on costs and profits and benefit from its application, without having to spend time learning a vast quantity of obscure techniques.

The subject is fortunately free of technological jargon, and its finer points can be taught to all managers and staff concerned with cost origination and control, irrespective of their basic technical knowledge.

The value concept has two principal objectives:

1    To reduce prime costs
2    To promote greater cost consciousness and improve departmental co-operation in cost saving

The most dramatic contributions so far have been to design, manufacturing, buying, packaging, marketing, distribution and servicing, principally in the engineering industry. But the value concept is

145

equally applicable to non-manufacturing businesses, such as advertising, accounting, and many other fields.

Packaging is an area in which value analysis can often pay very handsome dividends. By regarding packaging as a functional activity, it is often practical to redesign it entirely so as to enable packaging materials to be stored in less space, to improve its protective value and to reduce its basic cost. Transport charges may also be reduced in consequence by causing the overall consignment of packaged products to be less bulky and lighter in weight.

The concept was developed in the US from 1947 and has been applied to US military projects and aero-space programmes, where it has helped to improve functional reliability. Administrators of many British defence projects are now advising contractors to employ the technique in new development programmes.

Salesmen often criticise the design, serviceability or price of products they are selling. They are frequently asked to sell products that have not really been developed for the markets they are intended to compete in. Similarly, production staff criticise designers for failing to design products which can be economically made in the plant available. The value concept establishes a better understanding of the inter-relationship between supportive functions and between staff in different cost originating areas.

The whole concept depends upon the development and application of an attitude of "challenge" and a constructively critical evaluation of all the elements of cost associated with components, products and services. When it is explained so simply, many companies claim (some with justification) that they are always watching their costs critically and must therefore already be employing the value concept. But few, if any, are getting *maximum value* from the costs they are incurring, unless they have adopted the value concept formally by specific direction from the top. This requires the training of managers and other staff in the basic techniques and philosophy which have been developed to help value appraisal.

Training is intended first to awaken cost consciousness and then to teach staff to view all elements of a product from the cost *and* performance viewpoints rather than from each viewpoint separately. This is how the value concept differs from other forms of organised cost reduction.

It is clear that if:

$$\text{Value} = \frac{\text{Style, performance and reliability}}{\text{Cost}}$$

then the value concept can either improve quality for the same cost, or maintain quality for a reduced cost, but in both cases value is improved. Often, however, quality is improved and cost decreased simultaneously. One thing is fundamental: *quality and performance must be maintained and not deteriorate as a result of the cost reduction.* In other words, value must be enhanced.

## SOME CAUSES OF HIGH COSTS

It is surprising how often people sincerely and earnestly do things which create unnecessary costs without being aware of it; but when they are alerted to the advantage of viewing cost as a function of value, cost awareness is greatly heightened.

Although the largest element of cost in any product originates in the design department, many people outside the department can influence overall cost, and if unnecessary costs are to be eliminated it is essential that all these personnel shall not only be trained in the value concept but also intimately concerned with its application.

Designers seldom design things with the specific intention of making them unnecessarily expensive, but they often incorporate features that are in fact unnecessary and therefore add to the cost of manufacture without enhancing the true value of the product. The indiscriminate use of chamfers, radii and countersinks are good examples. They are added almost as conventions on a vast range of engineering components without contributing to the function or appearance of the final product.

It is instructive to review some of the basic common causes of high common cost. First, the design of any product almost certainly results from compromises—of function, reliability, manufacturing method, serviceability, and so on; but these aspects are seldom co-ordinated adequately and optimum value balance is seldom achieved.

Second, there are conflicting pressures on the man co-ordinating design and development. These are pressures of meeting completion dates (which may be unrealistic), of keeping design costs to an acceptable level, of designing within existing manufacturing resources, of satisfying styling requirements, and of producing something that is needed by the market and can be sold profitably.

Third, the people creating costs are in various departments, such as purchasing, manufacturing and design, among which there may be ineffective liaison and inadequate understanding of the common objective, simply because so many factors that should be related are in fact considered in isolation.

## VALUE ANALYSIS IN THE ORGANISATION

Many companies are so organised that the principal departments operate as substantially independent vertical groups with varying degrees of horizontal communication; this often causes internal friction and therefore wasted effort. So the value approach plays a vital role in bringing together representatives from the main departments to consider projects jointly rather than various elements in isolation or not at all.

The cross-fertilisation of ideas that arises from group activity is important in achieving the value aim because criticism, if it is to be helpful, must be supported by positive improved alternatives. These are more likely to arise from group study, where various departments are represented, than from individuals in isolation, for in many cases a man may see the pointlessness of something without immediately being able to offer a better alternative. On the other hand, improved alternatives seldom develop without the stimulus of objective criticism.

Working in a group, one man may challenge or criticise something and simultaneously stimulate another man to propose an improved alternative, or at least contribute ideas that may lead to one. Bringing men of different backgrounds and responsibilities together and focusing their attention collectively on a problem or product enables them to consider their various functional interests in relation to the product and its cost at one and the same time.

This activity need not cut across departmental authority because (as Figure 12:1 illustrates) the group of departmental representatives refers individual problems back to the appropriate departments for study and positive proposals which, in turn, are corporately assessed and recommended by the value group before executive approval and implementation, again departmentally.

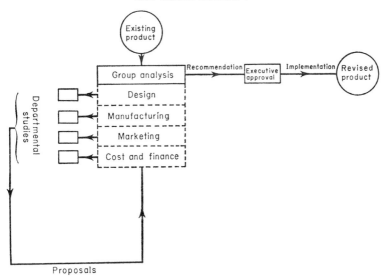

FIGURE 12:1    VALUE CONCEPT IN THE ORGANISATION
Lines of communication in value studies.


## APPLICATION AND TRAINING

The value concept may be divided into two categories of application:

1    Value analysis
2    Value engineering

The object of value analysis is to take existing products and improve their value by challenging accepted principles, materials, methods and components that are involved and by developing less expensive and improved alternatives. In almost every case an improved product is made at lower cost.

Greater foresight at the design stage will avoid unnecessary costs occurring in the first place. Value engineering is the term applied when a company functions in such a way as to ensure that unnecessary costs are avoided at the design stage, and maximum value is consequently conceived while the project is still on the drawing board. This can only be achieved when all the cost-originating personnel devote some of their time collectively to the objective.

149

In many companies much attention is focused on reducing labour costs by incentive payment schemes, when in fact the labour content may be a relatively small part of the actual sales value. In other cases, costs of production and sales are scrutinised very closely whereas the basic product design remains unchallenged. Yet design greatly influences production methods, costs and net profits.

When a company decides to adopt the value concept it should instruct the staff in the basic philosophy and techniques by seminar training. Seminars include practical working sessions on simple examples; and specific components and products should be taken from the company's normal product range as objects for value analysis.

This has the advantage of giving personnel the practical experience which is an essential part of a value analyst's training, as well as a real sense of achievement by providing some worth-while benefit to the company and reducing the cost of the articles examined without reducing their functional objectives. Provided the same performance is being achieved at lower cost, it can readily be seen that the value per unit cost is substantially improved.

Having done practical work in training sessions, staff from the principal departments—design, manufacturing, marketing and accounting—are usually keen to apply these principles in their daily work. Therefore, by focusing corporate skill, understanding and interest on a common objective, *an improved attitude is promoted to the benefit of the company as a whole.*

The training of a broad cross-section of staff simultaneously in their working environment is essential to the whole concept. They are able to appreciate the merit of the system most easily when they see direct and tangible benefits accruing in products with which they are familiar.

During training the fundamental principles of value economics should be taught and examples given to demonstrate the way in which various cost elements arise and how they may be controlled. The most rewarding phase of seminar working is when staff from different, often mutually suspicious, departments find themselves taking pleasure from reducing product cost by pooling their knowledge and ideas.

It is sometimes astounding to see how, in the seminar, a buyer's knowledge may be discovered for the first time by other departments' staff; the buyer assumes a greater importance in their eyes as a cost reducer or controller. Many industrial buyers are misused, being employed simply to place orders rather than to buy; but their contribution to the economic use of working capital becomes apparent when the value concept is adopted. Some of the most substantial permanent cost reductions come from training buying staff in value appraisal, and from seeking their aid from the early stages of product development.

Again, accounting staff often feel that they are excluded from making a positive contribution to a company's profitability, and indeed they are frequently regarded as an undesirable nuisance by many other departments. But, properly used, their assistance can be of considerable benefit to value improvement.

Value training thus uses every contribution from all departments to the best advantage. After all, the staff in these departments add to overhead costs, so why not encourage them to avoid creating unnecessary costs in the course of their work? In this way, they can be regarded partly as "direct contributors" to profitability rather than "indirects".

In addition to training their staffs, medium and large companies may appoint a specialist value analyst or train one of their existing staff in value techniques so that he can become a full-time value analyst and co-ordinate the whole value function. A smaller company may wish to have one of its staff combine this duty with his other work.

Training should be given by professional value analysts. Unless a company is large enough to employ fully experienced value analysts on its own staff—always assuming they are able to find them—it will have to rely on outside help. This has the advantage that the men running the seminars will be fully acquainted with the latest developments in materials, production methods, services, and so on, this being essential knowledge for the professional value analyst.

## TYPICAL EXAMPLES

Elementary examples of the logic that can be used in value appraisal may be helpful in gaining an understanding of the general approach. These examples do not demonstrate new departures in engineering economics, but they illustrate the need to apply simple logic in order to improve profits.

First, in analysing any product, it is possible to classify its component parts into two categories. A simple example would be a pair of scissors. The blades are primary components; the screw or rivet is a secondary component.

The proportion of primary and secondary components will vary with the complexity and type of product, and should be assessed at an early stage of an analysis to indicate the component category to which initial attention might be given and the degree of influence that may be brought to bear on the function of the product. In the case of a product where the ratio of primary to secondary components is low, initial attention can be given to the secondary components without serious risk to the primary function.

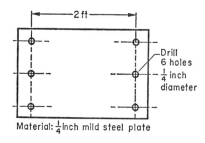

| Tolerance (inches) | Class of labour | Overhead rate | Cost for drilling |
|---|---|---|---|
| $\pm \frac{1}{64}$ | Semi-skilled | 100% | 2.3p |
| ±0.005 | Semi-skilled | 300% | 3.5p |
| ±0.0005 | Skilled | 500% | 11p |

Drill 6 holes $\frac{1}{4}$ inch diameter

Material: $\frac{1}{4}$ inch mild steel plate

FIGURE 12:2    COST OF TOLERANCE

Simple metal plate drilled with six holes. The accompanying table shows how the cost of drilling can be increased dramatically when closer dimensional tolerances are called for by the designer.

Second, consider manufacturing tolerances. These are easy to specify on a drawing board but often difficult and costly to achieve in practice. It is commonly said among value analysts that there is nothing so expensive as a tolerance! Consideration will show that only the tolerance which is essential to the functioning of a product should be specified, for unnecessarily close tolerances greatly increase manufacturing cost by demanding more expensive machine tools, staff, and inspection gauges. Rejection and therefore scrap rate will also be higher. Complete tolerance assessment is therefore essential in the value approach to product manufacture. This is simply illustrated in Figure 12:2.

Third, Figure 12:3 illustrates the cost of shaping various materials into a component. Again, the figure is self-explanatory and leaves no doubt that care must be taken to see that when a material is specified it really is the correct material from the functional and value viewpoint instead of being the result of a passing whim or fashion.

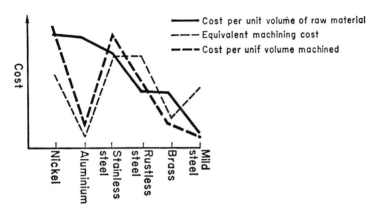

FIGURE 12:3    VARIATIONS IN PRODUCTION COSTS FOR ALTERNATIVE RAW MATERIALS

The advantage to be gained from low machining costs can outweigh high initial costs of raw material. Aluminium, for example, shows up very favourably as a material which, although relatively expensive in the raw condition, costs less per unit volume after machining than other less expensive materials.

The following example illustrates the substantial gains that can arise from value analysis.

In this case, the original concept in the design of a heat exchanger was to build a large primary chamber in the expectation that the surface area would permit the use of mild steel without excessive scaling. Evaluation trials, however, while giving excellent results as far as combustion and heat transfer were concerned, showed that the working temperature of the chamber was in places exceeding 550°C.

As mild steel cannot be relied upon to give satisfactory service above 450°C. it became necessary to consider a more sophisticated material—stainless steel—for all or part of the primary chamber, with a consequent increase in material cost not allowed for in the original estimate.

The problem was value analysed to determine whether alternative

153

materials were available. This necessitated an assessment of their performance, suitability for incorporation, and cost. A high chromium, low carbon steel was found that would resist 550°C. Its coefficient of expansion was compatible with mild steel, and it could also be welded satisfactorily to itself and to mild steel.

Another trial chamber was built with three sides of mild steel and one of the new steel and it proved entirely satisfactory in further trials. The comparative economics of these designs were:

Prime cost of unit to original design, but in
    stainless steel    .    .    .    .    .    £87.60 each
Prime cost of unit to revised design of composite materials    .    .    .    .    .    £38.35 each

Total saving = £39.25
or 55%

## VALUE POLICY

Distinction has been made between value analysis and value engineering, and it is seen that value analysis provides the ideal launching platform for the whole value system, as in addition to providing training facilities it does show some positive, short-term achievement and therefore improves costs and profit at an early stage. The ultimate objective, however, is value engineering and the training of all cost originators in the company so that they will automatically avoid building unnecessary costs into a product.

In the long run, it is cheaper to avoid building the cost in than it is to remove it afterwards, particularly as there may be considerable investment in tools, gauges, jigs and fixtures. Value analysis, therefore, must take account of the costs required to make changes in an existing product line, for example, if a whole spares stock is going to be seriously affected by changes, then the economics may be questionable. The cost of destroying existing jigs, fixtures, etc., and of creating new ones for redesigned parts must also be taken into account.

There will, therefore, be many cases when it is more economic to continue with a product of relatively poor value than to improve its value at the expense of overall economic considerations. Nonetheless, there are many products to which the value concept can be economically applied to considerable advantage.

Percentage cost savings have been quoted at various times but are not particularly meaningful unless related to specific products. However, in many cases individual components can be eliminated completely or redesigned to give cost reductions of 80 per cent or more in extreme cases. Total product costs have sometimes been reduced by as much as 20 per cent, but if a fair cross-section of products is reviewed it is probable that the overall cost reduction will be 7 to 10 per cent.

It is also possible that, by value analysing a product at the prototype stage, the benefits gained may not be confined to a straight reduction in costs, compared to the original design. The reduction in man- and machine-hours required per unit may be so great that the product can be manufactured within a shorter cycle, and be put on the market far sooner than anticipated. All this would be achieved at a lower capital cost than planned.

# Personnel Management, Industrial Relations and Training

# CHAPTER 13

# Manpower Planning

*by* E S M Chadwick

*Formerly Manager, Manpower Research and Planning,*
*The British Petroleum Company Limited*

In most cases, a company's performance can be measured by the return which is earned by the assets employed. It follows that any proposal to acquire new assets must be considered in the light of the additional return which can be expected. The decision must be influenced by the company's objectives and policies. Manpower is a valuable asset which deserves the same degree of careful planning and control as any material investment.

# 13 : MANPOWER PLANNING

Any company contemplating the purchase of a piece of plant or equipment costing, say, £150 000 would undoubtedly undertake the most careful study of its suitability for the purpose for which it was intended, of its capacity, the means by which that capacity could be utilised to the full, of its place in the scheme of production and of the expected return on the investment. Few companies apply the same level of consideration or criteria to manpower. Yet a simple calculation will show that, on present values, one graduate costs, on average, about £150 000 during a normal working span of about thirty-five years. The reason for this difference in approach lies in the traditional attitude to manpower as a cost rather than as an investment.

It may be argued that, unlike machines, people are adaptable and that the needs of manpower in the future, as in the past, can be met by recruitment when the need arises. But there is ample evidence to show that for some time to come there will be a shortage of manpower, particularly of the quality manpower which is being needed in ever-increasing numbers. In addition, changes in manpower requirements are likely to be much more rapid in the future than they have been in the past, when there was usually adequate time to make adjustments in skill requirements. No longer will a man be able to learn in his youth a skill which will carry him through the whole of his working life. It is probable that the young and the not so young will have to change their skill once, or even twice, during the course of their working lives.

Not everyone agrees that there is a shortage of quality staff. Some take the view that there is considerable underuse of existing talents and abilities, and that there is a large, as yet untapped, potential for the exercise of higher skills if only adequate training and education can be made available. This, in itself, is a very large subject. Suffice

161

to say that manpower planning must go hand-in-hand with activities directed towards the most effective use of manpower. Indeed, this is the purpose of manpower planning.

## ROLE AND CONTENT OF MANPOWER PLANNING

In its broadest sense, manpower planning can obviously cover the total activity of the personnel function—records, recruitment, selection, training and development, appraisal, career planning, management succession and so on. But it is important, both for analytical purposes and ultimately for executive purposes to disentangle these activities and think of them as a number of sequential phases. These can be considered in various ways, but it is convenient to think of three main phases:

1   *Development of manpower objectives.* Producing forecasts of the manpower necessary to fulfil the company's *corporate* objectives. In this phase, analysis, forecasting and the setting of targets will be in terms of total numbers, skill groups, organisational groups, total costs, etc. In other words, the development of a manpower strategy, linked with, in fact an integral part of, company strategy.
2   *Management of manpower.* In this case, the problem is of managing manpower resources in order to meet objectives, and the development in more specific and individual terms of plans for recruitment, training, development, succession, appraisal systems, etc.
3   *Control and evaluation.* The continual evaluation and amendment of plans in the light of achievement and changing circumstances.

The components of phase two of this progression are, of course, fairly familiar and in some areas of industry are often taken to be synonymous with manpower planning. Phase one, on the other hand, although obviously supplying the general context in which phase two must operate, has not yet developed the familiar practices and techniques of phase two.

It is the ultimate aim of manpower planning that these three

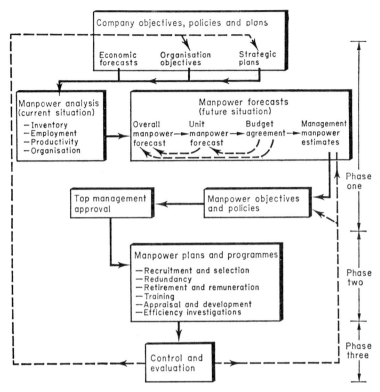

FIGURE 13:1   PROCEDURE FOR MANPOWER PLANNING
The three phases of manpower planning are shown in their logical
sequence together with the information feedback loop which must
result from the final phase of control and evaluation.

phases should be fully integrated (see Figure 13:1). This chapter
concentrates on phase one and on the forecasting of manpower
needs to meet the particular manpower objectives that are necessary
to attain broad company objectives. Unless this phase of planning
is well understood, it is clear that the vital second phase will necessarily take on an atmosphere of uncertainty, becoming an operation
concerned entirely with short-range tactics and having no particular
strategy in mind.

Within phase one, experience of manpower planning in companies
ranging in size from 450 employees upwards has shown that what-

ever the difference of size and background, seven major considerations have been common to all:

1    The necessity for the closest co-operation between those working on manpower planning and the rest of management. Manpower planning is a total management activity.

2    The growing importance of the cost of manpower in the day-to-day operations of every company.

3    The importance of manpower as an *asset* in the long-term operations of companies: an asset that can increase in value through careful utilisation.

4    The difficulty of recruiting and retaining high potential personnel who are in ever-increasing demand.

5    The rapidly changing distribution of skills available and required in each company.

6    The importance of the social environment and the outside pressures which may bear on a company and restrict its freedom of action in the manpower field.

7    The importance of the educational system, its output at each stage and the rise in the general educational standard of new recruits at every level.

## PLANNING TIME-SCALE

The planning time-scale can give rise to a great deal of discussion. However, in most situations, five years is a reasonable period for a company to look ahead. Such a period covers, for example, most types of apprenticeships, the period covered by *other* company plans and, in general, gives the appropriate lead time necessary to deal with most staff situations. There will, of course, be some exceptions to this. For example, except for broad costing forecasts, it will rarely be necessary to think so far ahead for unskilled and semi-skilled categories of staff, who can be comparatively easily and quickly recruited and trained for production. Occasional operating or organisational situations can also render some aspects of the future so unpredictable that, for the time being, planning has to be very short term; an impending major reorganisation, for example, or fluctuating events in sales or promotion policy.

It also remains true that for some activities and notably some individual career development plans, five years can be a comparatively short period. Consequently, in some individual cases in areas of phase two, a five-year planning period, though possibly only able to cover part of the plan concerning an individual, is a *practical* period for looking ahead in terms of the actual action contributing to the long-term aim.

## LIMITATIONS OF MANPOWER PLANNING

It is important to bear in mind what can reasonably be expected from manpower planning. The aim is the reduction of uncertainty, but the possibility of doing this varies inversely with time. The increasingly tentative nature of those forecasts covering the later years of the planning period must, therefore, be appreciated. It may be more appropriate to think of the five-year period as comprising a two-year plan (a plan implying action) and three-year forecasts.

Manpower planning deals with an asset, the individual components of which do not lend themselves to precise measurement and docketing and which often behave in a totally unpredictable manner. And it is dealing with this asset in a trading and technical situation which is also fluid and where targets and plans have often to be radically readjusted at short notice. Consequently, the manpower planning activity shares, in a particularly acute way, the essential characteristics of all planning in an uncertain world—it is a never-ending readjustment of expectations and aims to meet changing goals within a very uncertain environment. Its language and results will therefore be probabilistic in nature and will not be inflexible commitments to some postulated single course of events.

Above all, it is *not* a new and revolutionary approach to problems that have only recently been identified; indeed, many of its strands have long been common practice in many companies. The problem is to bring these practices together into a systematic approach that directs attention to the future and to the identification of potential manpower problems.

## METHODS FOR MANPOWER PLANNING

Two methods have been found useful and are the ones which are becoming most generally applied:

1     *Forecasting*—that is, the assessment of manpower requirements against company targets and objectives coupled with detailed analysis of manpower and identification of trends.

2     *Prediction*—the use of mathematical techniques to provide an insight into the dynamics of the manpower situation and to indicate the probable outcome of present, or possibly of alternative courses of action.

The second method is not an alternative to the first but a supplement. It is applicable only in the larger companies for the reasons which will be given.

## PREPARATION OF COMPANY MANPOWER PLANS AND FORECASTS

The starting point of any forecast or plan must be a careful analysis and description of the present position in terms both of the manpower currently employed and also of the needs and pressures that have led to this position:

### Present manpower

This can conveniently be expressed as:

1     Numbers and costs by sex, age, grade, length of service, function/department, profession/skill/qualification

2     Numbers related to sales, production, etc., or such other criteria as may be appropriate

### Present organisation and policies

The pressures that have produced the present manpower situation, including:

### 1  National considerations

(*a*) The general position of the company in relation to national policies, both economic and social

(b) The company's market share in relation to other companies

(c) The position in the labour market, national and local, for the various categories employed

## 2  Company considerations

Changes in:

(a) Organisation
(b) Manning schedules
(c) Volume and range of products
(d) Supply and distribution patterns
(e) Sales/production objectives

## Analyses of trends

Analyses of trends in terms of distribution of manpower between and within departments and functions, of movement and of costs, are essential to any attempts to make forecasts. These analyses can only be carried out if a systematic historical data bank is available. The retrievability of data related to groups rather than to individuals is not a familiar feature of staff work and data banks of this type are as yet all too rare.

## ANTICIPATED CHANGES

On the basis of the anticipated influence of company planning, and technological, social and economic change, forecasts can be made of the establishment of jobs necessary to carry out the company's business. An example of a summary of anticipated *total* changes is illustrated in Figure 13:2. This relates to a real company and summarises into a simple table a great deal of analysis along the lines which have been discussed and emerges from an examination of the interrelationships of the parts of their system.

It is interesting to note that, although the total establishment is expected to increase by 536, this is the net result of the creation of 1133 new jobs and the removal of 677 jobs. In addition to the 536 extra posts to be filled, a replacement of 3104 will be required to balance wastage. In all, this represents a considerable amount of

| | 1968 | 1969 | 1970 | 1971 | 1972 | 1973 | TOTALS |
|---|---|---|---|---|---|---|---|
| Establishment at beginning of year [* as at 1 July 1968] | 5129* | 5222 | 5482 | 5554 | 5593 | 5650 | — |
| Anticipated changes in establishment | 346 | 426 | 138 | 139 | 63 | 21 | 1133 |
| | 253 | 166 | 105 | 100 | 47 | 6 | 677 |
| Increased requirements due to shorter working hours | — | — | 39 | — | 41 | — | 80 |
| Establishment at end of year | 5222 | 5482 | 5554 | 5593 | 5650 | 5665 | — |
| Anticipated net changes in establishment | 93 | 260 | 72 | 39 | 57 | 15 | 536 |
| Replacements due to wastage | 264 | 552 | 566 | 568 | 576 | 578 | 3104 |

FIGURE 13:2     SUMMARY TABLE OF TOTAL MANPOWER CHANGES

The kind of summary which might result from a detailed manpower analysis conducted along the lines described in this chapter.

manpower movement over five years in an apparently stable manpower situation, since almost the whole of the 536 additional posts are the result of manning a new factory and an extension of the research activity.

## PREDICTION OF FUTURE MANPOWER

It has been found possible to use with advantage mathematically based prediction techniques in order to assist in policy decisions. These are, as has been stated before, supplementary to the planning and forecasting described in the preceding paragraphs, and are, in general, only applicable in companies employing fairly large numbers of the same category of staff.

The basic principle is that while individuals will act and react as individuals, there are discernible patterns of behaviour in groups of individuals. This is true provided each group is sufficiently large—

probably not less than 100—to avoid wide fluctuations by reason of unusual individual behaviour. The groups must also be homogeneous. For example, a group of graduate/professional engineers employed on a variety of functions in the company, ranging in age from 24 to 50, could not be considered homogeneous. On the other hand a group of graduate/professional engineers employed on production and aged 25 to 30 would be homogeneous, as also would be female typists aged 18 to 21 employed in the same factory or head office. What constitutes homogeneity can vary somewhat from organisation to organisation and it is for those concerned to define it for themselves from their own knowledge.

There is not space, nor would it be appropriate, to include a detailed description of these techniques here. The basic need is for a bank of historical data containing comparatively simple and the least equivocal information over a minimum of five years. From such a store of information, it is possible to extract such essential factors as turnover rates in whatever category is required, or probability of promotion between grades as related to age, length of service and qualifications. By establishing this picture of movements within the staff of the company, it becomes possible to consider forecasts of movements within the next five years, to assist in policy decision, to indicate the probable future consequences in alternative courses of action.

The approach has been to use the trends of the past five years to forecast the position within the next five years. This, of course, can only be done with a full realisation of the assumptions involved. Just because there has been a particular pattern over the past five years, it will not necessarily be the same for the next five years. The aim indeed is to examine the effect of a variety of trends and see whether the projected position achieved by these trends is satisfactory or not. The executive decision lies in deciding what position is desirable, what trend produces this position, and what action, if any, is necessary in order to produce that trend. There is no method for establishing a staff position which, in five years time, will *inevitably* be achieved; decisions can be made which will, in all probability, approximate to that position—the accuracy of the approximation depending, not only on the accuracy of the predicting method, but also on the unpredictable effect of outside influences.

Nevertheless, such analyses lead to a more complete understanding of the factors involved in producing a particular staff position and possible remedial action for undesirable predicted situations can be more readily assessed.

## SUMMARY AND CONCLUSION

The study of the totality of manpower by categories and skill groups (phase one) such as has been described has four main purposes:

1    The gaining of insight into and understanding of situations and the relationships that brought them about.
2    The assessment of the effect of the various factors—trading and production patterns, technological change and development, economic change and social change—on demand, supply and cost.
3    The assessment of those areas which are controllable by the organisation and those which are not.
4    The isolation of problem areas, present and future, which require action.

Manpower planning has a considerable contribution to make to the better utilisation of manpower and, therefore, to improve profitability through:

1    Better balancing of recruitment to needs in numbers, ages and skills; avoiding the loss of opportunities through lack of appropriate manpower; and the wastefulness of "over-braining" the organisation.
2    Making possible a planned and purposeful programme of retraining and development of existing manpower to fit them for the tasks ahead with emphasis on skill training.
3    Emphasising the need for rationalisation in keeping with changing technological capabilities, and the development of organisation structures based on modern needs.

It is often suggested that manpower planning is only relevant to large companies. This is not so. It has been successfully and advantageously practised in companies with a wide range of size, background and activity. It could indeed, be argued that the smaller company has the greater need; it is far more susceptible to change and to manpower shortages, lacking the flexibility which larger numbers can give. Its position is generally weaker in the labour market. The difference between the larger and the smaller company in this field is not of principle or of approach, but in the sophistication of the techniques employed.

Some of those techniques which have been found useful have been described in this chapter. But manpower planning is a complex subject embracing the whole field of management. There is no simple tidy package; it has to be tailored to the particular business. It calls for determination by all management to achieve results; it requires self-discipline to persevere in what, at the beginning, can be a large and sometimes frustrating task; it calls for the ability to interpret information, both internal and external.

It is something which is best learned by doing; and it is better to start simply, linking planning with an existing system, for example annual budgeting, and building from there.

But planning, whether corporate planning or manpower planning (it cannot be too strongly emphasised that without a corporate plan there can be no manpower plan) should become part of the normal conduct of business. It can provide a means of involving middle management in the setting and achieving of targets. An involvement that is vitally necessary if their interest is to be maintained and their capacities utilised to the full.

## CHAPTER 14

# *Job Evaluation*

*by* Tom Watson

*Senior Lecturer, School of Industrial and*
*Business Studies, University of Warwick*

Job evaluation provides a rational basis for the establishment of wage and salary differentials and simplified payment structures. It forms part of the system necessary to control manpower costs, whilst allowing determination of rates of remuneration through the normal processes of collective bargaining.

# 14 : JOB EVALUATION

Job evaluation is now used to grade the jobs of two-thirds of all employees in the US. It seems to have been an American invention and to have grown out of attempts to classify civil service jobs for payment purposes. Interest was slow to develop in the UK, but was much encouraged by the National Board for Prices and Incomes.[1] Job evaluation has also received attention from management consultants. Companies that use job evaluation will discover that it can help them to develop more effective wage-salary policies.

## THE NATURE OF JOB EVALUATION

Definitions of job evaluation abound. Two recent British definitions are better than most but seem to miss the essential nature of job evaluation.

> Job evaluation is a term used to cover a number of separate and distinct methods of systematically measuring the relative worth of jobs, employing yardsticks which are derived from the actual content of the jobs themselves.[2]
> Job evaluation is the process of analysis and assessment of jobs to ascertain reliably their relative worth. using the assessments as a basis for a balanced wage structure.[3]

If the claim to be able to measure the worth of jobs were strictly true, wage negotiation might be greatly simplified. Unfortunately worth cannot be measured: it can be estimated, it can be tested in the market place, experts can give opinions on it, it is even possible to devise tables or formulae which yield figures which are useful for

175

certain purposes. Some approaches are better than others, but none amount to measurement as we usually use that term.

Defining job evaluation as a method of comparing jobs on a systematic basis treats it simply as a technique and consequently misses a vital point. There is another way of considering job evaluation which is of greater relevance to directors: it is that a job evaluation scheme is both a statement of policy on wage or salary differentials and the means of implementing it.

Once job evaluation is seen as policy the technical mystery is swept away and its advantages and limitations can be examined more realistically, particularly in relation to the needs of smaller companies. While companies have some freedom to choose or design the job evaluation scheme which embodies their policy on wage differentials, they are also subject to the constraints of the labour market and the bargaining power of unions.

Clear-cut policies set the limits within which subordinate managers are' free to act. Routine decisions need not be referred to the board, but it remains in control because it has marked out the boundaries of managers' authority. Job evaluation does this, it defines the limits on the differentials to be paid for extra skill, extra responsibility, arduous conditions, and so on, thus simplifying wage decisions so that they can safely be delegated.

## AVAILABLE METHODS

Job evaluation methods differ in two main respects:

1 Jobs may be compared directly with other jobs, or comparisons may be made indirectly by comparing all jobs with scales worked out in advance.

---

FIGURE 14:1    OUTLINE OF JOB EVALUATION METHODS (*opposite*)
The five main types of job evaluation schemes are summarised. They are classified into direct and indirect comparison schemes, and the advantages and disadvantages of each are shown above the method summaries. They are also cross-classified into integral, analytic, and dominant element schemes and the advantages and disadvantages of each of these is shown to the left of the method summaries. Factor comparison is thus an analytic comparison scheme and has the features of analytic schemes described on the left—for example, assists objectivity—and of direct comparison schemes listed above—for example, flexibility of application.

# JOB EVALUATION

| Type of plan | Disadvantages | Advantages | Direct comparison<br>Job ⟶ Job | Indirect comparison<br>Job ⟶ Scale |
|---|---|---|---|---|
| | | | Jobs must all be known to evaluators or described in great detail. Review documentation may be weak | Time and cost of preparing scales. Scales may distort comparison of jobs if not well chosen and defined. May be too rigid |
| | | | Reduces preparatory work. Simplicity. Flexibility of application | Basis for decisions is integral to system and can be used by evaluators who do not know all jobs. Suitable scales may already be available. Wide range of jobs may be compared |
| Integral<br>Compares total jobs | Becomes more difficult as number or variety of jobs increases | Simple, avoids time and expense of analysis | Ranking<br>Rank order established by successive "slotting in" or "pair comparison". Usually, then grouped in grades and pay rates established | Grading<br>Each job is compared with descriptive examples or definitions of work which is representative of each grade. Appropriate rates established by survey |
| Analytic<br>Analyses jobs and compares them factor by factor | Requires more time and costs more. Effect of interaction of factors may be lost. Factors may be difficult to choose or agree | Concentrates attention on specific aspects of the job. Assist formulation and application of policy | Factor comparison Money scales for each factor developed from key jobs which serve as anchor points. Jobs placed on each scale in relation to key jobs; rate for job is total money awarded under all factors | Points rating<br>Jobs analysed and compared factor by factor with sets of definitions which determine points to be awarded. Appropriate rates established by survey |
| Dominant element<br>One element considered to be main determinant of pay is used for comparison | Experience of their use is limited at present. They represent important improvements in the assessment of responsibility, but they may leave out factors for which workers expect to be paid. They claim to be applicable to all types of work | | | Time-span of discretion<br>Analyses time taken to detect marginally bad decisions. Rate established from time-span and age on equitable wage curve<br>Decision band<br>Jobs are graded according to the type of decisions made |

2    Jobs may be compared whole, or they may be analysed into factors and the factors compared. In a few schemes a single dominant factor is used as an index of the value of the job.

The principal advantages and disadvantages of the main methods of job evaluation derive from these different ways of comparing jobs. There are five main methods:

1    Ranking
2    Grading or classification
3    Factor comparison, Benge plan, or weighted in money
4    Points rating, or weighted in points[4]
5    Time span on discretion,[5] decision band or Strathclyde method[6]

These are summarised in Figure 14:1 which also links the advantages and disadvantages of each group.

Many schemes combine features of two or three of the first four methods. The "direct consensus" and "profile" methods both incorporate ranking, which is achieved by comparing each job individually with every other job (method of pair comparisons). The "profile" method (and sometimes the direct consensus method) has features in common with factor comparison. The "HAY-MSL" method is, at basis, a sophisticated points scheme supported by an interfirm comparison service.

The differences between integral and analytic methods are made clearer by the examples shown in Figure 14:2, (integral comparison, the IAM grading scheme) and Figure 14:3 (analytic comparison, a typical "points" factor definition).

The NBPI reported on the extent to which these different methods are used in the UK. Their findings are summarised in Figure 14:4 which also presents comparable data from two earlier American surveys. The NBPI survey covered 2065 schemes. It found that points rating was the most favoured method with companies of all sizes, but that ranking and grading methods were used by a slightly larger proportion of small companies than large. The survey also found a trend towards the increasing use of analytical schemes, particularly points schemes.[7]

*Grade A.* Tasks which require no previous clerical experience; each individual task is allotted and is either very simple or is closely directed.

*Grade B.* Tasks which, because of their simplicity, are carried out in accordance with a limited number of well-defined rules after a comparatively short period of training (a few weeks); these tasks are closely directed and checked, and are carried out in a daily routine covered by a time-table and short period control.

*Grade C.* Tasks which are of a routine character and follow well-defined rules, but which require either a reasonable degree of experience or a special aptitude for the task and which are carried out according to a daily routine covered by a time-table and subject to short period control.

*Grade D.* Tasks which require considerable experience but only a very limited degree of initiative and which are carried out according to a predetermined procedure and precise rules; the tasks are carried out according to a daily routine which varies but not sufficiently to necessitate any considerable direction.

*Grade E.* Tasks which require a significant, but not an extensive measure of discretion and initiative or which require a specialised knowledge and individual responsibility for the work.

*Grade F.* Tasks which necessitate exercising an extensive measure of responsibility and judgment or the application of a professional technique (legal, accounting, statistical, engineering).

FIGURE 14:2    INDIRECT INTEGRAL COMPARISON: IAM GRADING
SCHEME

This scheme was developed by the Institute of Administrative Management (IAM). Its six grades cover clerical work from office junior to supervisory hands. The general scale shown here is supported by more detailed definitions of the grades in use in job families such as accounting, typing and secretarial work. Jobs are allocated to the grade having the definition which fits them most closely.

Some companies have spent considerable time in attempting to refine their job evaluation schemes and make them more exact. This has led to complex schemes becoming even more complex. This in turn has made them more expensive to administer and more difficult for employees to understand, which could lead to mistrust or even rejection of the scheme. Seeing job evaluation as a statement of part of a company's wage policy, rather than as a personnel management technique, will help directors to be realistic about the amount of complexity which is justified in the particular circumstances of their companies. It is sensible to design scales which help evaluators to overcome their personal biases, but boards will want to ensure that their policies are not obscured by technicalities.

---

## FACTOR 12—WORKING CONDITIONS

This factor considers the degree of discomfort to which the job holder is exposed—for example, heat, cold, weather conditions, dust, fumes, noise Consider only the physical working conditions

| DEGREE | CONDITIONS | POINTS |
|---|---|---|
| 1 | Occasional exposure to unpleasant conditions such as heat, fumes, etc, but generally protected from excessive exposure to dirt or bad weather conditions, etc | 5 |
| 2 | Frequent exposure to unpleasant conditions such as heat, fumes, wetness, dirt or weather conditions | 10 |
| 3 | Almost constant exposure to disagreeable conditions such as heat, fumes, dust, wetness, dirt or bad weather conditions | 15 |
| 4 | Constant exposure to highly disagreeable conditions such as corrosive fumes, excessive wetness, dirt, weather conditions, heat, etc | 20 |

FIGURE 14:3    INDIRECT ANALYTIC COMPARISON: TYPICAL POINTS
FACTOR DEFINITION

In an analytic job evaluation scheme jobs are considered factor by factor. This figure shows typical instructions for a fairly simple factor. It defines the aspect of the job to be considered, and. describes a range of working conditions. Each job is allocated the points corresponding to the degree description which most closely fits it. Points awarded for all factors are totalled and converted to money values.

| | NICB SURVEY U.S. ABOUT 1950 | CHICAGO SURVEY ABOUT 1950 | NBPI SURVEY 1968 |
|---|---|---|---|
| Ranking | — | 6% | 20% |
| Grading | 4% | — | 28% |
| Factor comparison | 10% | 8% | 5% |
| Points | 70% | 77% | 47% |
| Combinations and others | 14% | 8% | — |

FIGURE 14: 4    INCIDENCE OF JOB EVALUATION METHODS

The figures in this table are the percentages of schemes of each type found in each of the surveys.

Research has shown that about 95 per cent of the variation between the evaluation of jobs can be accounted for by four factors: mental requirements, physical requirements, responsibility, working conditions. In choosing or negotiating the factors to be used, most companies subdivide these four factors. Some subdivision probably helps precision; too much subdivision leads to the possibility of overlap and the danger that some jobs will be given credit twice over for some aspects of their work. About eight to twelve characteristics seems to be the most workable number, for example: the NEMA scheme.[8]

1   Education
2   Experience
3   Initiative and ingenuity
4   Mental or visual demand
5   Physical demand
6   Responsibility for equipment or process
7   Material or product
8   Work of others
9   Safety of others
10  Working conditions
11  Hazards

## SECRECY IN JOB EVALUATION

Some companies regard some policies as confidential while others are explicit and published. If policy truly guides the actions of a company it cannot remain unknown indefinitely: customers, suppliers and employees deduce policies (or the lack of them) from the action companies take. Clearly, however, there may be periods when policies are kept secret. Many companies feel it is unwise to publish their policy on wage and salary differentials. Boards should be realistic about what they can gain by secrecy and about the possibility of maintaining it. People talk about wages and salaries even when they are supposed not to, and the grapevine usually has a lot of comparative information. Moreover, gaps in the information available on the grapevine are usually filled with guesses, speculation, wishful thinking and sometimes malicious fabrication.

This inaccurate information produces the discontent which secrecy is supposed to prevent.

It seems unlikely that there could be secrecy about policy where differentials have to be negotiated with unions. Interesting light was thrown on this, however, by the 1968 dispute concerning the sewing-machinists at Ford, Dagenham. The report of the Court of Inquiry under Sir Jack Scamp[9] shows that while the unions participated with the company and consultants in the evaluation of hourly paid jobs, they did not know:

1    The weight of job characteristics in influencing the total points awarded to each job.
2    The way point values were turned into wage grades.

The company and consultants advanced reasons for this secrecy which were accepted by the unions and by the Court. Secrecy is therefore possible: but the possibility is usually limited. The company and the consultants have already said that disclosure should come in time. Moreover, the weighting to be attached to each job characteristic was computed from information which the unions helped to establish. If they had felt that it was worth the trouble they too could have applied the same statistical techniques by computer and have discovered the information that was being withheld. Presumably they were more concerned with the results, and these were sufficiently satisfactory for it to be unnecessary to check the scheme in detail.

What was gained by secrecy? The consultants advising Ford had devised a scheme which combined the best judgements of all the parties concerned. Despite this it was felt that people might still have strong misgivings about some of the results, even though their opinions had helped to determine them, and that this could lead to a "prolonged and sterile argument". The presence of reputable consultants was accepted as a guarantee of fair play, and in this case secrecy saved time and money. Other people have found that openness assists acceptance and the consultants concerned normally recommend it.

Secrecy is sometimes thought to be desirable while anomalies are being eliminated. The exposure of anomalies brings pressure to eliminate them and accelerate their removal. Moreover, this is probably achieved at no great extra inconvenience or cost. Eliminating anomalies in pay structures is only expensive if men are seriously underpaid; but if that is the case there will be some chance of losing them, with consequent addition of recruitment and training costs to the market rate for the job.

## UNION ATTITUDES

Some companies are concerned about union attitudes making job evaluation difficult to introduce. At an ILO conference in 1957[10] a Boilermakers' official said that neither his union nor any other metal trades workers' union in the UK had any intention of accepting job evaluation because employers seemed not to accept the principle of collective bargaining in relation to it. The TUC staff college is now teaching the subject to union officials and has published a booklet on it.[11] This reinforces the impression that trade unionists are not so much opposed to job evaluation as to its being used to avoid collective bargaining.

There can be no certainty of union support in any given case. Unions may demand the right to participate. On the other hand, they may prefer not to participate in the scheme, thereby reserving the right to challenge the results. In either case an assurance that no member shall suffer loss as a result of the introduction of job evaluation is a normal union prerequisite for the acceptance of results. The establishment of criteria which enable differentials to be determined in a systematic way is consistent with the basic trade union policy of the rate for the job. Some job evaluation schemes in the UK have been introduced because unions requested them.

Even when unions will not participate in a scheme, it can still be used by management to make sure that it is pursuing a consistent policy in its separate negotiations with different unions.

## INVESTMENT AND RETURN

The costs of job evaluation arise from three sources:

1    Work necessary to introduce job evaluation.

2    Adjustments to pay rates when the scheme is implemented.
3    Staff and continuing adjustments needed to maintain the scheme.

The costs of introduction will depend on the complexity of the scheme, and the number of jobs to be covered. Job analysis and evaluation would probably take about seven man-hours of management or consultants' time per job. Some companies have reported that preparatory work cost one-half per cent of the payroll cost. The NBPI recommended that industry organisations develop schemes. This has been done successfully in Sweden, Germany, the US, and this country, and it can obviously reduce preparatory costs by sharing them across an industry. Smaller companies particularly can benefit from having available ready-made schemes designed for their own industry.

The costs of adjusting rates are more difficult to estimate. A survey reported by the NBPI found increases ranging from 2 per cent to 12 per cent of payroll (two companies out of ninety-one reported "no increase" while eighty-three could not indicate the size of the increase).

The work necessary to ensure that rates are re-evaluated when jobs change or new jobs are created has been estimated in the US at about one-tenth per cent of payroll.

These costs are part of the price of control, the benefits will come in the longer term. It is rare for a company that has used job evaluation to abandon it, so it must be presumed that companies do manage to obtain and retain long-term benefits for themselves and their employees.

An important advantage that users of job evaluation seek is the possibility of simplifying wage administration as well as making it fair. Where wages have not been controlled and the pattern of differentials has grown haphazardly, it is quite usual to find a different wage rate for every ten hourly-paid employees. This increases administrative costs and increases the possibilities of unfair differentials which will be challenged. Job evaluation enables Ford, with 42 000 hourly-paid employees at eighteen main plants in England and Wales, to administer wages with five grades for men, and three for women. Another company in a different industry employed

15 000 and had over 1000 different wage rates. It found that job evaluation made it possible to administer wages more fairly and easily through a structure of nine grades. Good policies (including sound job evaluation schemes) enable a company to act consistently. Inconsistencies generate claims from one party that it is being treated less favourably than another and must henceforth enjoy parity of treatment. It is sensible to avoid leap-frogging claims from customers for bigger discounts by establishing terms of trade which can be applied consistently. It is equally sensible to avoid leap-frogging wage claims by establishing a system of differentials which can also be applied consistently.

The benefits of job evaluation can easily be dissipated if other aspects of wage payments—for example, overtime and incentive payments—are not under control. Job evaluation is concerned with the type of work, but not with the amount: it makes the assumption that each worker will be properly occupied through his working hours. It is therefore only part of a total wages and salary policy; it can be used to establish time rates, or base rates for payment-by-results schemes. Other policies, such as the use of measured day work, work-study-based incentives, or other managerial controls, are necessary if full control of manpower costs per unit of production is to be obtained. Conversely, of course, these other policies will not control total labour costs if a piecemeal process of bargaining over differentials allows base rates to drift.

Few companies, whatever their size, will choose to have no coherent policy on wage differentials. Job evaluation provides the means of establishing and implementing such a policy.

## REFERENCES

1    National Board for Prices and Incomes, *Job Evaluation,* report number 83, Cmnd 3772, and report number 83 (supplement), Cmnd 3772–1 (HMSO, 1968)

2    THOMASON, G. F., *Personnel Manager's Guide to Job Evaluation* (Institute of Personnel Management, 1968)

3    BRITISH INSTITUTE OF MANAGEMENT, *Job Evaluation— a Practical Guide*

4    These methods are described in detail in standard texts such as: LYTLE, C. W., *Job Evaluation Methods* (Ronald Press, 1964)

OTIS, J. L., and LEUKART, R. H., *Job Evaluation* (Prentice-Hall, 1954)

5   JAQUES, E., *Time Span Handbook*, 1964

6   HUSBAND, T. M., "How to Evaluate Jobs", *Management Today*, July 1968

7   NBPI, Report number 83 (supplement), pp. 8–9

8   National Electrical Manufacturers Association, USA

9   *Report of a Court of Inquiry into a Dispute Concerning Sewing Machinists Employed by the Ford Motor Company Ltd.*, Cmnd 3749 (HMSO, 1968)

10   *Job Evaluation*, General study report number 56, page 120, International Labour Office

11   *Job Evaluation and Merit Rating*, third edition (TUC, 1970)

# CHAPTER 15

# Attitude Surveys

*by* D Mackenzie Davey and P McDonnell

*Directors, MSL-Mackenzie Davey*

Board-room and senior management decisions which directly affect people employed in a company are often based on senior managers' "knowledge" of how those concerned will react, and of what will give them satisfaction. But senior managers are often aware only of the views that have been expressed by a vocal minority. Even in small companies, attitude surveys can throw up information about the feelings and needs of people which comes as a surprise to those at the top—and which can prove of the greatest value to them in making the key decisions.

# 15 : ATTITUDE SURVEYS

The term "attitude survey" is generally accepted in industry as meaning a *systematic* investigation of the attitudes of people in an organisation. The use of this technique is growing in the UK as its value as a practical management tool becomes steadily more widely recognised. Management decisions that are based on hunches about what is causing dissatisfaction among employees—or about what would be welcomed by them—can be expensive if the hunches are incorrect. This applies not only in terms of their general effect on morale, but also to monetary considerations.

For example, any management action that leads to an increase in labour turnover—or that fails to reduce an existing high level of turnover—can markedly affect costs. A number of studies of labour turnover have indicated that the cost per person can range from £100 to many thousands of pounds. Even when labour turnover is not unduly high, the existence of poor morale among employees (associated as it may be with high absenteeism, high accident rates, generally low efficiency, or—in extreme cases—strikes) can have significant effects on profit. An attitude survey can thus provide information which is just as necessary for the efficient running of a business as is much of the other data called for by management.

Surveys are sometimes restricted to particular groups, for example, the sales force. Often they cover all kinds and levels of employees, including management. When a survey is confined to shop-floor people, office workers often complain that they are not included; supervisors and junior and middle managers feel neglected if their subordinates' opinions and attitudes are sought, whereas they are not given a chance to voice their own opinions.

A survey may be concerned with a narrow range of topics. For instance, it may be directed towards finding out how people feel about specific company policies or practices such as pension

arrangements, a safety scheme, or the training provided for salesmen. It is more common, however, for a survey to be concerned
with all, or most, aspects of working for the company. The additional
gain from a comprehensive survey of this kind more than justifies
the relatively small additional effort or outlay involved in
conducting it.

## ARRANGING THE SURVEY

As a usual first step the survey and its purpose are announced in
advance to those concerned. This is done through house journals,
at meetings, by letters, or in various other ways. At this stage it
should be made clear that people taking part in the survey will not
be identified in the subsequent report (unless they wish to be named).
It is also essential to make clear that those conducting the survey
and analysing the findings are impartial.

Where only a sample of the relevant people are to be invited to
take part in the survey the basis of selecting the sample is explained.
It is also usual—and strongly advisable—to emphasise to participants that they will get some "feedback" of the survey findings.

The two basic survey methods are the interview and the written
questionnaire. Interviews may be conducted with individuals and/
or with groups; they may be non-directive or the interviewer may
ask specific questions. Written questionnaires also vary in style,
but usually call for the minimum of writing on the part of the participant. In many surveys a combination of interviews and questionnaires is adopted. Outlined below are two extremes of the range of
possible methods: completely open interviews with individuals,
and structured written questionnaires.

When a survey is conducted by means of non-directive individual
interviews it is often—because of the time involved—only possible
to invite a sample of the relevant people to take part. It is important
in this case to ensure that the sample is not biased. Interviews take
from fifteen minutes to one hour or more, depending largely on the
seniority of those involved. They are usually held on the company's
premises, in working hours.

At the beginning of the interview the individual is asked to talk
about any matters related to his work or to the company which he
likes or dislikes, or thinks are important, or about which he has

suggestions to make. The interviewer records the substance of the comments and the degree of emphasis attached to them.

This method has the advantage that it allows participants to express themselves freely about matters that are important to them, it can produce more detailed information than questionnaires can, and it often allows more subtle interpretation of the information obtained.

With the use of the written questionnaire, on the other hand, it becomes feasible to invite all who wish to do so to take part in a survey, thus ensuring that no one feels left out. Moreover, data obtained from questionnaires are usually easier and quicker to analyse than data from interviews. The questionnaires can be posted to people at their homes or filled in on company premises during working hours. As with interview surveys, the use of company time for this purpose helps to emphasise to participants that the management's intentions in conducting the investigation are serious.

Before the questionnaire is drawn up, a sample of people is usually interviewed—singly or in groups—to ensure that all matters of importance are included. In its final form the questionnaire usually allows people to answer the questions by simply ticking one of several responses that are provided.

The "questions" may in fact be in the form of statements such as: "My boss tells me what I need to know about my job," or: "This company has a poor reputation as an employer." In each case the participant is asked to tick a YES/NO type answer, indicating his agreement or disagreement.

Where a wide range of people within an organisation are taking part in the survey the questionnaire includes additional specific items for such groups as salesmen, supervisors and managers. In nearly all cases it also has an open-ended section in which people are invited to write any special comments or suggestions. With the exception of this section, questionnaire responses are usually particularly suitable to analysis by computer.

## ANALYSING AND USING THE RESULTS

Whichever survey method is used, the findings are analysed to indicate the levels of satisfaction within the various groups and subgroups. The analysis also allows comparison between different groups. Thus it may highlight differences between departments, or between people of different levels of skill, different lengths of service and so on, in the way they feel towards the various aspects of their work and its environment.

Figure 15:1 illustrates one of the ways in which data from an interview survey can be analysed and reported. In Figure 15:2 the findings from a typical questionnaire survey are shown, and one section of this has been subjected to more detailed treatment in Figure 15:3.

| ORGANISATION OF WORK | DEPT A | DEPT B | DEPT C |
|---|---|---|---|
| *Quality of equipment—representative comments*  Number interviewed | 32 | 44 | 38 |
| *Critical.* Machines worn out, need continual maintenance. Investment in new machines would increase production. Can't produce good quality work with our machines. Need better equipment. Frustrating when machines continually breaking down.  Number commenting | 17 | 29 | 2 |
| *Appreciative.* New machines make life easier. Higher production now: good investment by company. Work more enjoyable with good equipment.  Number commenting | 4 | — | 17 |

| | MALE | SECTION K  FEMALE | TOTAL |
|---|---|---|---|
| *The Work Itself*  Number interviewed | 50 | 40 | 90 |
| *Monotony of work.* Jobs are boring. There is no interest in the work. Jobs are soul destroying. Should be more variety in the work. They should let us change around more. My five-year-old child could do my job.  Number commenting | 4 | 22 | 26 |
| *Pressure of work.* The pace is too much. I am worn out at the end of the day.  Number commenting | 3 | 23 | 26 |

FIGURE 15:1   ATTITUDE SURVEY REPORT: INTERVIEW TYPE

One of several ways in which data collected from an interview type survey can be analysed and presented.

## ATTITUDE SURVEYS

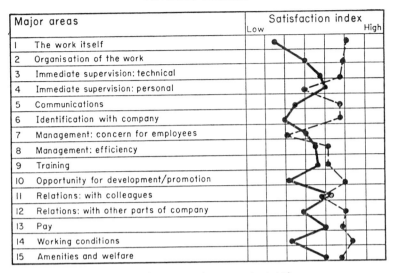

| Major areas | Satisfaction index<br>Low         High |
|---|---|
| 1   The work itself | |
| 2   Organisation of the work | |
| 3   Immediate supervision: technical | |
| 4   Immediate supervision: personal | |
| 5   Communications | |
| 6   Identification with company | |
| 7   Management: concern for employees | |
| 8   Management: efficiency | |
| 9   Training | |
| 10   Opportunity for development/promotion | |
| 11   Relations: with colleagues | |
| 12   Relations: with other parts of company | |
| 13   Pay | |
| 14   Working conditions | |
| 15   Amenities and welfare | |

———— Group A (45 participants out of 49)
– – – Group B (51 participants out of 56)

FIGURE 15:2    ATTITUDE SURVEY REPORT: QUESTIONNAIRE TYPE

After analysis, presentation of the results obtained from a questionnaire survey might be presented in a table like this.

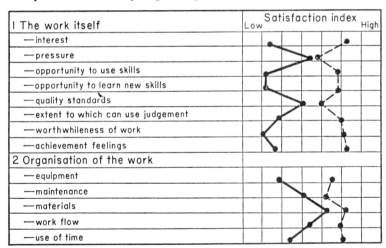

| 1 The work itself | Satisfaction index<br>Low         High |
|---|---|
| — interest | |
| — pressure | |
| — opportunity to use skills | |
| — opportunity to learn new skills | |
| — quality standards | |
| — extent to which can use judgement | |
| — worthwhileness of work | |
| — achievement feelings | |
| 2 Organisation of the work | |
| — equipment | |
| — maintenance | |
| — materials | |
| — work flow | |
| — use of time | |

———— Group A (45 participants out of 49)
– – – Group B (51 participants out of 56)

FIGURE 15:3    DETAILED ANALYSIS: PART OF QUESTIONNAIRE
SURVEY

These results are a more detailed presentation of part of the summary report shown in Figure 15:2.

193

Survey findings invariably include a good deal of information that is directly useful. A comprehensively conducted survey can reveal people's dissatisfaction or satisfaction with:

1   The work they do and how it is organised. The materials and/or equipment they use.
2   The training or retraining provided and the general opportunities for development.
3   The efficiency and personal skills of supervision and management.
4   The company: its reputation, its concern for employees, the security it offers.
5   The co-operation between various parts of the organisation.
6   The extent to which they are informed about the company's plans, and other aspects of communication.
7   The payment systems that are in operation.
8   The physical working conditions.
9   The amenities and welfare provisions.

Many causes of dissatisfaction are trivial in the sense that they can easily be put right once they are known to be sore spots. For instance, certain job titles may be embarrassing to those concerned. Others can call for more fundamental changes. Discontent with the opportunities for development provided for junior managers, say, may emerge as the critical factor in an excessively high turnover at this level.

To the outsider, many of the causes of satisfaction may also appear trivial: but such things as small privileges or the right to make certain minor decisions may be important to the people concerned. Knowing this can prevent management from thoughtlessly discontinuing these privileges or rights and thus upsetting morale. Again, the "odd jobs" done by some people in addition to their normal work may be seen by these people as providing welcome variety, and management may be unwise to "tidy up" the situation in the seeming interests of efficiency.

In some cases survey findings indicate that people are badly misinformed about certain matters. One survey revealed that people working in a particular section of an organisation firmly believed that their section was about to be closed down. In fact, the management had well advanced plans to expand this part of the company. Other surveys have brought to light failures of communication which were less extreme, yet seriously damaging to relationships.

Among the members of every organisation there is a great fund of experience, knowledge and ideas. Surveys can tap this. They frequently provide a large number of ideas and suggestions many of which are practicable and easily introduced. It is well known that people identify themselves with ideas that they have suggested and work hard to make them successful.

More generally, the findings of an attitude survey can provide a general picture of the state of morale in the organisation. In some cases, the analysis and interpretation of the findings point to a central factor underlying a number of seemingly unrelated matters which are causing dissatisfaction.

Suppose, for example, that there is a feeling by shop-floor workers that their problems are not appreciated by management. At the same time, bad relationships exist between certain parts of the works and the accounts department, with consequent lack of co-operation. All of these troubles, and various problems of communications, may be shown to derive from the fact that the main offices are physically separated from the works.

A survey can provide a useful tool for assessing people's reactions to changes that have been introduced. It can provide a basis for predicting how people will react to changes that are being considered. Advance knowledge of people's anxieties about the installation of a computer, for example, can help management plan its introduction in a way that will allay or minimise them.

A widely established benefit is that conducting a survey *in itself* gives a general boost to morale. People enjoy being invited to give their views and opinions, and by consulting its people the management indicates that it regards them as having a useful and responsible contribution to make.

After the findings of an attitude survey have been reported to senior management, participants should be given some feedback. At least the broad findings of the survey should be reported to them, and this can be done through various media. In addition, decisions must be made about what should be done as the result of the survey. (It is generally accepted that if no action follows a survey those who participated are likely to take a cynical view of management's motives in having it conducted.)

Where the evidence indicates that people are misinformed about certain matters all that may be needed is that management should take steps to tell people the facts. In other cases, minor action can remove petty irritations; or more basic thinking may have to be done when the evidence suggests that established policies or practices are causing serious discontent. But even when circum-, stances prevent the implementation of major changes, the reasons for this can and should be explained to people.

Supervisors and managers can profitably take part in deciding what action is appropriate. Indeed, involving them in discussing the implications of a survey report—"Why should *our* department be so dissatisfied with the way things are organised?"—can be beneficial to their own development. It can help to make them more sensitive to the complexities of people's attitudes and motivations.

One company in this country which has conducted a great many attitude surveys reports that its line managers now call for such surveys to help them do their jobs properly. The general indications for the future are that it will become the practice to conduct company surveys at regular intervals. The use of largely standardised written questionnaires will provide a relatively quick method of "taking the temperature", identifying problem areas before matters become serious, and obtaining information about those policies and practices which motivate people in a positive way.

## CHAPTER 16

# Incentive Payment Systems

*by* Ian L H Scott

*Research and Development Division, PA Management
Consultants Limited*

Directors are increasingly anxious to make use of new payment systems for industrial employees which will help to promote better management-labour relations, in addition to the obvious aim of increased productivity. There is no single ideal solution, and it is certain that money is by no means the only important factor. The key to improvement lies in harnessing the powerful motives of achievement, involvement, personal growth and competence:

# 16 : INCENTIVE PAYMENT SYSTEMS

For thirty years there was little change in the general pattern of pay-ment systems for industrial employees with one-third on piecework or direct output bonus schemes and two-thirds on ordinary day rates.

The percentage on other systems was almost negligible, except for a few pockets of measured day work and a handful of profit-sharing and share-of-production plans. However, in recent years, two trends have begun to develop.

1   Moves to replace piecework schemes by more stable payment systems.
2   Moves to justify increased earnings, for those previously on daywork, by productivity-related payments.

There has been so much publicity about the shortcomings of many of the old piecework schemes that even those who have not been involved, that is, the cases of trend 2, have begun to look for alter-native payment systems. There is mounting evidence of a desire for a new payment system which will encourage high levels of pro-ductive effort without raising the temperature of management/em-ployee relations—or, to put the matter more positively, will produce an atmosphere in which management and employees can work more amicably towards joint objectives.

## MONEY IN RELATION TO OTHER MOTIVATIONAL FACTORS

Perhaps the dominant feature of the search for new payment systems has been a desire for some measure of stability of earnings—not that many pieceworkers have not already achieved a pretty stable pay packet. Artificial restraint on earnings has been the experience under many a piecework scheme as also with badly maintained bonus schemes. The present desire is not for this contrived stability but for an inherent stability in a scheme which is both simple and effective.

There are two common mistakes in this widespread search for the ideal "scheme". One is the assumption that there is one general solution—there isn't. People are different, environments are different, objectives are different.

The second mistake is that money is the main motivation. Money is important, but it should not be expected to do everything. What goes wrong with far too many monetary incentive schemes is the abdication of supervision and management from the role of motivators, leaving everything to the rate-fixer, the bonus clerk and the pay packet.

For some individuals, the variable pay packets will do the trick—given that the rate-fixer is fair and strong. For other individuals (a surprisingly large proportion) money is necessary, and more money is desirable, but the strongest motivation to apply effort where the company needs it is less tangible. Words like achievement, satisfaction, involvement, personal growth, competence, prestige, fulfilment and so on are used to try to describe basic powerful motives.

These motives can be harnessed only by suitable organisation and good man-management. When this is applied, the money plays a consequential role—a confirmation that competence, growth and all the other factors have been achieved. It is under these conditions that relatively stable payment schemes might be appropriate, provided the multitude of other considerations point in the same direction.

## ENVIRONMENT AND SELECTION OF THE INCENTIVE PLAN

Assessment of the environment in which motivation is to be applied, and clarification of the real objectives, is an essential preliminary to embarking on any development of incentives, monetary and nonmonetary. The complexity of such an assessment is shown by one checklist—see pages 201–7. This is designed to draw attention to actions necessary by management for establishing an environment suitable for motivation, and also to highlight considerations which will affect the selection of the incentive plan appropriate to each group of employees. Figure 16:1 follows on pages 201–207.

| | Prelim action | | Type of incentive indicated | | | | | | |
|---|---|---|---|---|---|---|---|---|---|
| | | | | Monetary | | | | | |
| | Needs action | OK | Non-Mon | PBR | GMDW | HDR | SHOPP | Superv | |
| **1 The company's needs:** | | | | | | | | | |
| Maximum individual output | | | | | | | | | |
| Maximum team output | | | | | | | | | |
| Maximum flexibility, versatility | | | | | | | | | |
| Maximum machine utilisation | | | | | | | | | |
| Maximum materials yield | | | | | | | | | |
| Maintenance of service with fluctuating demand | | | | | | | | | |
| Effort from "isolated" operatives | | | | | | | | | |
| Quality improvement | | | | | | | | | |
| Acceptance of change | | | | | | | | | |
| Other | | | | | | | | | |
| **2 Security of employment:** | | | | | | | | | |
| Sales trend | | | | | | | | | |
| Likely scale of redundancy? | | | | | | | | | |
| Are operatives looking to present wealth or future security? | | | | | | | | | |
| Effect of pensions? | | | | | | | | | |
| Employment prospect within daily travelling? | | | | | | | | | |
| Distribution of ages? Men | | | | | | | | | |
| Distribution of ages? Women | | | | | | | | | |
| Level of employment locally: | | | | | | | | | |
| Skilled workers | | | | | | | | | |
| Unskilled workers | | | | | | | | | |
| Other | | | | | | | | | |
| **3 Organisation and communications:** | | | | | | | | | |
| Organisation structure: | | | | | | | | | |
| Recorded? Up to date? | | | | | | | | | |
| Published? To operative level? | | | | | | | | | |
| Conflicting loyalties? | | | | | | | | | |
| Check sample of operatives. Do they know who is responsible for: | | | | | | | | | |
| Discipline? | | | | | | | | | |
| Earnings performance? | | | | | | | | | |
| Technical direction? | | | | | | | | | |
| Work flow? | | | | | | | | | |

SITUATION ASSESSMENT CHECKLIST (Page 1)

| | Prelim action | | Type of incentive indicated | | | | | | |
|---|---|---|---|---|---|---|---|---|---|
| | | | Non-Mon | Monetary | | | | | |
| | Needs action | OK | | PBR | GMDW | HDR | SHOPP | Superv | |

| | Needs action | OK | Non-Mon | PBR | GMDW | HDR | SHOPP | Superv |
|---|---|---|---|---|---|---|---|---|
| **3 continued** | | | | | | | | |
| Do operatives know managing director: | | | | | | | | |
| By name? | | | | | | | | |
| By sight? | | | | | | | | |
| To speak to? | | | | | | | | |
| Is there a personnel manager? | | | | | | | | |
| Do operatives know him? | | | | | | | | |
| Does he handle grievances? | | | | | | | | |
| welfare benefits? | | | | | | | | |
| disciplinary measures? | | | | | | | | |
| Do supervisors abdicate | | | | | | | | |
| responsibility because of him? | | | | | | | | |
| Is there any social contact "up the | | | | | | | | |
| line"? | | | | | | | | |
| Casual | | | | | | | | |
| Company organised? | | | | | | | | |
| Is company policy, progress, | | | | | | | | |
| product pride, etc., promulgated | | | | | | | | |
| to all levels? | | | | | | | | |
| Through supervision? | | | | | | | | |
| Company newsheets? | | | | | | | | |
| Posters? | | | | | | | | |
| MD's announcements? | | | | | | | | |
| Formal channels? | | | | | | | | |
| Grievances: | | | | | | | | |
| Are supervisors trained to handle? | | | | | | | | |
| Do operatives know of procedure? | | | | | | | | |
| Shop stewards? How active? | | | | | | | | |
| Suggestion schemes: | | | | | | | | |
| How well administered? | | | | | | | | |
| Praise given publicly? | | | | | | | | |
| Employee attitude? | | | | | | | | |
| Management attitude? | | | | | | | | |
| Other | | | | | | | | |
| | | | | | | | | |
| **4 Working conditions:** | | | | | | | | |
| Physically attractive or | | | | | | | | |
| repugnant? | | | | | | | | |

SITUATION ASSESSMENT CHECKLIST (Page 2)

| | Prelim action | | Type of incentive indicated | | | | | | |
|---|---|---|---|---|---|---|---|---|---|
| | | | | Monetary | | | | | |
| | Needs action | OK | Non-Mon | PBR | GMDW | HDR | SHOPP | Superv | |
| **4 continued** Isolated or in social contact while at work? Travelling to work, convenient? Costly? Amenities: lavatories relaxation washing (at breaks) cloaks canteens coffee/tea Other — Quantity? Convenience? Conditions? Employee control? | | | | | | | | | |
| **5 Wages:** Local wage rates: Near the works In housing areas National wage rates for similar work Progressive wage scale — Exist? Promotion opportunities — Understood? Job evaluation/ Pay structure — Manifestly fair? Cost of living awards (automatic?) Other | | | | | | | | | |
| **6 Supervision:** Calibre? man-management training? (formal? by superior? none?) How motivated: financial? known objectives? feedback? Feel part of management— Informed? | | | | | | | | | |

SITUATION ASSESSMENT CHECKLIST (Page 3)

| | Prelim action | | Type of incentive indicated | | | | | |
|---|---|---|---|---|---|---|---|---|
| | | | | Monetary | | | | |
| | Needs action | OK | Non-Mon | PBR | GMDW | HDR | SHOPP | Superv |
| **6 continued**<br>Style<br>    Production centred/employee<br>      centred?<br>    Is style imposed by management?<br>    Other<br><br>**7 Employee attitudes and motives:**<br>Money:<br>    Community attitude to prestige,<br>      status?<br>    Individual need for extra cash?<br>    how pressing?<br>    Cash desire inhibitors?<br>    (e.g., mum takes all)<br>Informal groups<br>    Boundaries, leaders, "outsiders"<br>    Purpose<br>    Conflicts with:<br>      Unions<br>      Supervisors<br>      Other groups<br>      Individuals<br>Pride in work:<br>    Skilled or de-skilled jobs?<br>    Opportunity for progression upwards in skill, versatility<br>    Knowledge of finished job, purpose<br>    Short-term knowledge of results<br>    Responsibility for and freedom to plan work<br><br><br>Maturity:<br>    Catagory 1, vegetable<br>    Category 2, moronic (needing very close supervision) | Percentage of work force | | | | | | | |

SITUATION ASSESSMENT CHECKLIST (Page 4)

| | Prelim action | | Type of incentive indicated | | | | | | |
| | Needs action | OK | Non-Mon | Monetary | | | | | |
| | | | | PBR | GMDW | HDR | SHOPP | Superv |
|---|---|---|---|---|---|---|---|---|
| **7 continued** | | | | | | | | |
| Category 3, awakening but immature (needing immediacy of incentive) | | | | | | | | |
| Category 4, go-getting individualists (needing wide range of reward and quick feedback) | | | | | | | | |
| Category 5, sociocentrics (needing group targets, participative management, desiring stability or earnings) | | | | | | | | |
| Category 6, aggressive self-starters (needing clearly defined objectives and confirmation of achievements) | | | | | | | | |
| Category 7, self-contained self-starters (needing participative selection of objectives and good supporting organisation) | | | | | | | | |
| Other | | | | | | | | |
| **8 Unions:** | | | | | | | | |
| Which List? | | | | | | | | |
| Known prejudices? | | | | | | | | |
| Stewards: | | | | | | | | |
| How many? | | | | | | | | |
| Political affiliations? | | | | | | | | |
| How elected? | | | | | | | | |
| How often elected? | | | | | | | | |
| How long in office? | | | | | | | | |
| Check their knowledge: | | | | | | | | |
| Of firm's current position | | | | | | | | |
| Of management structure | | | | | | | | |
| Rivalry for membership? | | | | | | | | |
| Other | | | | | | | | |
| **9 Restrictive practices:** | | | | | | | | |
| List (staffing, demarcation, etc.) | | | | | | | | |

SITUATION ASSESSMENT CHECKLIST (Page 5)

| | Prelim action | | Type of incentive indicated | | | | | |
|---|---|---|---|---|---|---|---|---|
| | | | Non-Mon | Monetary | | | | |
| | Needs action | OK | | PBR | GMDW | HDR | SHOPP | Superv |
| **9 continued**<br>National, imposed by:<br>  Union?<br>  Employers' federation?<br>  Tradition?<br>Local (history? origin?)<br>Do operatives see restrictive practices as:<br>  Essential to security of employment<br>  Loyalty to union, group?<br>  Chance to hit at managements?<br>  An unnecessary, frustrating<br>    imposition?<br>History of attempts to remove RPs<br>Other | | | | | | | | |
| **10 Existing incentives:**<br>Piecework—how consistent?<br>  Tight or loose?<br>Direct bonus—how consistent?<br>  Tight or loose?<br>Indirect bonus—how consistent?<br>  Tight or loose?<br>Group bonus—how consistent?<br>  Tight or loose?<br>SHOPP, etc.—how consistent?<br>  Tight or loose?<br>Opinion on fairness:<br>  from large sample of operatives<br>  from shop stewards<br>  from first-line supervision<br>  from management<br>Can operatives work out own earnings<br>  hour by hour?<br>Are progressive targets available?<br>Does first-line supervision<br>  understand scheme?<br>Does first-line supervision handle<br>  the performance feedback? | | | | | | | | |

SITUATION ASSESSMENT CHECKLIST (Page 6)

| | Prelim action | | | Type of incentive indicated | | | | |
|---|---|---|---|---|---|---|---|---|
| | | | | Monetary | | | | |
| | Needs action | OK | Non-Mon | PBR | GMDW | HDR | SHOPP | Superv |
| **10 continued**<br>Does first line supervision accept responsibility for performance?<br>Merit rating? Performance appraisal?<br>Feedback?<br>By whom?<br>Targets set?<br>Do supervisors participate in a related scheme?<br>Is a "new look" needed?<br>Other | | | | | | | | |
| **11 Other Aspects:** | | | | | | | | |

ABBREVIATIONS:

OK       = Not relevant, or situation satisfactory—that is, will not inhibit effort

PBR      = Piecework, direct bonus

GMDW  = Graded measured daywork, stepped payment

HDR      = High day rate

SHOPP  = Share-of-production plans: Rucker (R), Scanlon (S), or profit sharing (PS)

Superv   = Bonus to supervisors (only?)

Non-Mon = Non-monetary incentives—knowledge of results (KOR), short interval scheduling (SIS), leisure (L), job enrichment, etc.

FIGURE 16:1    (Page 7)
STIMULATION OF EFFORT: SITUATION ASSESSMENT CHECKLIST

This list is used when assessing the "environment" and "employee attitudes/motives" as a preliminary to planning a "stimulation of effort" exercise. The columns on the right can be adapted for your own system of marking (say √, ×, or points) to show, for each factor: (a) whether the factor will need special attention to remove restrictions on stimulation of effort; (b) which of the main groups of incentive is indicated. There may well be other factors. Add them to the list.

The areas to be considered include:
—the company's needs and objectives
—organisation, communication
—history of management/employee relations, mutual trust
—working conditions
—wage levels, parity, anomalies
—supervisory calibre, style, motivation, involvement
—employee types, maturity, security needs, growth motives, their neighbourhood norms
—informal groups
—scope for job enrichment
—union customs, organisation, rivalries
—restrictive practices, and what they really mean to employees
—history of incentives.

Candid consideration of every one of these questions (and the answers), in relation to each small work group will bring most board rooms face to face with the many decisions and actions which should precede any attempt to select, let alone design, a new system of payment.

Preparing the ground for a new approach to incentives might well involve putting management's own house in order first, as well as negotiations and perhaps a "productivity deal" to clear away the debris of the past.

## RANGE OF INCENTIVE PLANS

The incentive "options" still include the whole range of payment systems:
—*Non-monetary incentives,* e.g. participation group management, targets and feedback results, "go home when you finish the day's work", short-interval scheduling, competition.
—*Payment by results*
—*Graded measured daywork or premium payment schemes,* which occupy a broad middle-of-the-road band between direct payment by results and the next category.
—*Measured daywork and high day rate schemes,* which demand both a labour force and management attuned to an "all-or-nothing" · philosophy (which may indeed be appropriate and attainable in some situations).

—*Share-of-production plans,* that is, payment based on sharing out a set proportion of the sales value of production or the added value. This can be simple to administer but on the other hand demands an appreciation of commercial fluctuations from even the least mature employee.

None of these groups of payment systems is entirely new. Each has its proper use. Indeed one could say that the first group, non-monetary incentives, will be used by good managers whether financial incentives are used or not.

## Graded measured daywork

The desire for an element of stability in earnings, while retaining a reasonable level of incentive effect, is leading to the increasing use of graded measured daywork. This is a form of wage structure which incorporates a monetary incentive. It generates a wage rate which reflects both the "rate for the job" and the typical performance of the individual.

A degree of stability in earnings is achieved because small fluctuations within a band of performance have no effect on the wage rate and changes in performance must persist before the wage rate is affected.

Performance is determined by comparison of measured results with measured standards. The common basis of performance is standard hours of work, but other requirements and results can be used.

The general structure of graded measured daywork permits considerable variation in the strength and directness of the monetary incentive. The details can be designed to have an effect close to direct payment by results, or to emphasise stability of effort and earnings as with normal measured daywork, or any level in between.

The basic requirements of a graded measured daywork system demand that:

1   Work is measured.
2   The level of earnings for normal hours at standard performance is set for each job category (typically a job evaluation exercise is a prerequisite). This level is expressed as a wage rate per hour. It is called "standard rate for the job".

3     Minimum and maximum rates per hour are set for each job category.

4     The performance above which the first increase above minimum rate is to be paid is set.

5     The performance above which maximum rate is to be paid is set.

6     The range of performance from that for minimum wage rate through standard rate to maximum rate is divided into bands of performance.

7     The range of wage rates from standard down to minimum and from standard to maximum is divided so that there is a wage rate for each band of performance.

8     Performances are monitored and notified to each employee regularly.

9     A fixed interval is set for wage rate reviews (commonly in the range from one to four weeks).

10     The band into which overall performance falls is the basis for determining the *future* wage rate of the employee.

11     The change to a new wage rate may be: immediate or deferred (common for downward moves) and automatic or subject to management discretion (in special cases only—sometimes allied to subjective merit assessment on other factors).

*Pros and cons of graded measured daywork* (GMDW). The factors listed below are generally true of "middle-of-the-road" GMDW. Some are of greater or lesser importance depending on the detailed design of the scheme, that is, whether close to direct PBR or close to ordinary measured daywork.

1     *GMDW emphasises stability because it:*

—helps to stem wage drift.
—produces fewer queries about individual work values.
—is good for *steady* high level of output.
—can replace other forms of stabiliser (and is often easier to understand).
—provides opportunity for good supervisors to work on

motives of achievement and prestige (emphasising promotion to next grade).

—is attractive to many family men.

—is less attractive to "go-getters" and to many women.

2  *GMDW reduces immediacy of monetary incentives because it*:

—is ineffective for supporting demands for maximum effort during peaks of fluctuating work load.

—is not good for encouraging a steep rise in performance.

—requires fairly mature outlook by operatives.

—requires good man-management by supervisors to maintain or increase effort during short-term difficulties.

—involves less bickering over "good and bad" jobs.

—produces less resistance to change.

—is probably unsuitable for girls on very short-cycle work.

—reduces the impact on the operatives of occasional faulty work; good quality control needed.

3  *Emphasises management responsibility*:

—if work volume fluctuates, management must be able to vary the hours worked.

—lost time must be paid for at a medium to high rate to maintain the benefit of stability: management must be in control of work flow.

—sometimes gives greater opportunity to increase the proportion of measured work in spite of new jobs.

—gives managers the opportunity to combine personal feedback with performance reviews (especially when warning periods are used).

4  *GMDW makes administration easier*:

—long-cycle jobs may be calculated on completion only.

—fewer queries over minor details.

—danger that absence of pressure from operatives will lead to laxness in maintaining a high proportion of measured work etc.

5    *GMDW offers something different:*
—opportunity to start afresh, to replace badly maintained ineffective schemes with a "new look".
—a motive appearing to be in the direction of salaries for all.

*When to use graded measured daywork* Remembering that one should be selecting an incentive plan to support good personal management by line supervisors and that it must be selected independently for each reasonably homogeneous group of employees, the suitability of GMDW may be summarised as follows:

1    *Conditions for which GMDW is more suitable:*
—variable work content (hard to quantify)
—long-cycle work
—frequent switching of operatives
—steady output required
—little waiting time
—stable labour force
—large variety of jobs
—good supervision
—mature operatives
—frequent changes of style, model
—management in control
—top limit needed
—stability of earnings desired
2    *Conditions for which GMDW is less suitable:*
—seasonal work load
—frequent new recruits
—maximum output required at times
—waiting time hard to control
—weak supervision
—immature operatives
—management unable to apply sanctions
—high earnings opportunities more desired than stability

*An example of a graded measured daywork plan.* The example below is of a "highly stabilised" graded measured daywork scheme.

It is possible to have more performance bands, to alter the hourly wage rates, to shorten the periods indicated, and to have only one warning period. However, the principles are the same, whatever the difference in detail may be.

The standard measured daywork rate is paid for standard performance, and is paid for all attendance hours. Individual performances are calculated and notified weekly, but the pay performance upon which wage level depends, is calculated at the end of each four-week period.

All work carries a measured daywork value. This indicates a target time, that is, the time within which the job must be finished to achieve standard performance. At the close of each week, or as work proceeds, the standard times for all work done are used to establish indices of performance for each employee. These are recorded on a performance card which shows both performance for the week and average performance for each four-week period.

The basis of any employee's hourly wage rate is the standard measured daywork rate for the work on which he is employed. In order to recognise long-term differences in level of performance between employees, five payment bands have been established for each type of work—see Figure 16:2.

| PERFORMANCE BAND % | VARIATION PAYABLE FROM STANDARD HOURLY RATE |
|---|---|
| Up to 85 | $-4p$ |
| 86 to 95 | $-2\frac{1}{2}p$ |
| 96 to 105 | standard rate |
| 105 to 115 | $+2\frac{1}{2}p$ |
| 116 and above | $+4p$ |

FIGURE 16:2    PERFORMANCE BANDS
Example of the application of payment rates coupled to measured performance bands.

213

Each man is paid at an hourly rate determined by his performance according to this table, with the following provisions:

1     A rise in performance exceeding his current performance band, sustained over one four-week period, is followed by a corresponding rise in hourly rate in the *following* four-week period.

2     A fall in performance below his current performance band over any one four-week period does not result in a fall in hourly rate until the man concerned has been formally warned and has been allowed *two further* four-week periods to improve his performance.

In this particular example these provisions mean that, while sustained improvements in performance are rewarded after one month, a fall in performance brings a corresponding fall in earnings only after three months, during which the employee is given every opportunity and encouragement to improve. The performance bands are sufficiently broad to prevent changes in earnings arising from minor fluctuations in performance. This gives the employee a level of earnings which is dependent on his own efforts and is also stable over a period.

Each week, management receives a labour utilisation report based

| PERFORMANCE BAND % | HOURLY WAGE RATE | PERIOD 1 | PERIOD 2 | PERIOD 3 | PERIOD 4 | PERIOD 5 |
|---|---|---|---|---|---|---|
| 116 and over | +4p | | | | | |
| 106 to 115 | +2½p | | | | | |
| 96 to 105 | standard rate | ――― | ――――――――――――― | ――― | | |
| 86 to 95 | −2½p | | ――― | | ――― | ― |
| 85 and under | −4p | | | | ――― | |

FIGURE 16:3    TREATMENT OF LOWERED PERFORMANCE

How a degree of stability is achieved by allowing a time-lag to occur between reduced performance and a corresponding reduction in the rate paid. In the chart the solid line represents performance and the dotted line the resulting variation in payment.

on the standard times and giving a summary of performance, non-productive work and non-productive time. A man's pay performance is calculated by crediting not only standard work but also extra work and idle time. Detailed and accurate reporting of this is a valuable feature of the scheme.

*Treatment of significant changes in performance.* The normal situation with both performance and earnings in the middle band—standard rate—is shown in Figure 16:3, period 1. In period 2 performance has dropped into the 86 to 95 per cent band, but wages continue at the original level with a "first warning" at the end of the period.

Performance in period 3 is even lower—but wages still continue as before with a "final warning" at the end of the period. The "period of grace" is almost over—performance during this period determines pay in the next period—and performance is still low; but wages nevertheless continue as before, before dropping in period 5 to the level determined by performance during period 4. In this way, when performance falls, the operative does not lose money unless he produces a low performance in three successive periods.

However, when performance rises, the rewards come more quickly, as shown in Figure 16:4. In period 2, performance has risen into the 106–115 per cent band. Wages continue as before

| PERFORMANCE BAND % | HOURLY WAGE RATE | PERIOD 1 | PERIOD 2 | PERIOD 3 |
|---|---|---|---|---|
| 116 and over | +4p | | | |
| 106 to 115 | +2½p | | ——— | - - - |
| 96 to 105 | standard rate | - - - - - - - - - - - - - | | |
| 86 to 95 | −2½p | | | |
| 85 and under | −4p | | | |

FIGURE 16:4    REWARD FOR INCREASED PERFORMANCE

As in Figure 16:3, the solid line represents performance whilst the dotted line indicates the related payment scale. In this case, the time-lag is seen to be shorter than in the case of reduced performance. The degree of time-lag, and the difference in rates of pay can be chosen to suit the particular situation and results required.

during period 2, but rise in period 3—therefore the rate can fall only after three successive periods of lower performance.

*Variations on graded measured daywork.* In other examples of graded measured daywork the "steepness" of the money incentive has frequently been greater than in the above case. It is not uncommon for the same delay to apply to both enhanced and diminished hourly rates following a change in performance. Some cases, often referred to as premium payment plans, emphasise a "contract" agreement to work in a higher band performance, subject to a trial period. There is then an implication that the only satisfactory solution if performance subsequently falls, for reasons within the employee's control, is to part company.

The details of GMDW can be varied considerably and obviously must be tailored to suit the specific situation. What is of utmost importance is to avoid perpetuating a condition in which line management abdicates all responsibility for motivation in favour of a "system".

# CHAPTER 17

# Planned Training for Higher Profits

*by* Eric Wheatcroft

*Training Manager, PA Consultants Limited*

The Industrial Training Act has provided companies with an obvious incentive to set up training schemes which are at least in accordance with the requirements of the appropriate training boards. The cost of such training can easily be measured against the return yielded by the recovery of money paid out as training levies. This approach, by itself, is far too narrow. The opportunity should be taken to shorten training times, improve skills and to introduce booster training to improve the productivity of mature workers. The fruits of training will then also be reflected in high profitability, arising from a more efficient labour force. Fortunately, a number of training boards are moving towards encouraging this attitude in their member firms.

# 17 : PLANNED TRAINING FOR HIGHER PROFITS

Top management's current upsurge of interest in operative training —itself a result of the Industrial Training Act—has rather naturally been directed to recovering the levy. The present trend away from the levy-grant system by the industrial training boards should awaken industry to the need to evaluate their training operations in real-life terms. Few industrialists yet seem to have taken a look at training in the round and related it to its basic purpose—to make an optimum contribution to productivity, cost reduction and profitability in the individual company.

In particular, the idea that training can be a controlled activity and that its results can be assessed objectively is slow to catch on. Specific controls (indices) are available, however, to direct the work of the training department, and any company should be able to use them.

This chapter describes a set of controls, their implications, and the action that should be taken to overcome any deficiencies revealed. Since their exact application will vary from firm to firm, no attempt is made to set specific figures to them. Their importance lies in the philosophy of training to which they individually and jointly give rise.

As the training boards move away from their role of tax gatherers and donators of largess, for which many firms seem to have cast them, to consultancy where they must earn their corn, they would do well to concentrate on helping firms to evaluate the real contribution which training can make. Some boards are already moving in this direction by making grants contingent on the assessment by the firm of its own training needs.

Any profit-making concern must take action to see that its training operations meet its own assessment of its needs and achieve the objectives set. How should it set about this? As always, the first step is to ask a question: Why do we—the XYZ Company—train people at all?

The answer need not be elaborate. All that is required is a broad statement of long-term objectives, such as any board of directors should be prepared to make on their aims and intentions in any sphere of their firm's operations. Inevitably, the answer will take the form of a statement of intention rather than of fact. However, in order to qualify these intentions, it is necessary to take the prediction a little further. The means of doing this is the manpower budget.

## THE MANPOWER BUDGET

Although an attractive concept, a manpower budget is not always easy to build up in practice. But this is no reason for not making the attempt. The first point to accept is that the responsibility for seeing that preparation of a manpower budget is attempted rests with the board of directors.

A manpower budget is a direct reflection of a company's overall long-term objectives. It must take into account the company's aims with regard to its markets and its products. Market forecasts covering a period of several years—the exact number is very much a matter of individual circumstances—will determine broadly the product policy to be followed over the period. This in turn will determine the resources required to manufacture, sell and distribute these products. Among these is manpower.

The manpower budget must, of course, take into account the effect of likely change in the economic, social and technological environment of the company.

Some of these changes can be foreseen and their effects assessed, but technical progress still occasionally makes nonsense on the forecast. Few can predict with certainty what will happen to any particular skill even in as little as five years' time. For instance, could the demise of the shipyard riveter and the rise of the welder have been foreseen? One of the objectives of having a training plan is to allow these changes to be assimilated when they arise. The manpower budget is therefore based on what can be foreseen; changes are dealt with as they occur.

## THE TRAINING PLAN

The manpower budget will in turn indicate the company's training needs. But, once again, the training plan will not be precise and rigid. It must, however, be *live*, it must be *adaptable*, and it must be an *intrinsic part of company activity*.

It must be live so that it can grow and develop with the company and it must be capable of shedding dead parts and replacing them with new parts.

It must be adaptable so that it can respond to changes in the economic, social and technological climate.

Finally, it must be an intrinsic part of company operations so as to assist rather than hinder business in achieving its objectives.

The training indices have been evolved to help the individual firm when it comes to consider whether its training meets these standards.

## PRODUCTIVITY STANDARDS

Perhaps the most important index is a *productivity standard*. Few trainees in this country are given any form of qualifying exam or test to ensure that they have in fact attained the productivity standard expected of them. As a result, many trainees reach a standard lower than that found in many Continental or American companies. Apart from this, a test has a beneficial psychological effect on trainees, in that it gives them a definite goal to work towards.

The problem does not stop there however. When production standards are set, it is almost always assumed that the experience and skill of operatives are identical, and that the group *average* is the appropriate level at which to set standards.

The basic need is to get management in all spheres—training, works and top level—thinking about standards in relation to training. From here, it is an automatic step to start thinking of something better.

Just as method study can raise standards by analysing and improving an existing method, so skill analysis and skill development can raise the overall standard of skill. The training centre must therefore aim to teach newcomers the methods of the best—not merely the average—operatives. The concept of skill development is also important for the booster training of experienced operatives, which is considered later in this chapter.

## TRAINING TIMES

The next index to be taken into account is the *training time* required to reach the right productivity standards. Here the most common danger is over-long training times. Yet the use of analytical training methods, for instance, commonly cuts the time taken for the trainee to reach the requisite level of skill to one-half or even one-third.

The dangers of over-long training times include not only wastage of training capacity and unnecessary delays in getting trainees on to production work, but may also be the cause of a high *trainee turnover ratio*, the next index.

## TRAINEE TURNOVER

This serves first as a guide to the efficiency of selection methods, since one obvious reason for a high turnover is bad—or non-existent —selection methods. The problem here is the conventional one of trying to turn a sow's ear into a silk purse. Obviously, a man or woman who does not possess the appropriate inherent skills—be they physical or mental—can never adequately respond to training.

Just as a sow's ear makes a poor silk purse, so a silk purse proves unsuitable raw material in a sow's ear factory. In other words, the *best* calibre man is not always the *right* man, and the setting of too high a standard can lead to as much frustration as the setting of too low a standard.

Another reason for losing trainees is bad training methods. Assuming the method is technically appropriate, this occurs most often when the trainee is given no encouragement to learn. The emphasis throughout must be on the progressive attainment of specific limited objectives. If a trainee is faced with a complex task which—he is told—must be mastered in its entirety, he develops psychological barriers which hinder subsequent progress. On the other hand, if training proceeds step by step, he takes pleasure in his mastery of the current stage and is eager to proceed to the next.

This psychological aspect of training will be considered again in relation to booster training.

So far three indices have been considered which will help to establish the efficiency of any training department. These indices act not only as controls, but are also dynamic in that they suggest where weaknesses lie and so indicate areas for action. Moreover, the three indices are relevant to any form of training—whether of youths, adult recruits or mature employees in need of retraining. But when the training of specialist groups—such as apprentices or mature adults—is considered, special factors apply.

## APPRENTICE TRAINING

The length of *apprentice training* is governed by national agreements, and thus the scope for shortening overall training times is often beyond the power of the individual firm. However, within these limits there is no reason why a large proportion of the apprentices' time should be wasted. Many apprenticeship courses consist solely of exposing the youth to experience in a number of departments, and little attempt is made to plan progress. Apprentice training has two objectives:

1    Basic training in a wide range of skills.
2    Specialised training related to the production job that
     the youth will eventually be doing.

Keeping this in mind, management must be prepared to control each stage of the apprentice course, making use of the three indices specified. The time to be spent in each department must be programmed and the standard to be attained must be assessed through the use of a qualifying test, thus giving the apprentice a specific goal to aim for.

In particular, outside courses must be selected with care. Many of the first year courses run by technical colleges or the Department of Employment—while admirable in themselves—tend to teach every apprentice to be a toolmaker. The standards inculcated are excellent, but may be too high for the needs of a particular firm.

In selecting apprentices the less obvious danger today is the insistence on recruiting only youths who are basically of too high calibre for the job. When such a youth is exposed to an unplanned course he quickly realises that it is simply filling in time, and either leaves or reacts with apathy.

As a result of changes in technology and the introduction of new materials, the skills required from the apprentice-trained craftsmen have paradoxically become simpler on the one hand and more complex on the other. For instance, the copying lathe replaces the free-hand turner and diecasting replaces machining, with consequent lesser demands on the men performing these operations. Against this the skills required by, say, maintenance staff in industries such as chemicals and electronics—not to mention any industry where machinery is highly automated—are becoming more complex. The latter type of job is now more akin to the technician's than the craftsman's.

Appreciating these changes, many of the more intelligent youths, who ten, twenty or thirty years ago would have become apprentice-trained craftsmen, are today more likely to take up a technician's job. Because of this there is a shortage of apprentice recruits in many companies, caused in part by the use of wrong selection methods and aggravated by inappropriate training methods. Therefore, so long as apprenticeship lasts in its current form the individual company must be prepared to define more closely the jobs which its apprentices are eventually likely to be doing, and recruit and train accordingly.

## MATURE OPERATIVES AND RETRAINING

So far, the only controls considered are those for newly recruited trainees, both operatives and craftsmen. The image of training is such that this part of training is often equated with the whole. Training for experienced operatives is of equal importance.

For the experienced operative two types of training must be planned. The first is conventional retraining in a second skill. This becomes necessary because of an intention to diversify or as a result of changing technology, or owing to product obsolescence caused by changes in consumer taste. In drawing up the overall training plan manpower budgets must take these factors into account and provide for the right amount of retraining.

# THE SPREAD OF PRODUCTIVITY AND BOOSTER TRAINING

There is, however, a second form of training for mature adults that is, if anything, more important. The scope for this type of training is shown by a further basic index—the *spread of productivity* within production departments. If, for example, the spread of productivity within a group of individuals ranges from 50 to 100 per cent then the scope for improvement can be measured with a high degree of precision. Booster training sets out to narrow this gap between the best and worst operative.

Potential increases in productivity resulting from booster training range from 10 to 50 per cent. This is the largest single opportunity open to industry and if implemented on a large scale could make Britain a fully competitive nation and go a long way towards eliminating the balance of payments problem.

Once again, analytical training is a tool specially appropriate for booster training. The best operatives are studied, their methods and skills analysed (and often improved). These methods and skills are then taught to the less skilled operatives, which has the effect of raising the productivity of the whole group near to that of the best, as distinct from the average, man.

The problem in booster training is not the technical difficulties of learning and developing new skills, but the psychological resistance to change that the operative will almost certainly show.

Everyone is familiar with the difficulties of breaking bad habits. It is not surprising therefore that operatives persist in habits of work that are obviously bad in comparison with another's methods. Booster training has the aim of breaking down bad work habits and replacing them with improved methods. This is one of the most difficult of the instructor's jobs, but when well done the results are gratifying to both trainee and instructor.

The relationship between instructor and trainee is in all respects personal like that of doctor and patient. The doctor must inspire in the patient the confidence that he will recover, but at the same time he must ensure that the patient takes the medicine.

The theme that emerges strongly in this consideration of operative training is the interdependence of all the indices. The starting point

| | | PRODUCTIVITY AND SAVING | TRAINING TIME REDUCED BY |
|---|---|---|---|
| Boats | | | |
| Boots and shoes | Closing | Saving $90 000 p.a. | |
| Carpets | Spinning | +22% | 66% |
| | Weaving | | 66% |
| | Mending | | 66% |
| Hosiery | Linking | +20% | |
| | Boarding | Defects—60% | 70% |
| | Pairing | +40% | |
| Knitwear | Most operations | +30% | 66% |
| Lingerie | Sewing | +30% | |
| Textiles | Battery filling | +20% | |
| | Weaving | +5% | |

(a) United States

| | PRODUCTIVITY AND SAVING | TRAINING TIME REDUCED BY |
|---|---|---|
| Electronics | +25% | 60% |
| Food | +31% (£21 000 p.a.) | 66% |
| Aero engines | +20% | 75% |
| Engineering | +13% | 75% |
| Hosiery | +33% | 60% |
| Weaving | +5% | 66% |
| Shoes | +22% | 75% |
| Paper | +20% | 50% |
| Garments | +22% | 66% |
| Carpets | £7 000 reduction in waste | |

(b) United Kingdom

FIGURE 17:1   INDUSTRY OPERATION RESULTS

How analytical training increased productivity—or made other savings. The figures in Table (a) are derived from work carried out by PA Consultants in the USA, where productivity standards tend to be higher than their equivalent in the UK.

is production standards, which must be based upon the perform-ance of the best operatives. The time spent under training must be sufficient to reach this standard, but must be no longer than this. Only recruits who are inherently capable of reaching the right standard should be selected. Finally, experienced workers who are below standard must be booster-trained to reach this standard.

The indices once correctly set will show whether objectives are being attained or not, but only the positive direction of management will ensure that training achieves the goals of increasing produc-tivity, lowering costs and raising profits.

## Analytical training

An analytical training programme is planned as a series of steps, arranged to form a logical progression. These steps are as follows:

1   *Basic exercises.* Pre-training of skills before production work is attempted. Simulators are used to isolate skills for separate practice and to provide easier perceptual cues.
2   *Job exercises.* Pre-training production skills on non-productive materials.
3   *Parts.* The production job is broken down into parts which are given repeated practice. This promotes con-centration and the ability to remember previous errors.
4   *Complete job.* Parts of the job are joined together pro-gressively until the whole job can be practised in one.
5   *Short run.* Repetition of the job cycle in short runs pro-vides continuity and the ability to maintain the pace over increasing periods.
6   *Longer runs.* Muscles become stronger, perception and judgement improve, enabling the trainee to operate sub-consciously. Co-ordination is developed.
7   *Full-day runs.* Stamina is developed to the point where the trainee can maintain 100 per cent performance all day.

# CHAPTER 18

# Group Training for Manager and Organisation Development

*by* Mel Berger

*Research Officer, Birkbeck College, University of London*

Most organisations are faced with problems of communication, commitment to decisions and co-ordination of plans. These problems often result in information gaps, grapevines and inter-departmental rivalry. Sound decisions are not implemented properly, and staff and managers are lost because the organisation is apparently unable to tap their abilities. Whilst control systems are frequently applied to optimise the use of money, machines and materials, little is done to optimise the use of human resources.

# 18 : GROUP TRAINING FOR MANAGER AND ORGANISATION DEVELOPMENT

In recent years there has been a growing recognition of "human" problems in industrial organisations. Skills of man management are increasingly seen as making an important contribution to organisational success. This has led to the introduction of training, often called "human relations training" or "group dynamics training", specifically aimed at helping managers to improve these skills. Teaching methods vary considerably. They range from case studies and role playing to simulated work situations and group training.

This chapter examines a variety of techniques for man-management training called group training. Group training differs from more traditional approaches such as lecturing, case studies and role playing in several basic ways. Group training aims to improve the skills of group members by focusing on the training group itself. Problems which arise out of the experience of working together are examined with the goal of improving the effectiveness of the group or the individual's effectiveness within the group. Thus people learn by their own experience; a process sometimes called "experimental learning".

By contrast, a case study or a role play involves a situation that is either fictional, historical, or real to someone other than the trainees. Sometimes people are required to pretend, and act out of character in the case. In group training, the group is its own ongoing case study and people are themselves. Group training places considerable emphasis on evaluating the performance of the individual, the group, or both. This generally leads to experimenting with alternative behaviours, procedures, and styles of working within the group.

Group training has become increasingly accepted as important to the development of man-management skills. Nowadays most managers are aware of some group training approaches but few know how to apply them within their own organisations or to assess their suitability for specific cases.

A number of quite different group training approaches are currently being used. These include group relations training, Managerial Grid, T-group training, Coverdale training, team training, study groups, action training, organisation laboratory and many more. The methods may differ in their emphasis on personal skills versus group skills and personal relationships versus work relationships. They may be directed by the group leader to a considerable extent, or such direction might be minimal. They can be slanted towards different learning objectives and different background experiences of trainees.

This chapter will explore three aspects of group training:
—Current interest and demand for group training
—Application in industry
—Implementation in order to improve group and organisational effectiveness.

## CURRENT INTEREST AND DEMAND FOR GROUP TRAINING

Education and training, in schools, universities, and industry has traditionally placed a great deal of emphasis on the learning of techniques, technical information and skills, and little emphasis on the learning of interpersonal skills, such as how to communicate effectively and how to work in groups. However, many of the changes which have occurred in the past decade place demands on people in organisations which can best be met by increased interpersonal, or man-management skills. Some of these pressures towards changing patterns of work relationships and social interaction are described below.

### Innovation

Industrial technology, that is work methods and machinery, changes over time. Although this has always been so, the rate of change has accelerated sharply over the past few years. This means that people must be able to adapt and cope with change more than previously. Technology is also more complex and interrelated; this means that there is greater need for trained specialists and these specialists must be able to co-ordinate their work with other specialists. These types of changes have influenced the structure and procedures of many organisations from being mechanistic, hierarchical, and authoritarian, towards being more flexible, specialised and participative. This trend has led to the need for effective co-ordination and problem solving, and the freedom to take initiative and to be creative.

Today's manager does not often have sufficient information to take decisions on his own and must rely more and more on specialists who understand the technology to supply and to co-ordinate the information. He must delegate technical decision-making to the specialist. His job thus becomes more one of long-term planning, policy-making, co-ordination, and control, rather than day-to-day decision-making and supervision.

Although the trend is towards flexible organisations and procedures, whether an organisation moves in this direction or remains more mechanistic depends largely upon technological and marketing needs. Organisations whose technology and markets are most subject to change (such as electronics, engineering and chemicals) have a greater need for flexible organisation and work relationships than industries with more stable technology (including food, hospitals and textiles for example).

## Personal attitudes and motivation

People are more educated, more informed of rights, more mobile, and more independent. This probably stems from a higher standard of living, not experiencing the scarcity of a depression, having increased educational opportunities, and having more information through the mass media. People are, therefore, less likely to be satisfied with passively following orders and rules and with doing routine, menial jobs. For many people, job satisfaction is as important as monetary incentives.

The economic situation is one of greater job alternatives. Therefore, if one is dissatisfied with his job he can more easily find another than in the past.

The government and society take greater responsibility for individuals. There is unemployment insurance, national health, and numerous pension schemes. Thus, the threat of starvation and discomfort from not having a job for a short period of time is not severe. Further, unions often protect the worker from arbitrary decisions. A secure job is no longer enough to satisfy many workers. Job satisfaction, recognition, and promotion opportunities are equally important. This is particularly true for skilled and educated individuals.

Thus, in order to achieve good and effective work relationships and to achieve optimal task effectiveness, people must work together in ways which often differ from the past. However, most people's background, training and education are insufficient to deal with the increased demand for man-management skills and the flexible relationships, structures, and procedures which are generally required. This gap often leads managers to deny the need for change, to blame others for problems, or to say that the new relationships and procedures go against human nature ("people cannot make decisions in groups", "the boss must always have the right answer"). It is not surprising that many are not able to adapt to new requirements and new demands; they simply have not been trained to do so. The rapid growth and acceptance of group training is a response to this training need.

## APPLICATION IN INDUSTRY

The past twenty-five years have seen the growth and development of group training and the refinement of specific group training approaches to meet different needs. There is currently a wide variety of approaches from which to choose. These may aim to improve the performance of the individual manager, an on-going work team or an entire organisational unit.

Up to about five years ago, most group training consisted of an individual manager attending a course in isolation from his normal work setting and work colleagues. It was found that this sometimes led to difficulties in transferring course learning to the job setting.

The response to this problem has increasingly been to train work units together and to link training to an overall development plan. This general approach is often called "organisation development" (OD). OD is an approach for encouraging exploration and planned development of managerial group and organisational processes. It involves the use of behavioural science knowledge and generally originates near the top of the organisation. Whereas management development aims at developing the skills of managers so that they may contribute more to the organisation, OD aims to create an environment which will facilitate effective contributions to the organisation. Thus, OD focuses on groups, work relationships, inter-group relations, target setting and planning.

Two short case studies will now be presented to illustrate different uses of group training for organisational development. Both involve the training for organisational development. One involves the training of all managers from a division of a large company; the other describes a training situation in an on-going work unit.

## Managerial Grid case study

This case is based on an article by George Clark and describes the use of a popular training method—Blake and Mouton's Managerial Grid training—in one division of a large company.

The Managerial Grid consists of six phases. The first is aimed at educating the manager about the Grid approach itself, including working in groups effectively, facilitating interaction between groups, and the effect of various management styles.

One of the central Grid concepts is managerial style which can be described along two dimensions. These are:

1    Concern for production (including production of new ideas, creativity and decision-making)
2    Concern for people

Five principal styles can be derived from these two dimensions (see Figure 18:1).

On this initial phase, people learn about their own managerial style. Discussions and exercises are also featured which aim at the understanding of team effectiveness, the value of reviewing group performance, and inter-group dynamics such as conflict and stereo-typing. Further phases apply the grid technique to on-going work groups, to the interface between groups, to overall business strategy, and to diagnosing business improvements.

The division decided to use phase 1 of the grid in order to facilitate the implementation of an agreement between the company and

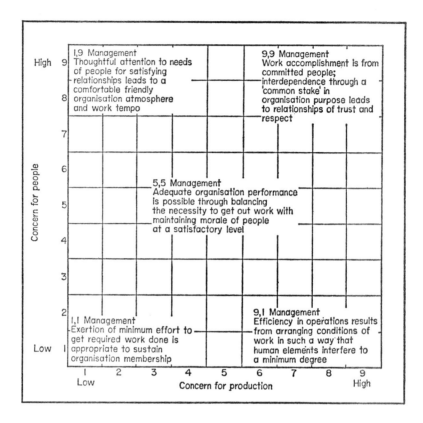

FIGURE 18:1    THE MANAGERIAL GRID

The grid allows comparison between two managerial dimensions
—concern for production and concern for people. From this comparison five principle styles of management are derived

(Reproduced from *The Managerial Grid* by R. R. Blake and
J. S. Mouton, by kind permission of the authors.)

the union. The objectives of the training programme were to help
managers to rethink their methods of managing and to implement
the new agreement without undue staff difficulties.

It was considered essential that top management in the division
should understand the programme and be committed to it before
beginning the programme. To do this, three top managers attended

a phase 1 seminar run by an outside organisation for managers of different companies. Several other senior managers also attended externally run Grid seminars. From these, several were selected to be trained as instructors for the in-company seminars. It is worth noting that great care in training in-company trainers and concern for commitment from the top went into the overall programme. Only when this had been achieved did the bulk of managers go through the training. In all, about seventy managers and supervisors attended the in-company training seminars. In many cases, this was followed by on-the-job projects and by work with on-going work teams.

Reactions to the seminars were generally quite good. The applicability of the learning to the job, however, often seemed to depend on whether managers had opportunities to put the training into practice. Also, where there was follow-up with the managers and their work teams, the lessons could be better put into practice. It was felt that more follow-up in work teams would have increased the effectiveness of the overall programme.

The impact of the seminars was assessed both subjectively and quantitatively against yearly targets. A subjective evaluation by those involved indicated that increased frankness, openness, and skills in dealing with conflict were important factors in enabling useful discussions to be carried out with both junior management and manual workers. A quantitative evaluation which compared organisation performance figures with yearly targets indicated that:

1    Nearly 17 per cent fewer people were required than would have been the case under previous manning schedules.
2    There was a direct saving at the rate of £3600 per £100 000 salary bill.
3    There was an indirect saving at the rate of £11 000 per £100 000 salary bill.
4    Annual voluntary labour turnover dropped from over 30 per cent to 13 per cent.

It was not possible to ascribe the results entirely to the Grid training as a change in salary structure and some changes in work procedures were also introduced as part of the management-union agreement. However, it was strongly believed by those involved in the programme that the training played a major part in the surpassing of targets.

## Management team case study

The second case study is based on a recent experience of the author in the use of group training for a work team. I was invited by a member of the management development section of a large company to conduct a training programme for a top manager and his team. The team consisted of the divisional senior manager and ten middle managers who worked in different areas of England. They, in turn, had four to six subordinates and several supporting staff.

The objectives of the training, as specified by the senior manager, were to: improve the effectiveness of the work group in conducting discussions and in making decisions, to improve communications between team members, and to increase the solidarity and interdependence of the team members.

The senior manager had previously attended two T-group seminars and had a good understanding of group dynamics and of how he wanted his team to work together. His difficulty was in applying these skills to a group without similar skills, without much experience in working together, and who were fairly dependent on him for direction. He felt, and I agreed, that it would be useful if the team spent some time on their own during the workshop, in order to learn some basic skills of working in groups and to develop some independence from the boss.

The workshop was planned to last for three days and the senior manager would not be present for the first day and a half. Before any detailed planning of the course, I interviewed each of the managers to be involved to discuss the types of problems they faced on the job and their expectations of the training workshop. Frequently mentioned problems pertained to relationships with subordinates, the usefulness of monthly team meetings, technical support services, and MBO which had been introduced recently. Following these interviews, the workshop was planned in detail.

During the first day and a half of the workshop, the group spent the major portion of their time working on some of the more frequently mentioned work problems (as determined by the interviews).

The discussion of any one problem was limited to a specified length of time and the group was expected to reach conclusions or recommendations by the end of the discussion. This was done to approximate normal work pressure and to ensure that the group didn't get bogged down on any one problem. Two standard group dynamics exercises were also used to illustrate specific points about effective group work.

During each discussion and exercise two members were assigned to observe the method by which the group tackled the task. Following the discussion they criticised the group work and then the entire group considered how they could improve the group's effectiveness in the next discussion. In this way the group learned from its own experience and members became more aware of the dynamics of team work. There were also several short lecture/discussions about group dynamics, rational decision-making procedures, leadership, and communication. The first day and a half resulted in the group learning a lot about working together and shared work problems, and in the feeling of being a work group rather than isolated individuals.

On the evening of day two the boss arrived and there was a joint discussion about integrating him into the group. This led to an examination of work relationships in the group and how they could be improved. This task was a group decision and it took the form of criticising the performance of one another within the context of their group meetings. The specification of context was important in order to exclude second-hand and private information.

On the third day, the group including the boss worked together on job problems. This was the acid test for the group—could they all work together in a productive manner? Interestingly, the problem chosen for discussion was the implementation of MBO. The result of the discussion was several practical decisions as to how it could be implemented in a way which was satisfactory to everyone. Thus, the course ended on a note of success.

The team's work efficiency was considerably increased as a consequence of their three days together and members felt themselves to be part of a team. These benefits remained during future monthly meetings. It was also reported that several managers had been able to apply their learning to situations with their subordinates so that they were now more effective managers of their own units.

These two cases illustrate different approaches to group training; they differed in the type of work relations dealt with and the degree to which the programme followed a prescribed structure. In both cases considerable preparation went into the planning and implementing of the course including precise clarification of learning objectives and obtaining commitment from key top men in the organisation.

## IMPLEMENTATION

Based on the previous case experiences, several guidelines can be specified for managers considering the introduction of group training.

### Preparation of a training programme

It can take a good deal of time to plan and prepare a training or development programme. The first step is to diagnose development needs, preferably by discussion with the people who will be involved in the programme. From this it will be possible to set specific objectives. For example, the objective may be to change existing management practices, to train new managers, to increase the efficiency of group decision-making, to improve communication, etc.

It is important to obtain commitment from as high a level in the organisation as possible by maintaining a close liaison with them throughout the programme, by encouraging them to go on a stranger course in order to find out for themselves the benefits of the training, or by setting up a pilot course or discussion day (just) for them. These steps, if successful, should lead to involvement and commitment of those who will take part and to support from top management. This, in turn, will increase the likelihood of the success of the overall programme.

### Fitting training to the organisation

The training approach should not be too dissimilar from the existing organisation climate and structure. Organisations in environments which are relatively unpredictable and changeable usually have the greatest need for group training. These organisations cannot rely on standard procedures and must be able to make good decisions at all managerial levels based on specialist information and on changing circumstances. An organisation which is rigidly structured and which has fairly fixed well-defined procedures would probably find a highly structured training approach more acceptable to the individuals involved. On the other hand, an organisation with a more flexible structure and with flexible procedures would probably find a moderately structured approach most acceptable.

Where the training approach is not seen as acceptable or valid by the trainees, regardless of its "objective" merits, there is likely to be considerable resistance to the programme. Since group training involves people and the complexities of human nature, without goodwill and commitment, resistance to change is likely to greatly reduce the learning potential of the programme.

## Selection

Training will be most successful where organisations take responsibility for careful selection, preparation and follow-up of potential group members and where training departments take responsibility for selecting and training trainers.

## Evaluation

Periodic monitoring of the training programme is advisable to ensure that the development objectives are being met. This may necessitate experimentation with slightly different training approaches.

## Follow-up on the job

Although training courses are the usual starting point in improving managerial skill, follow-up with on-going work units is important in order to gain maximum benefits. Without follow-up managers may encounter difficulties in implementing new ideas and in changing their approach because of lack of support by their work associates or fear of trying new things or because of lack of confidence in their own expertise. Follow-up, even on a voluntary basis, ensures that managers or work units who desire to make changes will get sufficient help and guidance. This may take the form of team training, process consultancy, or project work.

## An organisation development sequence

Some organisations have developed an overall organisation development sequence. Initially top managers may go to stranger groups in order to sample group training approaches. The company then may run a series of in-company courses aimed at introducing new ideas, techniques, man-management approaches, and a common language. From this, training of work groups and the implementation of other development activities may follow. Training a work group is most likely to succeed if key members have had a previous group experience.

Although it is usually helpful to have outside expert advice in the early stages of a programme, it may be more economical and often more effective to train people inside the company to conduct the actual training programmes. In some cases, it has been found useful to have one or two external consultants who work with the internal trainers or consultants on a regular basis. The training of internal trainers does require both time and money. Often, this involves sending them on external courses in order that they learn basic skills of working in groups, increase their understanding of group processes, and learn in depth the impact they have on others. Some large organisations have set up their own in-company trainer development programmes.

*Section Four*

# Marketing

# CHAPTER 19

# *Product Profile Analysis*

*by* T R Angear

**Consultant, McAlley Associates**

The vital path of new product development is littered with costly failures, even among the best run concerns. Companies are giving increasing attention to early stages of the product development cycle, with special emphasis on screening and profit analysis. Although there are pitfalls to watch, product profile analysis scores high for its systematic approach.

# 19 : PRODUCT PROFILE ANALYSIS

The development of new products poses a real dilemma for management. On the one hand, a continuing flow of new products is essential to sustain long-term growth and, in some cases, even survival. Who has not heard the proud boast of a company chairman that 50 per cent of his company's turnover (they seldom refer to profit) is derived from products that did not exist five years ago? On the other hand, the high failure rate of new products, particularly in the consumer products field, is almost legendary. Management literature is full of references to mortality rates, as high as nine in ten in some cases, and to such phenomena as the "decay curve of ideas"—an assumption that at least fifty drawing board ideas are required to produce one commercial success.

This is true of even the most successful and professional marketing companies. A C Nielsen has reported that in 1969 the British housewife was able to choose from 288 different home laundry products (brands, types and sizes) compared with a mere ninety-two alternatives in 1947. This is a very real achievement by Lever, P & G and Colgate. And yet, the closely related field of toilet soaps has proved a very much tougher proposition for these manufacturers with such brands as Lyril, Espri, Dove, Caress and Sunlight now part of history.

Expensive failures are by no means the prerogative of the detergent industry, however. Rank's excursion into bowling alleys and Singer's attempt to market washing machines are examples of how the best run companies can come badly unstuck.

Fortunately, management is rapidly realising its shortcomings in the area of new product development. Rationalisation is taking place through administrative reforms and improved decision-making procedures. In particular, much closer attention is being paid to improving decision methods at each stage of the new product development process—*search, screening, profit analysis, product development, test marketing* and *commercialisation.* There is greater realisation of the need to make a series of conscious decisions as to whether a product should be pursued or abandoned.

Over the last decade management has tended to concentrate upon the *last* three stages of the product development cycle. They have developed improved research methods for concept, placement and copy testing, refined the various analytical tools for reading test markets and have made greater use of management techniques (e.g. PERT) for co-ordinating new product activity. And yet, in many product fields, the failure rate is still unacceptably high.

In future we are likely to see very much greater attention directed towards the first three stages of the development cycle—*search, screening* and *profit analysis.* This will follow from management's increasing awareness of two important cost factors:

1    Rapid escalation of development costs following the profit analysis stage—an exponential increase in some markets with high R & D market entry costs.
2    High opportunity costs of too many test market failures —principally the deterioration of relations with distributors and retailers and the diversion of Head Office sales and marketing effort away from a company's main profit lines.

## THE CHECKLIST APPROACH

Product profile analysis is a quantified checklist approach to new product development. It has been developed and implemented by McAlley Associates as an aid towards improving the quality of decisions during screening and profit analysis. It is designed to:

1    Evaluate and enumerate all new product concepts against a common decision framework.
2    Arrive at a rank order of priorities for co-ordinated R & D and marketing effort.

The common framework is a set of key factors evolved from the three most relevant disciplines—*marketing, operations (R & D, production* and *purchasing)* and *finance.* Within each discipline every factor is weighted according to its importance to a company's agreed strategy. Then each new product idea is evaluated against each factor on a five- or seven-point scale.

The essential starting point for successful PPA is an agreed corporate and marketing strategy. This should define the long-term objectives of the company in terms of sales and profits, return on investment and/or earnings per share. It must also indicate both the kind of markets in which the company intends to operate and the degree of financial risk it is prepared to undertake. Without these parameters it is impossible to draw up a checklist of key factors.

## AN EXAMPLE OF PPA IN ACTION

### Establishing corporate strategy

The **XYZ** Pharmaceutical Company is an independent British company manufacturing a range of patent medicines, analgesics and upset-stomach remedies. Established for over 100 years, its products are household names and are used as remedies for a range of illnesses—both real and imaginary. Sales and profits rose steadily until the late 1950s when the introduction of more efficacious, heavily advertised products by American drug companies caused sales to level off. Rising raw material costs and administrative overheads brought about a steadily worsening profit position which was aggravated by an abortive attempt to market, under licence, an expensive range of women's hand creams and facial cosmetics.

The company confined its sales entirely to the chemist trade and operated a twenty-man sales force which called on approximately 5000 active retail and wholesale accounts. It had recently increased its R & D staff and possessed good know-how in the areas of skin-care and hair-care.

A team of management consultants had reviewed the company's strengths and weaknesses and recommended a corporate marketing and financial strategy to the recently strengthened board of management.

With some modifications to the strategy, the board defined its future business as that of *personal health, hygiene and beauty* and set specific five-year objectives in terms of improving earnings per share and raising the return on capital. It identified a major gap between current projected performance and its five-year targets and placed prime emphasis on the development of new products (both internally and through acquisition).

The board established a new product development team to co-ordinate this activity. Conscious of its specialist R & D skills, the company was determined to break into growth markets like shampoos and personal deodorants—most of which require good distribution in grocery outlets to provide the scale economies for heavy press and television advertising. It recognised that the cost of market entry was high but was determined to isolate and attack specific market segments (and accept a second or third market share position), rather than go for brand leadership and meet the major toiletry manufacturers head-on.

## Choice of marketing factors

The new product development group needed to screen the forty or fifty product concepts that had been raised via R & D projects, brain-storming sessions and agency contributions. It decided to apply product profile analysis and drew up a list of eight marketing factors considered the most relevant to the agreed marketing strategy. These were then weighted on a scale of nought to ten according to their relative importance. The results are shown in Figure 19:1.

| FACTOR | WEIGHTING |
| --- | --- |
| Market size | 8 |
| Growth potential | 6 |
| Grocer/chemist market breakdown | 10 |
| Vulnerability of competition | 5 |
| Distribution channels | 4 |
| Product superiority | 9 |
| Line extension | 3 |
| Price flexibility | 7 |

FIGURE 19:1  TABLE OF RELEVANT MARKETING FACTORS

These are the eight marketing factors considered most relevant by the XYZ Company. Their new product development group have assigned a weighting number to each factor according to its relative importance

250

This weighting schedule reflected the company's prime interest in large, grocery-important toiletry markets with good growth potential even though access to these markets would require new (and expensive) methods of distribution. It was its intention to market products with a sufficient performance plus over competition to allow for premium pricing. The company saw little advantage or benefit from the use of "umbrella" brand names from its existing lines—most of which were in stagnant, semi-ethical markets.

## Compiling a product rating scale (marketing)

Having established the factor weightings, the new product group set up an objective, seven-point rating scale for each factor (See Figure 19:2). They defined the framework of the scales as closely as possible and then rated each of the new product ideas on these scales. This entailed considerable library research into published data on market sizes, growth rates etc. and a fair amount of "guestimating" on the part of totally new product ideas. The team were genuinely surprised, however, at the amount of competitive information that they found in the company—most of which had been lying unused for years.

## Calculating market profile totals

At this stage, each product had been considered against the eight marketing factors, and eight corresponding product ratings derived. It was then necessary to take into account the weightings assigned to the different marketing factors. This was achieved by multiplying each product rating figure by the appropriate weighting number in order to arrive at a "marketing score".

Figure 19:3 shows the marketing profile score calculations and results for two potential products. It is seen that two entirely different products received almost identical total scores by this method.

The new product development group compiled a table of forty-five products, and arranged them in order of the total market profile scores achieved. The maximum possible score was 364; the actual results ranged from 150 to 275.

| FACTOR | EXCELLENT 7 | VERY GOOD 6 | GOOD 5 | FAIRLY GOOD 4 | FAIRLY POOR 3 | POOR 2 | VERY POOR 1 |
|---|---|---|---|---|---|---|---|
| Market size (RSP) | £1½M upwards | £1M – £1½M | £800 000– £1M | £600– £800 000 | £400– £600 000 | £200– £400 000 | £0– £200 000 |
| Growth potential 3 year average | 11 per cent upwards | 10 per cent p.a. | 5 per cent p.a. | 3 per cent p.a. | 2 per cent p.a. | 1 per cent p.a. | Static |
| Percentage grocer/chemist turnover | 100/nil | 80/20 | 60/40 | 50/50 | 40/60 | 20/80 | nil/100 |
| Vulnerability of competition | No market leader(s)— "sleepy" management market under-developed | | ............Average ability ............ moderate spenders | | | | ............Rock solid good "marketeers" heavy spenders |
| Existing distribution channels | No change | | ............New and old ............ | | | | ............Complete change |

| | Absolutely unique | Superior: difficult to better | Superior but imitable | Better plus gimmick | Slightly better plus gimmick | "Me too" plus gimmick (e.g. two-stage perfume release) | Complete "Me too" |
|---|---|---|---|---|---|---|---|
| Product superiority | | | | | | | |
| Line extension | Complete umbrella—"awareness" advertising only | | | Use existing brand names: new advertising | | | New name new advertising |
| Pricing flexibility | Complete freedom no price leadership/new market | | | Consumers have average awareness of price brackets Some trade pressure on margins | | | Cartel or permanent price war |

FIGURE 19:2   PRODUCT RATING SCALE—MARKETING

This seven-point scale has been designed so that each potential new product can be assigned a "product rating" according to its expected performance against each of the eight marketing factors.

| Factor | Factor weighting | EFFERVESCENT TOILET CLEANSER TABLET | | | ODOUR-FREE AEROSOL DEPILATORY | | |
|---|---|---|---|---|---|---|---|
| | | Product rating | = | Score | Product rating | = | Score |
| Market size | 8 | 7 | = | 56 | 6 | = | 48 |
| Growth potential | 6 | 5 | = | 30 | 6 | = | 36 |
| Grocer/chemist turnover | 10 | 8 | = | 80 | 2 | = | 20 |
| Distribution channels | 4 | 2 | = | 8 | 6 | = | 24 |
| Line extension | 3 | 1 | = | 3 | 1 | = | 3 |
| Product superiority | 9 | 4 | = | 36 | 6 | = | 54 |
| Vulnerability of competition | 5 | 2 | = | 10 | 6 | = | 30 |
| Pricing flexibility | 7 | 5 | = | 35 | 6 | = | 42 |
| **Total** | | | = | 258 | | = | 257 |

FIGURE 19:3    MARKETING PROFILE SCORE TABLE

Here are two examples of product market profile calculations carried out by the XYZ company. Each individual score has been derived by multiplying the product rating by its corresponding factor weighting. Addition of all eight scores for each product yields the market profile total

## Product profiles—operations

The new product team were tempted to assign R & D priorities immediately but were instructed by the board to submit the same list of products to an operational (R & D, production and purchasing) screening procedure. They therefore assigned a code name to each of their product ideas and prepared a short statement as to what each product was expected to do. "Knockout", for example, was a three-layer cold tablet, with each layer coloured differently and containing respectively an analgesic, an expectorant and a decongestant. The team also provided an estimate of first-year sales.

The R & D people were asked to prepare a short list of ingredients needed for each new product. This information, compiled for the benefit of the purchasing department, enabled the operations team to start their own product profile analysis.

The operations director identified six key factors in his area of responsibility. He assigned weighting factors and set up a similar rating table to that of his marketing colleagues (see Figure 19:4). His main concern was over the lack of available land for factory

| FACTOR WEIGHTING | | EXCELLENT 7 | VERY GOOD 6 | GOOD 5 | FAIRLY GOOD 4 | FAIRLY POOR 3 | POOR 2 | VERY POOR 1 |
|---|---|---|---|---|---|---|---|---|
| Equipment | 5 | Use existing | Add small items | .......... | Some new some old | .......... | Many major new items | All new |
| Factory space | 9 | Use existing—no alterations required | Minor modifications only | Some redesign of layout required | New construction within existing building | Extension to factory required | New factory on existing site | New factory on new site |
| Manufacturing experience | 4 | Know the process backwards | .......... | .......... | Familiar with at least half the process technology | .......... | | Completely new technology |
| Labour | 3 | Fully automated production | Less than 250 labour-days per annum | .......... | Around 1250 labour-days per annum | .......... | Over 2500 labour-days per annum | Entirely manual |
| Raw material supply | 6 | Common material. Stable supply. Supplied on demand | .......... | .......... | Relatively scarce. Some variation in supply. Order lead-time around 6 months | .......... | | Scarce material. Highly variable supply. Long order lead-time (over 18 months) |
| Research and development | 8 | Pilot product available | Confirmatory testings only | .......... | Familiar with chemistry: no experience of formulations | | New field: some published information | Entirely new field |

FIGURE 19:4   PRODUCT RATING SCALE—OPERATIONS

This is the table produced by the XYZ Company's director of operations in order to calculate product ratings from the aspect of R & D, purchasing and production extension. He could build an extension to the present factory or add more storage capacity in a new warehouse but more ambitious plans would require a new factory on a new site—the nearest available land being forty to fifty miles away.

He was also acutely aware of his cramped laboratory facilities and of the long lead times required to recruit and train suitable research staff. On the credit side, there was a good pool of available labour in the area, especially part-time women employees who would be invaluable on the finishing floor during special sales promotion periods.

The operational profiles acted like a shower of cold water on the marketing department's euphoria. Many of the marketing men's "way-out" ideas—which scored well on their checklist—scored badly on the operational list. Some products were estimated to require at least three years of applied research, others would involve complex effervescent technology with the attendant problems of air conditioning and humidity control. In fact, the product which was ranked first by the marketing people ranked only ninth on the operational list while the operations group's first choice came close to the bottom of the marketing list. A salutary experience all round.

## Product profiles—financial

Personal feelings notwithstanding, the marketing team were pleased at the progress made to date and were resolved to develop a set of financial criteria as a final stage in their feasibility analysis. Taking the combined marketing and operational scores they worked out approximate ten-year marketing plans for each of the top twenty products—estimating sales levels, gross margins and advertising expenditures.

The finance director wished to evaluate each new product investment against three main criteria, which he weighted as follows:

| | | |
|---|---|---|
| 1 | Investment in fixed assets (£0–£2M) | weighting = 5 |
| 2 | Investment in working capital (£10 000–£500 000) | weighting = 3 |
| 3 | DCF yield (0–50 per cent) | weighting = 10 |

The most important factor was the discounted cash flow yield. Historically, the company had used either the return on capital or payback methods of investment appraisal. These had proved misleading, however, in that they had failed to take account of the effect of taxation on both profit and capital expenditure, the "earning" life of the various projects and the time pattern of the flow of future earnings. The DCF method was also convenient in that, having formulated a basic company objective of achieving a minimum 15 per cent return on capital over the next five years, it was able to take this figure as a cut-off point for all investment appraisal decisions.

The finance director evaluated the twenty projects according to his three factors, using the familiar seven-point scale approach. While there was less variability in the finance profiles than in the marketing or production profiles, it was clear that (as one would expect using the DCF method, projects with a slow profit growth following heavy launch advertising commitments were viewed less favourably than those generating profit in the early years.

## Product profiles—marketing, operations and finance combined

Once the profile analysis had been completed it was possible for the new project development team to draw up a complete list of product profiles in which the assessments made by the marketing, operations and finance experts were combined. The products were once again placed in order of their scores; the first five product results are shown in Figure 19 : 5.

It should be noted that, because the product profiles were arrived at by straight addition of department profiles, a further weighting was built into the evaluation study. The maximum possible scores for each department were: marketing 364, operations 245, and finance 126. The product profile was therefore weighted in the ratio of 3 : 2 : 1 in favour of marketing.

## Management interpretation of product profile analysis

Given the results of product profile analysis, company management was left with the problem of the cut-off point. How many of the

| Product description | MARKETING | | OPERATIONS | | FINANCE | | PRODUCT | |
|---|---|---|---|---|---|---|---|---|
| | Profile Score | Rank Order | Profile Score | Rank Order | Profile Score | Rank Order | Profile Score | Rank Order |
| "*Knockout*"—three-layer cold preventative tablet | 245 | 7 | 215 | 2 | 110 | 3 | 570 | 1 |
| "*Checkout*"—flash dispersal anti-diarrhoea tablet | 265 | 2 | 205 | 3 | 90 | 5 | 560 | 2 |
| "*Cleanout*"—effervescent toilet cleanser tablet | 258 | 4 | 175 | 10 | 120 | 1 | 553 | 3 |
| "*Sprayout*"—odour free, aerosol depilatory | 257 | 5 | 195 | 4 | 85 | 6 | 537 | 4 |
| "*Washout*"—wash-off cream containing herbal extracts | 270 | 1 | 180 | 9 | 80 | 8 | 530 | 5 |

FIGURE 19:5   FINAL PRODUCT PROFILE SCORES

Here are the five top-ranking products identified by the XYZ Company's use of product profile analysis. Twenty products were included in the complete table, but the portion shown here illustrates the combination of marketing, operations and finance profile analysis into total output profile score

twenty projects should it develop over the next five years? Should marketing decide how many or should the finance department? In fact, the board decided that:

1    The company would take on as many development projects as its R & D department could reasonably handle (in this case the top *twelve* product profiles)
2    R & D priorities for these twelve projects were to be set by the *marketing* department.

After six months of exhaustive study the XYZ Pharmaceutical Company had determined its short list of development products, assigned research priorities and formulated a five-year, new product development programme. This plan was thoroughly consistent with its corporate, marketing and financial plans for the next five years.

## PROS AND CONS OF PPA

The above example serves to illustrate how product profile analysis can be made to work. The problem situation facing the company is an all too familiar feature of British industry at the present time. The strategies employed by the XYZ Company are by no means copybook or correct but the systematic approach has much to commend it.

In practice, product profile analysis has a number of operational advantages over less objective methods of appraisals:

1    By involving the three main functional departments at an early stage of analysis, personal involvement, commitment and communication are measurably improved.
2    The numerate appraisal technique forces management to think objectively, provides an effective antidote to the "jackpot complex" of many marketing departments and neatly sidesteps the well-intentioned suggestions of the managing director's wife.
3    It ensures that management makes a conscious "go/no go" decision across a range of alternative projects before heavy development costs are incurred.
4    It automatically assigns research priorities.

As with all new techniques, however, PPA has some possible pitfalls. There is a tendency for the profile scores to assume a spurious accuracy and certainty which is unjustified in the light of the approximate (and often pure "guestimate") input information and the fairly arbitrary choice of weightings. This is particularly true of the financial analysis which needs to be continually refined as the projects develop. Input data needs to be constantly monitored and updated—ideally in the form of quarterly review meetings—and it is imperative that the chief executive takes an active role in all the negotiations. In particular, the new product team must have his continuing support and direction.

It is also essential to adopt an empirical approach to the allocation of factor weightings and to make necessary adjustments in the light of experience. This applies both to the judgements of critical factors within departments and to the weightings applied to the scores of each department. These weightings should be devised with as much care and precision as possible and should be openly discussed at the regular review meetings referred to above.

## OTHER APPLICATIONS OF PPA

The PPA approach to new product development has a number of other interesting developments and applications. For example, once factor weightings and rating scales have been agreed, it is a simple matter to write a computer program to provide an instant profile score for any new projects that need to be evaluated. This is particularly useful for the updating procedure in that it avoids time-consuming manual compilations.

The method of using weighted factors can also be employed at the pre-test market stage. A number of advertising agencies and specialist consultancies are developing models for predicting the success or failure and ultimate market share of new products. The factors are chosen after an exhaustive study of the reasons why other similar products have succeeded in the market place and such important parameters as packaging, weight of advertising and repeat purchase patterns can be quantified. This information provides an essential "feedback" to the product rating scales outlined above and should eventually bring about changes in a company's marketing strategy.

The technique is also of considerable value in the field of

acquisition search. Having systematically evaluated its own strengths and weaknesses, an acquisition-minded company can set up an acquisition profile (marketing, operations and finance) of the kind of company it is looking for. This profile should then list the *complementary* qualities required in a candidate company to produce the all-important *synergy* that is expected from a successful merger. The search for a suitable company can then follow exactly the same screening method as for new products.

# CHAPTER 20

# Market Research by the Input–Output Method

*by* Kendall Carey

*Product Manager (Belting), BTR Leyland*

Input–output is a new tool for market research based on the recording of purchases and sales between industries. Already it shows promise as being one of the most effective methods. The French, for example, produce input–output tables twice a year for seventy-seven different industries, and Britain has made a start with forty-six industries. The more detailed these figures are, the more valuable they will become for industry and business.

# 20 : MARKET RESEARCH BY THE INPUT–OUTPUT METHOD

Wassily Leontief (Henry Lee Professor of Economics, Harvard University), the originator of input–output analysis, defines planning as: "The organised application of systematic reasoning to the solution of specific practical problems." Market research, as one of the major constituents of business planning, can be similarly defined. In solving marketing problems, the chief need is a knowledge of the interactions taking place within the economy.

Without this knowledge researchers are in the position of an architect trying to design a building without knowing the physical properties of the available materials. Moreover, the continuing series of economic crises, and the measures taken by the government to counteract them, have made directors only too aware of the need to estimate the effects of action outside their control on their operations. Input–output analysis, by tracing the transactions within the economy, has thus already become an essential research tool.

## APPLICATIONS FOR INPUT–OUTPUT TABLES

In determining the most profitable path for his company to follow the market researcher is concerned fundamentally with two forecasting problems.

1   He must forecast the sales of his company's present and potential products.
2   He must estimate the likely costs of production, and hence the profitability.

Sales forecasting involves identifying the factors influencing the markets to which the products are sold. In the case of packaging these might be consumer tastes, technology (for the electronics industry), or perhaps export prospects (for sales to heavy vehicle producers).

A basic input–output table is presented in the form of a matrix—see Figure 20:1. Industries are listed on the left-hand side of the table, and also along the top in the same order. Reading horizontally, the figures given in each box show the output of the industry on the left of the table distributed among the purchasers of this output. Alternatively, reading vertically the figures show the various inputs from each industry to the industry heading the column. Usually the table is extended to give each industry's contribution to total consumption, capital formation and other categories of final demand, and the contribution of labour and profit to each industry.

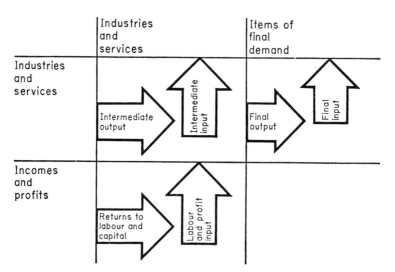

FIGURE 20:1    BASIC CONCEPT
The fundamental construction of an input–output table.

In Figure 20:2, which is taken from the inter-industry Transactions Table, the mechanical engineering industry sold £19.7M to the coalmining industry and £13.7M to the cotton and man-made fibres sector. Reading downwards, the industry paid £3.6M for coal, £3M for cotton and man-made fibres, and £4.4M for paper and board products. Since the output of an industry excludes its sales to itself, the box at the intersection of its row and column is left blank. The usefulness of the table depends on the degree of

| £ million    Purchases | Coal | Mechanical | Cotton and | Paper |
| sales    by | mining | engineering | man–made | and |
| by | | | fibres | board |
|---|---|---|---|---|
| Coal mining | — | 3.6 | 7.2 | 11.2 |
| Mechanical engineering | 19.7 | — | 13.7 | 9.3 |
| Cotton and man–made fibres | 0.8 | 3.0 | — | 3.1 |
| Paper and board | 0.6 | 4.4 | 3.2 | — |

FIGURE 20:2    EXAMPLE OF AN INPUT-OUTPUT TABLE
Extract from the inter-industry Transactions Table.

definition of the industry groups. It is possible to draw up an input–output matrix for actual products, but the complications of data collection would make it unlikely that such fine definition could ever be achieved on a national scale. However, tables have been produced for the United States economy with over two hundred headings; a sufficiently large number to interest even small firms.

An input–output table identifies first the initial purchasing industries and so enables a comparison to be made with the company's sales to these industries. This comparison is also an indicator of the distribution of competitors' sales. For example, Figure 20:3 shows the widely distributed sales of paper and board products throughout forty-two customer industries.

Apart from the concentrated demand from the printing and publishing industry, the markets for paper and board are widely scattered and many companies aim their promotion equally widely to take advantage of this. However, this is seldom as profitable as operating a segmented marketing policy. For example, in Figure 20:3, seven industry groups buy two-thirds of production, with thirty-five groups accounting for the remainder.

Thus a paper-producing company can plan its marketing policies and decide, in the knowledge of the major markets, to concentrate on two or three of the user industries, of which it has particular knowledge or with which it has good relations, thereby getting the best possible return on its selling or promotion costs.

The input–output table takes this a stage further and enables the market analyst to assess the indirect demand for a product generated by the next stage of consumers and so on until the demand is ultimately traced to its share in final demand, namely, consumption,

| CUSTOMER | £M |
|---|---|
| Coal mining | 0.6 |
| Quarrying | 2.2 |
| Coke ovens and coal-tar products | 0.1 |
| Chemicals and dyes | 5.4 |
| Drugs and perfume | 5.7 |
| Soap, polishes | 10.2 |
| Oils and greases | 1.1 |
| Paint and plastics | 1.9 |
| Iron, steel, milling | 0.4 |
| Tin-plate and tubes | 0.2 |
| Non-ferrous metal | 1.1 |
| Motor cycles | 2.6 |
| Aircraft | 2.5 |
| Railway rolling stock | 0.2 |
| Shipbuilding | 0.4 |
| Mechanical engineering | 4.4 |
| Electrical engineering | 7.9 |
| Radio and telecommunications | 4.2 |
| Hardware | 2.0 |
| Precision instruments | 2.7 |
| Miscellaneous metal manufacture | 1.7 |
| Cotton and man-made fibres | 3.2 |
| Woollens and worsted | 0.8 |
| Hosiery and lace | 2.5 |
| Other textile | 0.8 |
| Textile finishing | 0.9 |
| Leather and fur | 1.1 |
| Clothing | 2.9 |
| Boot and shoe | 2.0 |
| Cereal foodstuffs | 18.8 |
| Other manufactured foods | 30.6 |
| Drink and tobacco | 12.7 |
| Timber | 0.7 |
| Printing and publishing | 85.7 |
| Rubber | 2.3 |
| China, glassware | 1.9 |
| Building materials | 12.8 |
| Miscellaneous manufacturers | 7.0 |
| Building contracting | 12.0 |
| Gas and water | 0.4 |
| Electricity | 0.1 |
| Services | 51.0 |

FIGURE 20:3    SALES OF THE PAPER AND BOARD INDUSTRY

Out of some forty-two customers, only seven account for two-thirds of the paper and board total sales.

(*Source: Input–output tables for the United Kingdom, HMSO*)

exports or investment. The industry groups which will find the input–output tables most relevant in this respect will be those operating farthest from the consumers, and therefore having the highest ratings in Figure 20:4. The order of rating is based on information extracted from the preliminary table for 1963 which shows the percentage of an industry's output sold through intermediate buyers.

| INDUSTRY | INTERMEDIATE OUTPUT % |
|---|---|
| Mining and quarrying (other than coal) | 88 |
| Metal manufacture | 83 |
| Coal mining | 71 |
| Other manufacturers | 65 |
| Chemicals | 59 |
| Mineral oil refining | 57 |
| Gas, electricity and water | 44 |
| Agriculture, forestry and fishing | 37 |
| Services | 26 |
| Engineering and allied industries | 20 |
| Textiles | 17 |
| Food, drink and tobacco | 10 |
| Construction | 8 |

FIGURE 20:4    PERCENTAGE OF OUTPUT SOLD THROUGH
INTERMEDIATE BUYERS

This kind of table is useful to the market researcher in tracing demand beyond the direct customer to the eventual end user.

The use of the input–output table is not, however, confined to calculating demand. It enables the effects of changes in government policy to be calculated for a particular industry. For example, knowing the extent to which each of these "layers" of demand affects the demand for the particular product in question, a change in consumption resulting from an increase in purchase tax can be followed back through the system until its effect upon a particular company's business is determined.

A knowledge of the indirect demand for a product also enables an assessment to be made of the merits of "back-selling", namely sales representation or advertising directed at the customer's markets.

Back-selling can be done by a single company on its own, when it will try to make people familiar with the product by name. Sometimes the identity of the product is lost or irrelevant, for example a flue in a gas refrigerator. In this case, gas refrigerators can be promoted by all manufacturers of flues, the object being to expand the total market and increase sales without necessarily changing market shares.

## MARKET FORECASTING

Input–output tables can assist forecasting in two ways. First, forecasts for consumption or the output of the construction industry can be applied to the table. Second, by comparing tables over a period of time, assessments can be made of the rate of change of technology and consumer tastes. Ideally the two methods should be combined, but since technology and tastes change relatively slowly the first method alone is satisfactory for short-term forecasts.

Reliable forecasts of the likely growth in the sectors of final demand, such as those produced by the National Institute of Economic Social Research can be applied to the input–output table and the resultant changes are traced through the inter-industry transactions matrix to yield forecasts for a particular industry. One considerable advantage that this method has by comparison with forecasting on the basis of past trends plus experience is that compatibility between the various aggregate elements—for example consumption and public authority spending—is assured and the detailed forecasts that emerge are therefore consistent with the overall trends.

The table also enables the effects of an increase in the demand for the products of one particular industry to be assessed. Figure 20:5, derived from the input–output table, shows both the direct and indirect demand generated by £100 of final output by the motor and cycle industry. The meaning of direct and indirect requirements is perhaps best illustrated by the motor industry's use of rubber products (category 38). The £4.20 required direct would consist largely of tyres but £0.30 of other rubber products such as seals and washers are also necessary for the production of items classified as the output of other industries.

Thus if it is forecast, for example, that exports of the motor industry will increase by £20M this would, on average, result in a direct demand for mechanical engineering products of £900,000 and an indirect demand of £320 000—that is 200 000 × 4.5 and 1.6 respectively.

Similarly, from the more recent 1963 information it can be deduced that a £30M increase in the turnover of the construction industry will, on average, generate a demand of £600 000 for quarry products. Industries such as construction, which are well documented with detailed statistics on sales and orders received, can therefore provide indicators on which forecasts for the supply industries may be based.

The applications of input–output analysis so far mentioned have all been static in the sense that a table for a single year has been manipulated to yield information and forecasts. However, possibly the most unusual and interesting uses of the method are for making forecasts of technological and taste changes through comparisons of tables for different years.

Changes in technology in user industries are of greater importance to the market analyst, since if they are rapid a market can literally disappear in a few years. In these cases rapid diversification is essential, either to keep up with the change or to move into new areas. The rate of change of consumer tastes is similarly important to consumer goods producers and suppliers to these industries. It should be emphasised that the technological change referred to here is not the change in the technology available, resulting from research effort, but the rate of assimilation of new technologies by the economic system.

The procedure by which these rates are assessed is simple to explain, but in practice it requires the use of a computer. Direct comparisons of one table with another of later date would yield wrong answers. For example, the levels of GNP will differ and prices will have changed. So they must be adjusted for compatibility. A team at the Harvard Economic Research Project carried out these adjustments to tables for the American economy for 1947 and 1958 and were able to make direct comparisons of the changing inputs required by the various industry sectors.

They found, for instance, that 33 per cent more labour would have been required to produce the 1958 final demand with 1947 technology and that of the inputs to the communications industry, plastics and electronic components showed increases of from 33 to 82 per

| INDUSTRY GROUP | DIRECT REQUIREMENTS £ | INDIRECT REQUIREMENTS £ | TOTAL REQUIREMENTS[1] (GROSS) £ | NET OUTPUT[2] AS PER CENT OF GROSS OUTPUT % | TOTAL REQUIREMENTS[3] (NET) £ |
|---|---|---|---|---|---|
| 1 Agriculture, forestry and fishing | — | 0.1 | 0.1 | 56.8 | 0.1 |
| 2 Coal mining | 0.3 | 2.4 | 2.7 | 71.8 | 1.9 |
| 3 Other mining and quarrying | — | 0.5 | 0.5 | 41.3 | 0.2 |
| 4 Coke ovens and coal tar products | 0.1 | 1.5 | 1.6 | 17.9 | 0.3 |
| 5 Chemicals and dyes | 0.7 | 1.3 | 2.0 | 43.4 | 0.9 |
| 6 Drugs and perfumery | — | — | — | 44.8 | — |
| 7 Soap, polishes, etc | — | 0.1 | 0.1 | 28.1 | — |
| 8 Mineral oil refining | 0.2 | 0.5 | 0.7 | 10.0 | 0.1 |
| 9 Oils and greases | 0.1 | 0.3 | 0.4 | 21.4 | 0.1 |
| 10 Paint, plastic materials, etc | 1.7 | 0.4 | 2.1 | 40.1 | 0.8 |
| 11 Iron and steel-melting, rolling and castings | 11.9 | 3.8 | 15.7 | 40.8 | 6.4 |
| 12 Iron and steel—tin-plate and tubes | 0.5 | 0.5 | 1.0 | 27.4 | 0.3 |
| 13 Non-ferrous metals | 3.5 | 1.7 | 5.2 | 31.7 | 1.6 |
| 14 Motors and cycles | 100.0 | 0.4 | 100.4 | 42.6 | 42.7 |
| 15 Aircraft | 0.2 | 0.1 | 0.3 | 59.4 | 0.2 |
| 16 Railway rolling stock, etc | 0.1 | 0.4 | 0.5 | 44.2 | 0.2 |
| 17 Shipbuilding and marine engineering | 0.1 | 0.2 | 0.3 | 52.3 | 0.1 |
| 18 Mechanical engineering | 4.5 | 1.6 | 6.1 | 54.9 | 3.4 |
| 19 Electrical engineering (general) | 3.0 | 0.6 | 3.6 | 51.9 | 1.8 |
| 20 Radio and tele-communications | 0.5 | 0.6 | 1.1 | 47.2 | 0.5 |
| 21 Hardware and hollow-ware | 2.4 | 0.7 | 3.1 | 43.3 | 1.4 |
| 22 Precision instruments, jewellery, etc | 0.2 | 0.1 | 0.3 | 52.6 | 0.2 |
| 23 Miscellaneous metal manufactures | 5.8 | 0.8 | 6.6 | 43.1 | 2.9 |
| 24 Cotton and man-made fibres | 0.4 | 1.1 | 1.5 | 38.6 | 0.6 |
| 25 Woollen and worsted | 0.1 | 0.2 | 0.3 | 30.7 | 0.1 |
| 26 Hosiery and lace | — | — | — | 36.9 | — |
| 27 Other textiles | 0.7 | 0.4 | 1.1 | 35.5 | 0.4 |
| 28 Textiles finishing and packing | — | 0.2 | 0.2 | 55.3 | 0.1 |
| 29 Leather and fur | 0.3 | 0.1 | 0.4 | 30.4 | 0.1 |

| | | | | | | |
|----|-------------------------------------|------|-----|------|------|------|
| 30 | Clothing | 0.1 | 0.1 | 0.2 | 36.6 | 0.1 |
| 31 | Boot and shoe | — | — | — | 36.7 | — |
| 32 | Cereal foodstuffs | — | 0.1 | 0.1 | 28.4 | — |
| 33 | Other manufactured foods | — | — | — | 17.9 | — |
| 34 | Drink and tobacco | 1.5 | 0.1 | 0.1 | 14.9 | 0.7 |
| 35 | Timber and furniture | 0.3 | 0.4 | 1.9 | 38.2 | 0.4 |
| 36 | Paper and board | 0.1 | 0.7 | 1.0 | 44.8 | 0.4 |
| 37 | Printing and publishing | — | 0.6 | 0.7 | 54.8 | — |
| 38 | Rubber | 4.2 | 0.3 | 4.5 | 37.2 | 1.7 |
| 39 | China and glassware | 0.5 | 0.2 | 0.7 | 56.3 | 0.4 |
| 40 | Building materials | 0.1 | 0.5 | 0.6 | 45.4 | 0.2 |
| 41 | Miscellaneous manufactures | 0.6 | 0.3 | 0.9 | 43.7 | 0.4 |
| 42 | Building and contracting | 0.3 | 0.7 | 1.0 | 50.9 | 0.5 |
| 43 | Gas and water | 0.3 | 0.6 | 0.9 | 42.9 | 0.4 |
| 44 | Electricity | 0.6 | 1.1 | 1.7 | 48.8 | 0.8 |
| 45 | Services | 9.1 | 8.8 | 17.9 | 74.1 | 13.2 |
| 46 | Public administration, etc | — | — | — | — | — |
| 47 | Imports | 2.0 | 8.6 | 10.6 | — | 10.6 |
| 48 | Sales by final buyers | — | 0.5 | 0.5 | — | 0.5 |
| 49 | Taxes on expenditure *less* subsidies | 0.4 | 1.8 | 2.2 | — | 2.2 |
| 50 | Gross domestic income | 42.6 | — | — | — | — |
| | **Total** | 100 | — | — | — | 100 |

1 In terms of gross output
2 Includes depreciation
3 In terms of net output (*plus* depreciation)

Crown copyright 1961

FIGURE 20:5    REQUIREMENTS PER £100 OF FINAL OUTPUT BY THE MOTOR AND CYCLE INDUSTRY

Analysis of the requirements which are generated by each £100 of sales made by the motor and cycle industry. The supplies listed under "direct" are those items not used by other industries, such as tyres. Indirect supplies refer to products such as seals, washers, which are also used by other industries.

cent. Comparisons of consumer tastes can be similarly analysed by comparing the different industry inputs to final consumption.

## COST ANALYSIS AND FORECASTING

The techniques already mentioned are equally applicable to the problems of forecasting product cost, which is a compound of labour, technology and material requirements. The demand estimates, resulting from the market analysis, indicate the likely investment requirements in stocks and production machinery. The rate of technological change in an industry indicates the rapidity with which the machinery will become obsolescent, and, as the changing labour requirements make manpower forecasts possible, appropriate steps can be taken in training and recruiting. In addition, material input costs can be estimated from the demand forecasts of the main industry groups using the same materials. Thus if demand forecasts for copper-using industries show a rapid increase in supply, the price of the material to all users can be expected to rise; so it may thus be worth while investing in research to find alternative materials.

## INPUT–OUTPUT TABLES IN THE UNITED KINGDOM

The extent to which the inter-industry tables can be usefully employed in industry depends largely on the amount of detail provided. In the United States, tables are provided detailing eighty-six industrial groups including separate categories for farm machinery equipment; construction, mining and oil-field machinery; material-handling machinery and equipment; metal-working machinery and equipment; special industry machinery; general industrial machinery, and machine-shop products.

The analyst in the United Kingdom, in a similar industry, is limited by an entry for "mechanical engineering" in the detailed breakdown or simply "metal manufacture" in the more recent summary tables.

Preliminary input–output tables have been prepared in the United Kingdom for the years 1948, 1950, 1954 and 1963. The data collected during the 1968 Census of Production will also be assessed for input–output purposes. The year 1954 was selected for a more detailed analysis resulting in the publication of "Input–Output Table for the United Kingdom 1954" covering forty-six industry groups. The most recent publication is the Summary Table for 1963 included in the report on National Income and Expenditure 1967 obtainable from HMSO at 37½p. These tables follow the same outline as the 1954 preliminary tables so that both sources may be used for comparison, but only fourteen groups are shown.

A full table with 46 groups will be published for 1963 in due course; this number compares with 34 prepared in West Germany, 76 in Italy and 83 in the USSR. Some fifty countries have some form of national table and a single integrated table has recently been published for the European Economic Community.

The French, with seventy-seven categories, have taken up input–output analysis with enthusiasm producing tables twice a year brought up to date, not by a complete census, but by current statistical data readily available. This updating method is also used by the Central Statistical Office in the United Kingdom in preparing the preliminary tables. Quite obviously, the supply of input–output data needs to be improved in the United Kingdom before this type of analysis can be used as a precise planning tool in business. However, in market planning, the greater the variety of sources of information the better. Half a loaf is better than none and on this basis input–output tables are already worth studying.

## CHAPTER 21

# Cost and Value in Pricing Policy

*Management Information Executive, British Printing Corporation*

Pricing policy should be an essential part of marketing strategy but British industry in general has not given it the attention it deserves. With both domestic and industrial buyers becoming increasingly price conscious pricing policy is now more crucial than ever. Whatever is spent on promotion, if the price is wrong the product will not sell.

# 21 : COST AND VALUE IN PRICING POLICY

Over recent years there is little doubt that industrial and domestic buyers have become more discriminating in their buying, and that price enters into all buying decisions. In addition, with the emphasis on price restraint, whether government inspired or voluntarily imposed by the CBI, businesses have suffered a loss of pricing flexibility. It is also probably true that in British industry at large pricing policies have not been given the attention that they deserve; therefore in the future more sophisticated approaches to pricing will be required than have been required in the past. Before going on to discuss these more sophisticated methods, it will be useful to give an outline of the traditional approach to pricing.

## TRADITIONAL PRICING METHODS

In the majority of British businesses prices are decided primarily on the basis of cost, plus a percentage for profit. Only after the price of a product has been arrived at in this way is it compared with the market price for the product, or other products, which will be competitive with it. The reason for the prevalence of this practice is probably because it was the method of pricing manufactures enforced during wartime. Two principle methods are used to cost manufactured products: absorption costing (or "on costing") and marginal costing (or "direct costing").

### Absorption costing

With absorption costing, whatever its form, all the costs associated with a business are related to the output of manufacture, and are said to be absorbed at the time that the products are sold.

In general, the costs directly associated with the manufacture of a product are collected together, such as the costs of the material contained in the product and a labour or machine cost related to making the product. To arrive at a cost for pricing purposes, the other expenses of the business such as general production expense, administrative expense and selling expense are apportioned to the products to be manufactured to give a unit cost. The unit cost is normally arrived at by dividing the total of the production, administrative and selling expense by the normal volume of output.

If more than one product is manufactured a common unit of production such as a labour hour is used to apportion the production, administrative and selling expense to products.

When a cost for a unit of product has been arrived at, a percentage is added to provide the business with a profit. The unit cost and the added profit then becomes the price or price target. It is at this stage that competitors' prices are examined to see whether the product can become or will remain competitive on price. A graphical example of this method is shown in Figure 21 : 1.

When a company has a large product range, and where products

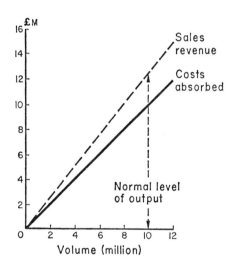

| | (000) |
|---|---|
| Normal level of output | 10000 |
| Production, admin and sales expenses total | £2500 |
| Unit material and labour cost | £0.75 |
| Unit cost of production, administration and sales expense ie £2500 divided by 10000 | £0.25 |
| Total unit cost | 1.00 |
| Profit %–25% | 0.25 |
| Unit price | £1.25 |

FIGURE 21:1    ABSORPTION COSTING

In the absorption costing method, the factory cost of each unit produced is found by dividing the total costs and expenses by the number of units produced. If this is done for different volumes of production, the results could be plotted on a curve similar to that shown. This is obviously dangerously misleading, since a profit is assumed even when only one unit is manufactured.

do not all use the same manufacturing facilities, the production expense (overhead) has to be analysed and apportioned to all the work centres. It is then necessary to recover (or "absorb") these expenses against the products made, or partly made, in each centre. This procedure is complex, and the basis of apportionment often has to contain arbitrary elements.

This method is used in most industries but is rarely found in food, tobacco, drink, chemical or other process type companies.

## Marginal costing

Marginal costing comes nearer to the economist's ideas about the costing of manufacture, in so far as the costs charged to a product are only those which can be related to the cost of making one more. In other words, the costs charged to the product are those that can be directly identified with the cost of making a unit, such as the cost of raw and packaging materials, labour and sometimes machine costs.

Under this system the difference between the selling price and the marginal cost of a unit is considered to be a contribution to the total of the production, administrative, and selling expenses and profit. This method is illustrated in Figure 21 : 2, using the same data introduced in the previous example of Figure 21 : 1.

It is difficult to use marginal costing in most industries because marginal costs are hard to define and the indirect expense is often far greater than the marginal costs. However, this method is widely used in food, tobacco, drink and chemical industries.

## Comments on absorption v. marginal costing methods

In industries such as the jobbing industry (a jobbing industry can be defined as one in which goods are made to order), it is undesirable to use marginal costing. In most other industries however, there is little doubt that for pricing purposes marginal costing is superior to absorption costing. The reason for this is that the determination of selling prices must be the concern of the senior executives of a business, and in particular marketing executives; what they require is a way to see what impact changes in volume and unit price have on profitability.

If Figures 21:1 and 21:2 are compared, it can be seen that the latter shows the situation more clearly. In the case of absorption costing the only thing that can be seen is the profit which would be made at a volume of ten million units. It cannot show the profit made

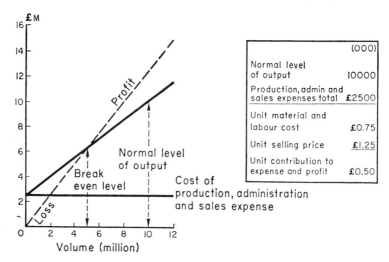

| | (000) |
|---|---|
| Normal level of output | 10000 |
| Production, admin and sales expenses total | £2500 |
| Unit material and labour cost | £0.75 |
| Unit selling price | £1.25 |
| Unit contribution to expense and profit | £0.50 |

FIGURE 21:2    MARGINAL COSTING

The data used to compile this curve is identical with that used for the absorption costing example of Figure 21:1. In this case, however, separation of fixed overhead costs and expenses allows the unit cost to be assessed in relation to volume of production. This, in turn, enables the manufacturer to establish the "break-even" level of production.

for any other level of sales. This is because the absorption cost line is related to one level of volume only.

Another point is that the graph of Figure 21:1 is misleading because it suggests that a profit—that is, the difference between the absorption cost line and the sales revenue line—is made even after only one unit has been sold. A further misleading impression is given because after a sales level of ten million units has been passed, the profit for each unit is £0.50 (since the indirect expense has been fully recovered at the level of ten million units, whereas the chart shows the absorption cost to continue at £1 a unit.

Figure 21:2 however, shows much more clearly the effect of volume on profit. For instance it can be seen that the production, administrative and sales expense is recovered when five million units have been sold at a unit price of £1.25. After this break-even point a profit is made of £0.50 for every unit sold; and no profit is made before the break-even point is reached.

Using marginal costing, a chief executive or marketing manager can relate volume targets to profit targets. Another advantage is that because the gap between the direct cost and the price that may be given to the product, is greater than that for absorption costs, management is forced to look more closely at the market, in order to decide on price.

The marginal cost also requires that probable demand be assessed and the level of fixed expenses related to a given range of output. For instance, in the example illustrated it is assumed that the indirect expense of £2 500 000 applies to a range of up to twelve million units of output, without serious variation. However, before a marginal cost and revenue chart can be constructed, a price for the product must be decided. If the price is to be realistic it must be based on the value of the product to the user or consumer, and not merely at a level which will arithmetically generate the desired profit.

## PRODUCT PRICING IN RELATION TO CONSUMER VALUE AND DEMAND

While the cost of manufacturing and marketing products and the administrative costs of a business cannot be entirely ignored in pricing decisions, ideally the price for a product in a free market must be what consumers are prepared and are able to pay. Assessing how the product will appeal to its consumers and the way in which demand levels at different prices are determined, can raise complex problems.

### Value of a product to the consumer

The value a consumer places on a product will depend upon the intrinsic and objective value of the product and his subjective reasoning towards it. The intrinsic value of the product covers the material content and the workmanship, skill, novelty or unique method used in making it. The objective value will be based on the intrinsic value and the product's performance, delivery period, beauty, uniqueness, and so on.

The subjective reasoning applied to the product will include the image of the company selling it, the status quality of the product, vanity appeal and so forth. All the qualities which make up the appeal of the product to the consumer are assessed in terms of how a consumer would favour a new product as opposed to an existing product.

The market research needed for this, however, is expensive, since to be reliable a large sample of potential consumers is required. It is mainly used only by consumer product companies. Engineering companies do use industrial market research, but many are unable to do so because they sell a vast number of products in small quantities.

Wilfred Brown and Elliot Jacques have developed an approach to product analysis pricing which covers ways of measuring and assessing product values without market or industrial market research. Their method was developed as a glacier metal project, and the method has been applied to the Glacier Metal Company, a company which has some of the problems of pricing encountered in the engineering industries.

## Demand analysis

Once the product's value to the consumer has been assessed, the next stage is to find the probable demand for the product. In the case of a new product which is to enter an existing market, information will exist about a ruling market price, or range of prices; so also will information about demand levels at different prices. Indeed, the issuing of target prices and product specifications will often precede the development of a new product.

With an entirely new product pioneering a new market, market research can determine acceptability of price and quality. However, entirely new products require more sophisticated techniques of demand analysis. The practice normally followed is to use market research information to assess the probable profitability of the product, and if it appears to be successful, to undertake a trial and to evaluate the information obtained from the trial.

When a price has been chosen (target price) which gives a level of demand both attainable and profitable, tactical factors are considered before the price is finally decided. The type of tactics to be followed will depend on whether the product is a pioneer or a market follower, and whether the company is a market leader or not.

A pioneer product may be launched at a price below that which the market would accept, in order to keep competitors out, or a high price may be chosen with the intention of reducing it when competitors enter the field.

A market follower may be priced at a lower price to obtain an entry into the market or at the ruling market price and depend on better organisation or advertising to get a foothold in the market.

Once the final price has been decided, the profitability of the product can be ascertained by deducting expected costs from the expected revenue. Thus, profitability is arrived at by working backwards from the market price and demand to costs, rather than from the costs of the product upwards.

# PRICING POLICY FOR EXISTING PRODUCTS

In addition to the pricing of new products, a company must obviously have a policy directed at the pricing of its existing products. In the consumer field two considerations are important in such a policy. These are price stability, and the role of promotional strategies in relation to price.

## Price stability

Stability of price is desirable for many obvious reasons. The price of a product is more likely to remain stable if it has been based on consumer demand rather than on costs, and there are several factors which provide reasons for changes in prices other than costs: they include the movement of competitors' prices and the prices of alternative products.

If the product has been on the market for some time, these factors will have been forecast and appraised as a part of the annual planning process. In other words, the key to pricing stability is to identify all factors affecting prices and to adopt a planned approach to price fixing.

## Promotional strategies in relation to price

A promotional campaign could involve the offer of attractive free gifts, the opportunity to purchase valuable articles at reduced prices, or a straight "money off" offer. Whatever the type of campaign, the company will have a specific objective in view. These objectives might include the wooing of consumers from a competitor's product, the extension of sales outside a recognised season—for example, soup in summer—or simply a straight increase in normal sales.

Whichever way a product is promoted, or whatever objective is in view, the effect of an incentive offer is to persuade the consumer to buy the product without altering its normal market price. So promotional strategies can be used to boost demand for the product, enabling the company to make higher marginal profits without increasing or decreasing the market price.

Therefore in formulating pricing policies, promotional activities are considered as ways of keeping prices stable, by generating a higher demand or maintaining the current level of demand for the product.

—— CHAPTER 22 ——

# Customer Cost Analysis and Marketing Information Systems

*by M Arnott*

*Metra Oxford*

Company profitability can be significantly affected by better information about the differences in costs between servicing different kinds of customers. Adding a further dimension to costing, CCA is vital to companies selling to highly concentrated retail organisations. It provides a profit-oriented approach to marketing at both tactical and strategic levels for all companies selling to over 1000 customers.

# 22 : CUSTOMER COST ANALYSIS AND MARKETING INFORMATION SYSTEMS

Wide variations can be found in the costs of servicing different customers. When taken together, the variable elements of redistribution, selling, order processing and credit costs can make significant differences to the net profit contribution of customers. With information on these points, marketing decisions and price negotiations can be placed on a firmer footing. Customer cost analysis provides the base for a marketing information system that will allow marketing management systematically to improve company profitability.

## PRICING PROBLEMS

The power of the organised buyer is today posing real profit problems to many manufacturers. Most companies would accept it as self-evident that accurate product costs are essential for a rational pricing system. This does not imply a "cost plus" pricing policy. If anything, accurate costs are needed even more with a market pricing policy where small or even negative margins may apply for periods of time. In these cases the risks of making a loss because of inaccurate cost information are correspondingly higher.

Accurate product costing, where a range of products is manufactured, depends upon estimating those unit costs which vary significantly from product to product; or to put it another way, those resources which are used in significantly different proportions by different products must be identified and accurately costed.

The evidence produced by recent Metra studies underlines the need for modern marketing management to add a further dimension to costing, customer cost analysis, which is the determination and allocation of specific customer variable costs.

289

## CONCENTRATION OF BUYING POWER

The trend in retailing is towards the multiple outlet. A recent Nielsen Researcher for example estimates that multiple stores account for 41 per cent of turnover in grocery (for branded packaged goods it is known that these shares are even higher) and that the top ten multiples alone account for 29 per cent. Co-ops account for a further 15 per cent.

This ever increasing concentration of retailing activity has led to a centralisation of buying, further accentuated by the advent of the symbol groups. In particular, it has led to the establishment of a price negotiating machinery between manufacturing companies and representatives of multiples and symbol groups. Nowadays, many manufacturers effectively set the price for a sizeable percentage of their total output by individual negotiation with a small number of retailer representatives. The assumption that costs do not vary significantly from customer to customer could prove very expensive, but a negotiator needs more than this realisation: he needs accurate estimates of the extent to which costs vary from customer to customer in order sensibly to negotiate a price.

## ORGANISING BETTER COST INFORMATION

Customer cost analysis is a procedure that requires an interdepartmental approach to company working although the ultimate responsibility must be that of the marketing director. The production department will be responsible for the provision of basic financial information on variable product costs of separate items in the range. Distribution should supply variable costs of salesmen's time. Accounts will provide information on variable costs of order processing and credit. The task of the marketing director, or his department, is to assemble these different items into an integrated picture and to draw from it conclusions on the general effectiveness of the trading policy of his organisation and of any alterations required to increase profitability.

Four areas have been isolated in which costs vary significantly from customer to customer. These are:

1   Redistribution—the cost of moving goods from a warehouse to a customer, either to individual retail outlets, or another warehouse
2   Selling—the cost of the salesman's time, and other selling costs which vary directly from customer to customer, such as promotional allowances
3   Order processing—the administrative costs of analysing orders and producing invoices
4   Credit—the cost of waiting for payment for goods delivered

Credit costs can normally be monitored by the existing accounting machinery, but usually additional efforts have to be made towards estimating the first three costs.

It is necessary to relate the variable elements of redistribution, selling and order processing costs to at least two main variables i.e. the number of orders placed, and the quantities ordered. In general these two variables are readily available from existing order processing systems. Two further things need to be done: first to establish the cost relationships and calculate the parameters involved, and second to set up a system to monitor sales and cost information on an on-going basis.

The variable redistribution costs are estimated from vehicle and labour costs and a sample of delivery points. Taking into account average speeds, distances, unloading times and, in extreme cases, unsuccessful attempts to deliver, the costs per delivery, and per case delivered can be estimated. In general, costs which vary with the geographical locations of customers are not included as customer variable costs, although in particular instances this may be necessary.

To measure selling costs it is necessary to obtain information on frequency of visits and duration of visits to customers. In some cases this is already in existence; otherwise a sample of customers served by a sample of salesmen will provide reliable information. Self-recording sheets are sufficient for this purpose provided a reliability observation check is built in to a limited number of cases. There are nearly always significant differences between the average time spent visiting different customers, but usually these are not related to the size of order taken.

## Absence of obvious patterns

If a graph is plotted of order size against time spent on each visit, the points on it may be scattered widely, with no particular relationship emerging. Figure 22:1 illustrates the findings of one such analysis.

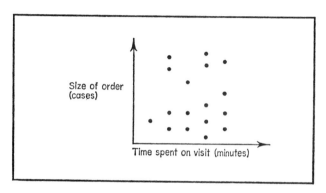

FIGURE 22:1    RELATIONSHIP BETWEEN SALESMAN'S TIME AND SIZE
OF ORDER TAKEN

An observed pattern showing how quite often there is no clear
relationship between order size and time spent on a visit.

As can be seen, there were long visits for small orders, short visits for large orders, and in general, no systematic relationship appeared. This is because time spent depended crucially on the practices of different customers rather than on the amount they ordered. For instance there were small customers who required the salesman to spend a long time checking stock for them, setting up displays, talking about the weather and so on. On the other hand some big customers required the salesman to do little more than actually take down the order.

An annual cost per salesman is calculated from average salaries, bonuses, car costs, etc, and hence an average cost per sales call is determined. From data on the number of sales calls resulting in an order, and the number of orders received where no sales call is made, an average sales cost per order is derived, which varies between customers. Merchandising activities are assessed on the same basis but related to a longer time period.

Finally, a cost per order is found for the order processing system. Since many systems are by now largely computerised, this

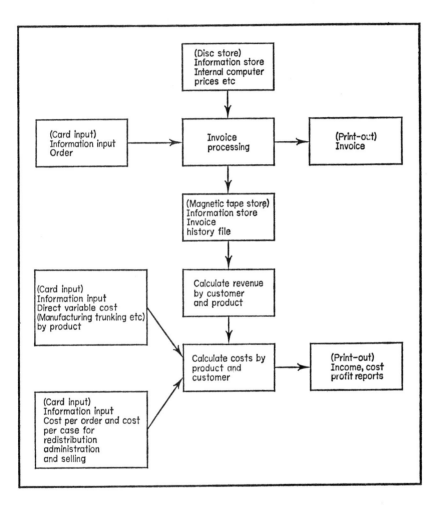

FIGURE 22:2     OUTLINE FLOW CHART OF COMPUTER ANALYSIS
This flow chart illustrates the way in which information from
existing in-house procedures is merged with new data to yield
customer-specific costs.

consists primarily of computer time and card punching time plus stationery and other easily identifiable direct variable costs.

These cost parameters are analysed by means of a computer program which extracts the relevant information from tape files of order and invoice information. An outline flow chart of the process is shown in Figure 22:2. But there is no reason why customer variable costs should not be monitored from a manual system. Using sampling techniques, a fairly cheap system can be devised. Particular attention is focused on the company's most important customers. In some cases as few as twenty customers account for over 50 per cent of total turnover.

## Large differences in profitability

Considering all customer variable costs together, very significant differences are found in the costs per case for each customer, and the effect on profitability is remarkable. Examples of the magnitudes of the differences found in one case are given in Figure 22:3. Index figures are used, based on 100 for Customer 1 in each case. The figures relate to net profitability, and allowances for all overhead costs are made.

| CUSTOMER | | | PRODUCT | |
|---|---|---|---|---|
| | A | B | C | D |
| 1 | 100 | 100 | 100 | —100 |
| 2 | 85 | 72 | 68 | —700 |
| 3 | 73 | 52 | 45 | —1 250 |

FIGURE 22:3    ANALYSIS OF PROFIT FOR EACH CUSTOMER CASE
When all customer variable costs are considered together, significant differences are found in the costs per case for each customer. This table displays the results of analysis for three customers, with customer 1 given the index 100 for each product. It is seen that product D was actually making substantial net losses.

As can be seen from Figure 22:3, product D was actually making a (net) loss. It can be seen that the losses for customers 2 and 3 were quite substantial. The identification of losses such as these could by itself pay for a study of this type. For products A, B and C, it can be seen that customers 1, 2 and 3 were significantly different in their profitability. Even in these (by no means extreme) examples, are instances where a case of product sold to one customer makes twice as much profit as it would if it were sold to another customer.

The remaining customers, who will normally number thousands after the key accounts have been dealt with individually, are dealt with in a similar manner but grouped into meaningful categories by size, type of business or organisation, area, sales region and so on.

## EVALUATION OF DISCOUNTS

As an example of the use of this type of analysis to the price negotiator, we look at the effects of special discounts on the profitability of different customers, and calculate the increases in units sold necessary to maintain budgeted net profit. In the case of one company studied analysis of two key customers gave the results shown in Figure 22:4.

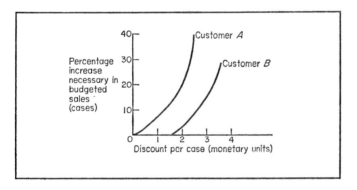

FIGURE 22:4    DISCOUNT GUIDES FOR NEGOTIATIONS
These curves show the percentage increases in sales that would be necessary to cover different discounts on the same product for two customers. Such curves should be used by key account salesmen.

In this case for customer B an increase of around 5 per cent in budgeted sales is necessary to retain budgeted net profit if an extra discount of two money units is given, whereas for customer A an increase of around 30 per cent is necessary. The time period considered in this example was that of the promotion. This sort of information is clearly of great value to the negotiator if he is to make profitable decisions based on the best information available.

The value of an analysis of this type is multiplied enormously where the information gained is used to set up an on-going monitoring system. The foundation of such a system will be the data base accumulated during the course of the initial customer cost analysis study. The main outputs will provide management information relating to control and to planning decision taking. The benefits to be derived from basing a marketing information system on a customer cost analysis study are significant because contribution is taken as the yardstick rather than turnover, which has already been shown to have weaknesses as a profit indicator on a between-customer basis.

## A PROFIT-BASED MARKETING SYSTEM

The integrated system will build on the flow chart shown in Figure 22:2. However to transform the system into a dynamic rather than a static one a greater level of analysis and an on-going method of input relating to selling expenditures will be required. The main factors on which more detailed information inputs are needed include:
—call frequency
—call duration
—call role or function
—special promotions, including discounts, displays and offers
—category of representative

Because of the complexity of the task and because of the vast amount of data that would otherwise have to be handled it is normally necessary to work on a sample basis. A sample of the total population however would not prove useful. It is necessary initially to divide the total population up into groups that can be distinguished meaningfully according to their performance or behaviour on some important criterion such as net contribution to profits and overheads *and at the same time* which can be identified and acted on operationally by marketing management through their instruments such as advertising, salesmen, promotional deals and so on.

This is usually done by means of a computer segmentation program such as AID (Automatic Interrelation Detector). The program works on the principle of taking the key variable to be explored, in this case net contribution, and seeing which characteristic of the population (such as turnover, floor area, product mix bought, age of manager or location best splits the population into two groups. These are composed in such a way that the individual units of the population allocated to each group are as alike as possible according to the key variable, net profit, and that the two groups themselves are as different from each other as possible. This process is then repeated for each of the two groups thus obtained and repeated again. Each segment will be exclusively defined by a unique series of identifiable characteristics. The process is illustrated in Figure 22:5.

By analysing the data in this way, the groupings that emerge can then be viewed as homogeneous entities within which all the important variables have been eliminated. This type of analysis has been found to be applicable to companies with as few as 1000 customers.

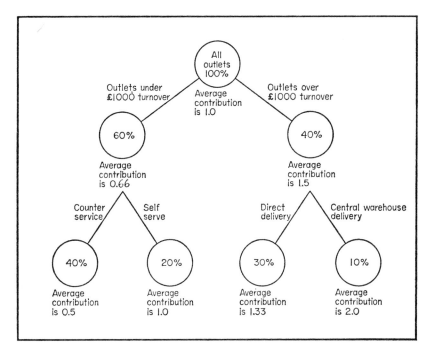

FIGURE 22:5 OUTLETS SEGMENTED ACCORDING TO
PROFITABILITY RATHER THAN SALES

This example of a segmentation shows how particular combinations of customer characteristics can lead to quite different levels of contribution.

## COST-EFFECTIVE MARKETING

The next step is then to examine within each segment the effect of applying different types and levels of marketing activity. Usually this can be done by using existing data such as promotional budgets, salesmen's call reports and so on. Sometimes, however, it is necessary to supplement the existing data by incorporating one or two additional points in the existing activity-reporting and recording system.

Because each segment can be regarded as reasonably homogeneous the "response curves" which can be drawn for different types of activity can be treated as reasonably independent of market variables and related to the effects of the marketing activity itself. This is illustrated in Figure 22:6.

This particular response curve suggests that net contribution within this segment does not improve substantially beyond the point of six merchandising calls per outlet per year. Response curves should be drawn for other important marketing activities. For example relationships between special promotions and return, between salesman category and return, between product mix and return and so on.

With this type of information marketing management can set out to test such apparent "facts" by changing items such as calling rates within segments and by closely observing the results. With a series

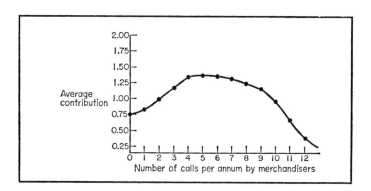

Figure 22:6    Response curve for merchandising calls
within a segment

Too many calls, although they may yield incremental sales, can reflect adversely on contribution.

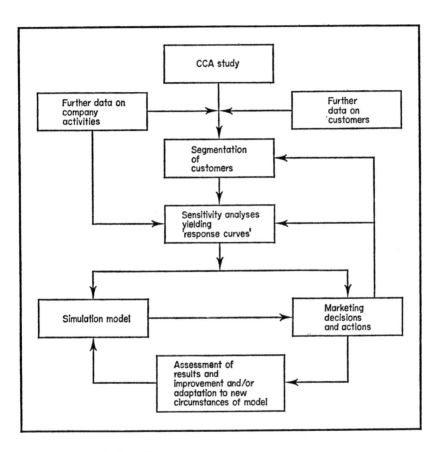

FIGURE 22:7    DEVELOPMENT OUTLINE FOR A PROFIT-ORIENTED
MARKETING MODEL

This simplified flow chart shows the broad stages in developing a
model for marketing. The feedback loops are necessary to make
such a model of real value to management, and to keep it updated.

of response curves for different types of marketing activity conducted within a set of identified market segments, marketing management is then in a position to maximise profit.

## A PRAGMATIC AND SIMPLE MARKETING MODEL

At this stage it is often useful to construct a simple simulation model so that the multiple interactions represented by the different response curves can be handled within a complete framework. This can be necessary because it is total company marketing operations that usually are at issue. This model can then be used to test the effects of single decisions or of integrated marketing plans. Because the information system on which they are based is on-going, the parameter values in the model are in their turn subject to regular updating and improvement.

At this stage of development it is then possible to introduce other elements of marketing planning into the model; short-term forecasting for example.

Step by step, a marketing information system is thus set up. Such a system allows marketing management to plan for profit more accurately and to control implementation more precisely. A general representation of the process for setting up such a system is shown in Figure 22:7.

# CHAPTER 23

# Sales/Operations Planning and Control

*by* Harold H Norcross and John R Poyser

*A T Kearney Limited*

How can the objectives of particular divisions and functions within the company be subordinated to the overall objectives of the business? To take sensible decisions affecting such vital areas as customer service, utilisation of resources, inventory investment and employment levels, the board room can benefit immensely from a new strategy now being used by a growing number of companies of all sizes in the United States.

# 23 : SALES/OPERATIONS PLANNING AND CONTROL

US businessmen live in an intensely competitive economy, in which the pressure to improve management methods is probably greater than anywhere else in the world. Competitors grow in number and

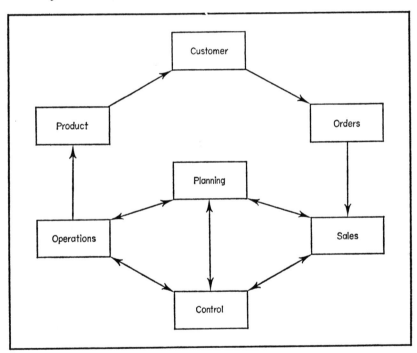

FIGURE 23:1    BASIC TERMS—SALES/OPERATIONS PLANNING AND CONTROL

*Sales*—customers and products start the cycle.
*Operations*—resources (people, plant, equipment, materials and money) are needed to produce goods and get them to the customer where and when he wants them.
*Planning*—establishes the way resources are to be used to achieve company objectives
*Control*—makes events conform to the plan.

they get smarter, faster and tougher. This competitive pressure has caused many US companies in recent years to develop and install a new approach to planning and controlling the diverse activities performed by marketing, production, inventory and distribution functions.

This new approach, now used by some of the most advanced US companies, is known as sales/operations planning and control (SOPC). It is based on the philosophy that information is a prime management resource, and must be provided through either sophisticated computer applications or integrated clerical procedures, or a combination of both, depending upon the volume and frequency of data to be handled. A few large European companies have started to use SOPC, making full use of American experience. This includes taking advantage of the lessons to be learned from American mistakes.

SOPC takes a corporate, top management approach. It is a comprehensive management information system, designed to integrate and co-ordinate all the individual systems required to forecast demand and plan operating levels; to control order intake, production schedules and inventories; and to produce, store and distribute products to customers. The basic terms, *sales, operations, planning* and *control* have the significance explained in Figure 23:1.

## OBJECTIVES

The various companies which have installed SOPC have all had increased profitability as their underlying goal. However, they have had different apparent motivating objectives, some of which are:

1   *Competitive customer service.* This means competitive reliability for on-time shipments, competitive delivery lead times, ability to provide advance information on delays which will cause late shipments, ability to answer inquiries rapidly.

2   *Dynamic inventory management.* This means planning and using inventories as one of the tools to achieve improved customer service, while at the same time reducing inventory investment and space requirement and increasing the annual inventory turnover rate.

3   *Optimum use of plant and equipment.* This means trans-
    forming a slow, sluggish flow of production into a nar-
    row swiftly moving stream of goods through the plant,
    thereby avoiding unnecessary capital outlay for ad-
    ditional facilities.
4   *Reduced costs.* This means reduction in different types of
    costs such as for holding inventories, for direct and in-
    direct labour, for clerical activities and distribution in
    the market.

Regardless of which is the motivating objective, usually all are
achieved in a complete SOPC installation, and each contributes to
increased profitability.

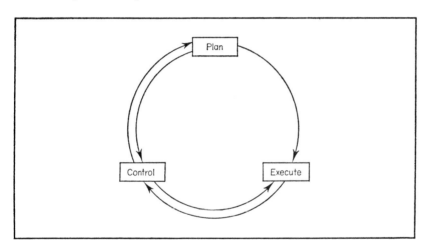

FIGURE 23:2   ELEMENTS OF SOPC
SOPC contains three basic elements:

1   Plan to meet set objectives.
2   Carry out the plan.
3   Control activities to ensure that the results conform
    to the plan.

## ELEMENTS

The SOPC management information system has three principal
elements: basic planning, execution of plans, and controlling performance (Figure 23:2).

**1** *Basic planning* is the act of determining the requirements to achieve corporate goals, as opposed to individual functional goals. It requires merging, adjusting and consolidating preliminary functional plans (such as sales forecasts and order backlogs, production plans, inventory plans and financial policies) into a single, corporate plan of action called the sales/operations plan (SO plan) (Figure 23:3).

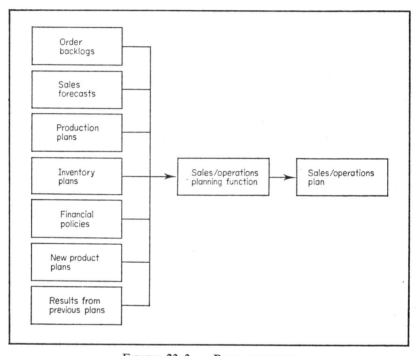

FIGURE 23:3    BASIC PLANNING

Plans for various company functions and objectives must be merged into a single corporate plan of action—the sales/operations plan.

This SO plan establishes the framework within which final functional planning is performed, and it provides a basis for measuring both functional and corporate performance. It is usually prepared every month for each month of a selected span of months. Frequency of preparation and time-span covered vary with manufacturing lead time.

**2** *Execution of SO plans* is accomplished by detailed day-to-day planning and performance of the work required in the order/

manufacturing/shipping cycle, all in accordance with the overall plan. It requires a high degree of interfunctional co-ordination supported by streamlined and integrated systems, procedures and communications and with computer applications where appropriate (Figure 23:4.)

**3** *Controlling performance* is the art of making actual results conform to the SO plan. It is accomplished through the combination of a structure of decision-oriented exception reports, appropriate decision rules to be applied to reported information, and people who are trained to use these control tools in taking effective actions (Figure 23:5).

This SOPC management information system makes use of techniques which have been tried, tested and proven in many individual functional systems applications. In this sense, it is not new; what is different, however, is the combining and tailoring of all of these techniques into a complete, beginning-to-end management information system, which uniquely meets the specific circumstances of a particular company.

A further difference lies in the basic planning element, which is the keystone of the entire system. While everyone plans in some way, SOPC planning uses a highly disciplined planning cycle and techniques performed by a small, specially constituted planning organisation. Keyed into the entire system, the superior SO plans result in demonstrably more effective execution and performance and improved achievement of company goals.

## INSTALLATION OF SOPC

Top management must take the responsibility for introducing an SOPC management system. This is because of the complex interfunctional relationships which are involved, and the corresponding need for functionally neutral guidance throughout the implementation period.

In a big company the programme to introduce SOPC may be planned in four stages:

Stage 1 is problem definition. It consists of a brief study across all of the areas involved in order to identify the major requirements for further detailed investigation and analysis. The end result is a

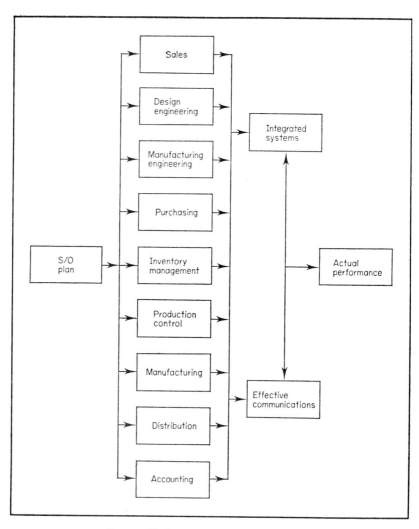

FIGURE 23:4    EXECUTION OF SO PLANS

Execution of the sales/operations plan requires a high degree of co-ordination between functions, supported by systems, communications and (where appropriate) computer applications.

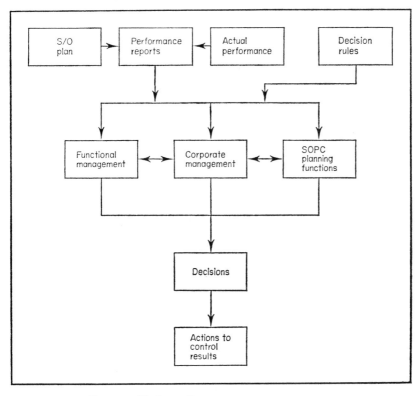

FIGURE 23:5 CONTROLLING PERFORMANCE

In order to make actual results conform to the sales/operations plan, control must be exercised through a combination of expectation reports and effective decisions.

project guide-book which defines the projects to be completed in the second stage.

Stage 2 is overall design of concept and systems, including recommended changes in policies and responsibilities and preliminary designs of individual functional systems.

Stage 3 is implementation. It consists of detailing all the approved recommendations developed in the second stage, and installing them in actual practice.

Stage 4 is follow-up, which is necessary to ensure that the new SOPC system does work and does produce the expected results.

The SOPC programme in a big company may be organised formally into four levels:

—A steering board, consisting of top functional managers and chaired by a neutral top executive, to review and approve recommendations.

—A programme manager to direct the day-to-day activities.

—Project team leaders to supervise project studies.

—Project team members to carry out the detailed tasks within each project.

If an outside management consulting firm is employed to assist in conducting the programme, it should be represented on the steering board, and its consultants may function as co-programme manager and as project team leaders. The project team members, however, should be company employees.

In medium-sized and small companies SOPC can also be applied with advantage. The support of top management is still needed in such companies; however, the planning and implementation can be simplified and the job can be done in much less time.

## APPLICATION EXAMPLES

Perhaps the SOPC concept can best be illustrated by briefly outlining its applications in several companies ranging in size from very large to very small, and representing a variety of industrial manufacturing processes.

### Large steel company

A large steel-producing company was suffering a reduction in its share of the market for flat-rolled products because of customer service deficiencies. Less than 50 per cent of shipments were made on time; customers were not notified that shipping promises would be missed until after the promised date had passed; enquiries concerning either current order status or potential new order capability could not be answered promptly.

The installation of a complete SOPC system has remedied all of these deficiencies. Over 90 per cent of shipments are now made as originally promised, and the new flow of information provides answers for all enquiries within a maximum of two hours. Actually, the improved shipping-promise reliability has sharply reduced the number of order-status enquiries. The company's market share has increased significantly.

By-product benefits include reduced inventories of in-process materials, reduced manufacturing lead times, and reduced overall costs. Significantly, too, a new customer service philosophy now pervades the entire management organisation, and overall morale has been greatly improved.

## Medium-sized manufacturing company

A medium-sized company producing high-quality metal office furniture was faced with its second major capital investment for plant expansion within a four-year period. In 1965, the plant had been expanded by 50 per cent (500 000 square feet), to provide a total of 1 500 000 square feet. Manufacturing management, late in 1966, predicted the need for an additional 1 000 000 square feet to produce sales forecasted for the 1969-71 period.

A study verified this prediction, but it also demonstrated that a very large proportion of total space was devoted to holding materials in process. If new procedures could be introduced to compress the quantity and volume of these materials, the space released could be used for manufacturing operations.

A full-scale SOPC installation provided the answer. Even before completion of the installation, materials were flowing faster and space utilisation was improved. Capital expense for additional space was postponed; the company gained a significantly higher return on investment.

## Small manufacturer

A small company producing a variety of saw-blades for both industrial and home-workshop uses had two main production divisions: one manufactured shelf products in large volumes on straight-flow production lines; the second was essentially a job-shop, producing to customer order and specifications in job-lot quantities over common work centres.

The company was experiencing common customer service problems: poor on-time shipping performance, late notification of shipping delays, and long delivery lead times. In addition, there were labour problems and excess employment costs due to un-controlled fluctuations in manpower needs.

It was determined that these problems were most severe in the made-to-order product division. Therefore, this division was tackled first in order to provide maximum benefits as early as possible, and to establish a model for later adaptation to the other division.

In this instance, the SOPC installation used mostly manual-clerical procedures, with only limited application to unit-record data processing equipment. This relatively simple installation, how-ever, proved to be what was needed to achieve the desired improve-ments in customer service.

## Large manufacturer of machine tools

One of the largest manufacturers of machine tools in the world found that its investment in inventories was growing faster than its sales volume. Annual inventory turnover was at only a 1.6 rate. Further, even though inventories were excessive, the company was unable to meet shipping promises—both for completed machines and for spare parts. In other words, there were too many unneeded items and not enough needed ones.

The full-scale SOPC installation required a very sophisticated computer application to control the 100 000 active part numbers. In this instance, too, it was necessary to develop a completely new bill of material structure to achieve the necessary degree of mech-anisation . . . a difficult, time-consuming and costly job, but worth all it cost and more. A recent review in one of its divisions indicated the annual inventory turnover rate has climbed to 2.2 and is expected to reach 2.5. Inventories are $10M lower than they would have been at the 1.6 rate, and this amounts to annual savings of $2M in carrying costs. Furthermore, inventories are balanced, and the on-time shipping performance has greatly improved.

## Paper-producing company

One of the largest producers of coated papers for both publishers and the merchant trade believed that it needed a new and larger finishing department, in order to maintain competitive customer service and to reduce damage to finished goods stored in over-crowded areas. A feasibility study was undertaken to establish the size and shape of a new department, and to determine the related economics. This study was never completed, because it was concluded part of the way through that if the company were to manage the existing facility properly, it would not need a new one.

What was needed was a complete SOPC programme, covering paper-making operations as well as the finishing department. By the time the installation was finished, the objectives had largely been achieved. Finished goods and in-process inventories were reduced, thereby relieving space congestion and reducing damage to paper stocks. Customer service was similarly improved. In addition, an unexpected side benefit occurred: new methods for planning the trim of the paper machines were developed which resulted in reducing trim loss and savings of over $100 000 annually.

The installation used mostly manual procedures. However, as the company progresses further in its use of a new computer, there will be more SOPC applications to EDP which will further improve the operation of the system and reduce costs.

## CRITERIA FOR ADOPTING SOPC

In all these case histories, and many others which could be cited, there is a common thread of SOPC principles. However, in every instance it has been necessary to adapt these principles in a tailor-made installation which uniquely fits the circumstances and objectives of the individual company.

This new approach to business logistics has clearly paid dividends in the US—more competitive customer service, better utilisation of resources, lower inventories, lower costs and higher profits. It may be asked whether British industry could benefit by American experience with SOPC. One way to test is to ask several questions:

1 What percentage of shipments are made on time? Is this competitive? When is the customer informed about shipment delays?

2 How long are delivery lead times? Are they competitive? Are they flexible for handling unusual customer requests for fast service?

3 What purposes do inventories serve? Are they used to

shorten lead times, reduce costs, and reduce operating fluctuations? Do they take up too much space? Are there losses due to deterioration or obsolescence? Are turnover rates too low—and carrying costs too high? Are there stock-out delays?

4    Are there several fluctuations in operating levels? Are overtime costs too high? Is productivity too low? Are costs high for laying-off and re-hiring? Is there usually an end-of-the-month rush to ship?

5    Are there good reports of actual performance compared to plan? Are they used effectively to control results? Is actual performance improving at a satisfactory rate?

The answers which can be given to these kinds of questions will determine whether or not Sales/Operations Planning and Control is needed.

*Section Five*

# Production and Distribution

## CHAPTER 24

# Scheduling Resources by the Critical Path Method

*by* Dennis Lock

In order to deserve the description "successful" any industrial project has to satisfy three basic conditions:

1    The technical specifications must be fulfilled
2    The budgets must not be exceeded
3    The work must be finished on time

The last two of these conditions are inextricably linked. "Time is money." There are many reasons why late completion of a project can inflate the eventual costs. Late delivery is also dangerous because of the disruption to resources set aside for other projects and the loss of customer goodwill. If profits are to be safeguarded, effective planning and control are essential.

# 24 : SCHEDULING RESOURCES BY THE CRITICAL PATH METHOD

Until the late 1950s most projects were planned with bar charts. These were simple to construct and interpret and they provided a clear visual display of the timescale. As with production loading charts, project bar charts could also be used to plan the allocation of resources. The drawback was that it was never possible to take into account the interrelationships of all the activities comprising a major project. This was primarily a problem of notation.

As projects grew more complex, the need for more effective planning methods became apparent. The result was the evolution of a family of methods in the USA which were used to great effect in controlling and co-ordinating large-scale military development programmes. These techniques belonged to the network analysis family, and one of the most effective of them all is the critical path method (CPM).

## ARROW DIAGRAM

The heart of any network analysis technique is the arrow diagram, or network itself. This replaces the older bar chart, from which it differs in several important respects. Figure 24:1 shows a very simple network. Each circle represents some programme event, such as the start of work on one aspect of a project or the completion of a particular task. The arrow joining the two events

FIGURE 24:1    SIMPLE NETWORK
Each circle represents a project event. The arrow joining any two events denotes the activity which must take place in order to progress from the first event to the second.

denotes the activity necessary to progress from one event to the next. These activity arrows are always drawn from *left to right*, by convention, but they are *not drawn to scale*, and their length has no significance.

Another network is shown in Figure 24:2, this time containing four activities. The numbers written within the event circles are for reference purposes, enabling any event or activity to be identified without ambiguity. Thus the arrow leading from event 1 to event 4 is described as: "activity 1 to 4". Further identification is provided in practice by writing a verbal description of each activity below its arrow. In this example, event 4 cannot be considered complete until all three activities leading into it have been finished.

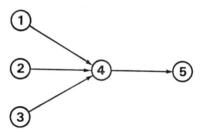

FIGURE 24:2     NETWORK RESTRICTIONS
The activity leading to event 5 cannot begin until all activities leading into event 4 have been completed.

The dependence of the final activity on preceding work is clearly highlighted.

Figure 24:3 reveals a slightly more complex situation, where the configuration more closely resembles a network. There are three possible routes to completion at event 6. One of these lies through the dotted arrow or "dummy". Dummy activities do not represent any actual work, but they are used to link events which are interdependent. In this case, the start of activity 3 to 6 is dependent not only on the completion of activity 2 to 3, but also on activity 1 to 4.

The notation so far described is sufficient to define the logical sequence of activities for any project, however large, showing the interrelationships between different project tasks. The process of constructing an arrow diagram forces the planners to think out clearly all the steps to completion, and assemble them in the correct

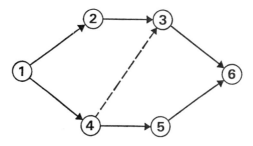

FIGURE 24:3     DUMMY ACTIVITY

Activity 3 to 6 cannot begin until activity 2 to 3 has been finished. The dummy arrow from 4 to 3 adds a further restriction, so that activity 1 to 4 must also be finished before activity 3 to 6 can start.

order. This is very similar to a production engineering exercise, and the resulting network, even without subsequent time analysis, can prove invaluable as a sort of "project process sheet". The planners must, of course, be competent to foresee the overall progress of the project, and for this reason networks are often constructed by senior members of the design or production staff.

## ESTIMATING THE PROJECT DURATION

Once the network has been drawn it is necessary to make an estimate for the duration of each activity in order to arrive at the probable duration for the whole project. The units of time used will be a matter of choice, and could be hours, days, weeks, or any other quantity provided that the same unit is adhered to throughout. In every case the estimate must be for duration, or "elapsed time", and the number of man-hours involved is not taken into account at this stage.

### Time analysis—the critical path

The estimates are written immediately above the activities to which they refer. This has been done in Figure 24:4, using weeks in this case. By adding up the estimates from left to right along each path through the network, it is possible to find the earliest time at which each event could be achieved. Where there is a choice of paths, the

321

longest must be taken, so that in Figure 24:4 the dummy arrow 4 to 3 has delayed the earliest possible completion time for event 3. The earliest completion times are written above each event circle. Earliest completion time for the project is seen to be week 7 at event 6.

Consider event 5 of Figure 24:4. The earliest possible completion time has been calculated at week 4, leaving three weeks available for the subsequent activity 5 to 6 before the end of the project at week 7. But this activity only requires one week, so that the start could be delayed until week 6 without detriment to the overall timescale. This result can be written on the network underneath the event circle. The latest possible completion time for every other event is found by working through the network from right to left, subtracting each activity duration from the latest possible completion time for the event which it immediately precedes.

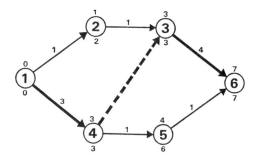

FIGURE 24:4    TIME ANALYSIS

The addition of estimates for the duration of each activity is followed by calculation of the total project duration and location of the critical path.

The difference between the earliest and latest possible times for each activity is called the "float". There will always be at least one chain of activities through a network where the earliest and latest times for each activity coincide. These activities with zero float form the "critical path". Any delay in carrying out a critical activity must delay the project. It is obvious, therefore, that critical activities demand closer control during a project than those which have considerable float. By highlighting the difficulties in this way, network analysis is a good example of a management by exception technique.

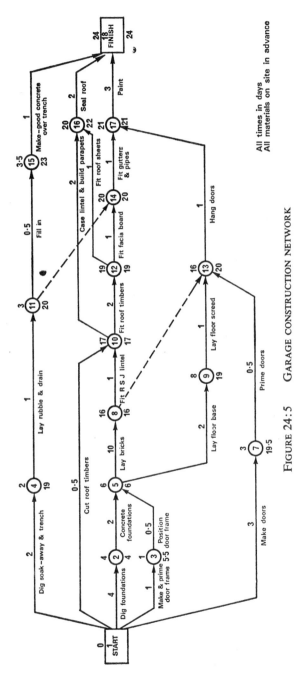

FIGURE 24:5    GARAGE CONSTRUCTION NETWORK

Although this network indicates a project duration of twenty-four days, resource limitations could delay some activities and prolong the project.

323

## CPM AND THE COST-TIME RELATIONSHIP

In Figure 24:5 a slightly more substantial project has been introduced in order to demonstrate some of the ways in which a network can be used. In this example, a garage is to be built for a private house. Remember that the network, as in the examples already given, is drawn without regard to the resources available.

Suppose that the indicated completion time of twenty-four days for the garage is unacceptable to the customer, and that unlimited resources can be brought to bear, including the use of heavier hire plant. These additional resources, however, are going to cost more money. It is possible, for some activities, to obtain a cost-time relationship similar to that shown in Figure 24:6. The optimum method for completing a job costs less. Extra money can be brought in to "crash" the activity to a shorter duration or, conversely, if the job is delayed for too long, overhead underrecovery will push up the costs again.

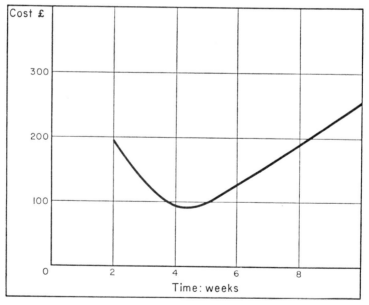

FIGURE 24:6 COST-TIME CURVE

The lowest point of the curve corresponds to the best method of carrying out a specific task. The cost will increase if the job is delayed, because of overheads. Extra money could, on the other hand, be spent to shorten the timescale on a crash basis.

The results obtained from time analysis can be used to decide the deployment of extra money to best effect in reducing the project timescale. If the activities along the critical path are crashed to achieve the required delivery date, any further money spent in crashing non-critical activities would have no overall effect on time-scale and would, therefore, be wasted.

In practice, it is usually found that as the process of re-estimating is carried through, the critical path does not remain static but changes as one activity after another is subjected to crash action. The art of planning for minimum project cost, consistent with the desired timescale, is to concentrate expenditure and effort on critical activities only.

## RESOURCE ALLOCATION

Unless unlimited resources exist for a project, the allocation of space, men, money and materials will have to be included as part of the planning routine. Networks cannot be used by themselves to indicate resource requirements. They can, however, be converted into bar charts. If coloured strips are used for the activities to indicate the types of resources needed, the day-by-day resources usage can be found using Gantt loading chart principles. The method simply involves the addition of all the strips of each colour for every vertical column on the chart.

Figure 24:7 shows a bar chart derived from the garage network of Figure 24:5. In this diagram, which is drawn to scale, all activities have been shown starting at their earliest possible times, and the sequence respects all the network restrictions. The resource requirements are shown at the foot of the diagram, and are displayed more dramatically in Figure 24:8.

If the available resources were limited, the uneven pattern predicted by the schedule of Figure 24:7 might not be acceptable to the contractor. If, for example, only one labourer and one skilled man could be used, the schedule would have to be rearranged accordingly. Some activities would have to be delayed until a man became available to carry them out. In this particular example it is possible to reschedule the project by shuffling the activities around on the bar chart until the resource histogram of Figure 24:9 is achieved. All the original network restrictions have to be observed, but not all the

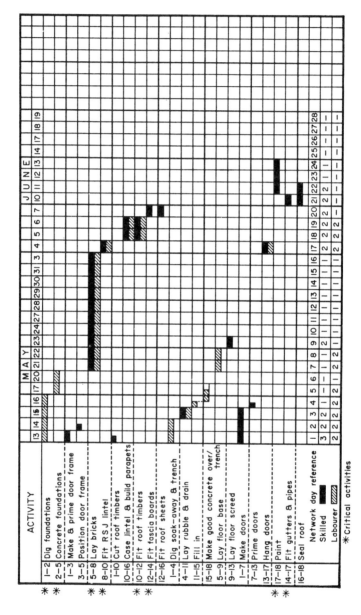

FIGURE 24:7   BAR CHART CONVERSION OF GARAGE NETWORK

This bar chart has been constructed by drawing all network activities to a timescale with each activity shown starting at the earliest possible time.

326

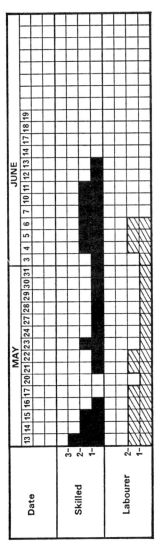

FIGURE 24:8    GARAGE PROJECT RESOURCES BEFORE SMOOTHING

This histogram emphasises the uneven resources which would be needed to achieve the schedule shown in Figure 24:7.

FIGURE 24:9    GARAGE PROJECT RESOURCE-LIMITED SCHEDULE

If the bar chart of Figure 24:9 were to be rescheduled to take account of resource limitations, a smooth histogram would result but completion would be delayed.

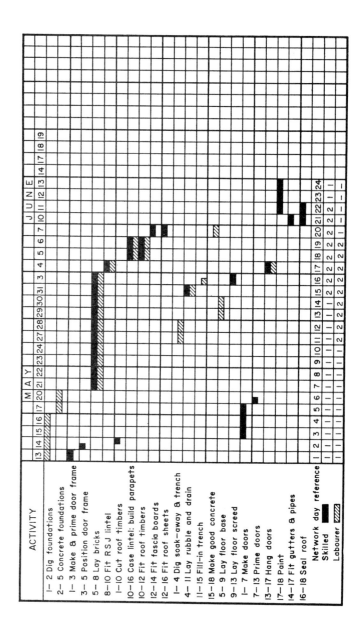

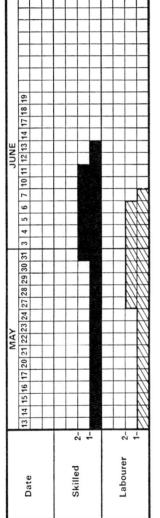

FIGURE 24:10    TIME-LIMITED RESOURCE SCHEDULE AND HISTOGRAM FOR GARAGE

Compare this schedule with that shown in Figures 24:7 and 24:8. The resource usage, as demonstrated by the histogram, has been smoothed without extending the overall timescale. This has been made possible by using the known amount of float available for each activity when carrying out rescheduling to remove resource peaks.

activities will start at their earliest possible times and the overall duration will be longer. This type of schedule, where the delivery time of a project is sacrificed to take account of limited resources, is called "resource limited".

In competitive markets, most companies are not afforded the luxury of extended timescales to cope with resource restrictions. Some level of planned overload often has to be accepted, and the peaks are accommodated by the use of subcontract facilities. Whilst the resource-limited schedule may be unacceptable, the unsmoothed schedule based on earliest possible starts for all activities is also inconvenient and inefficient. The answer lies in a compromise, where the original timescale requirements and network restrictions are observed, but activities are shuffled around to remove unwanted peak loads.

In Figure 24:10 a compromise schedule has been produced. All unwanted loading peaks have been removed by rearranging activities on the bar chart. In every case the network restrictions have been obeyed. Moreover, critical activities have been left at their earliest possible starting times, and no other activity has been delayed beyond the amount of float available. In this way, the overall predicted timescale of the original network has been held. This type of schedule is known as "time limited".

## SCHEDULING BY COMPUTER

If a network comprised some hundred activities or less, all the steps leading to a time-limited or resource-limited schedule could be carried out with pencil and paper. Larger networks become too complex to handle without the aid of a computer.

No attempt to use a computer can be made without the existence of certain basic facilities. These are:

1 Computer hardware of sufficient capacity
2 A suitable program or "software package"
3 Competent operating staff at the computer with network training
4 Good communications between the planner and the computer

There is no need for any company within the UK to be without these facilities, thanks to the efforts of several computer bureaux and software houses. Powerful programs exist which can perform all the steps described above, and link up project costs into the bargain to give a cost-time schedule.

Use of the computer eliminates much of the tedious clerical effort associated with scheduling. More important, the schedules which are produced will be flexible and easy to change, should project circumstances alter in any way. Schedules can be up-dated to take progress into account. It is also possible to mix projects in the computer, so that several are scheduled at the same time, drawing from a common pool of resources. These resources will be allocated by the computer according to the amount of float available for each activity.

This type of multi-project scheduling has another advantage, which provides the board of a company with a powerful tool for making market decisions. If a computer has been set up with a complete file of all projects being carried out within a company, the whole of the work load is represented. Any possible future orders can easily be converted into very coarse simple networks, and introduced into the actual schedule to test their possible effect on plant loading. By comparing different results between alternative order possibilities, the board is able to decide which customer should be attacked as providing the most desirable type of work to fit a given situation.

Computer printouts can be edited and sorted to suit the particular needs of an organisation. Some programs allow the user freedom of choice in the page layout. Each department in a company can be presented with schedules specific to them, containing no irrelevant information. Overall reports, but with only key activities shown, can be prepared for higher levels of management. Care must be taken to arrange all printouts in a form most likely to be of use to their recipients. Acceptance of critical path scheduling throughout a company will be made more difficult if the results are badly presented. A typical set of reports for one department might include:

1    A total day-by-day statement of resources required.
2    A report for each separate project showing the day-by-day resource requirements.

3    A report for each project listing all activities except dummies, sorted in order of their scheduled starting dates. This type of report would include useful information about each activity, such as the scheduled and latest permissible finish dates.

4    Cost reports, showing the value of resources which have been scheduled.

The cost of the computer will depend on the charge rates of the bureau used (or the time taken on the company's own machine), the size of the networks and the number of times that rescheduling is carried out. Errors in input information can add to the expense by creating the need for error runs. A typical charge for time analysis and resource smoothing is about £50 for a 500-activity network, although there are many variations. A very useful survey is available which compares many of the existing bureau services. (CAMPBELL, J. Y., *Computer Program User,* Report number 5, Loughborough University of Technology, 1968).

## INSTALLING CPM

Any board of directors faced with the decision to spend money to implement planning by network will need to know how much it will cost and what return they will see for the investment. To many, network analysis will be known, by reputation, as a good thing, but the details will be obscure. Fortunately, it is possible to quantify the expenditure fairly accurately in advance. It is also feasible, and indeed desirable, to get one's feet wet by easy stages. As a rough general guide, total expenditure on computer-based network scheduling need not add more than $\frac{1}{2}$ per cent to factory cost, and might typically add only $\frac{1}{4}$ per cent. The return is not quantifiable, but will be apparent from improvements in delivery performance and a smoother work sequence. The savings achieved will be hidden in the overhead figures, but the confidence generated, both in the customer and the contractor's staff, will soon become apparent.

Once agreement has been reached to go ahead with CPM, one individual must be chosen to take charge of the operation. He may be a consultant, a specially recruited expert or one of the existing staff who can be given special training. Short seminars are frequently given by a variety of trade institutions and research associations. Some experience must be gained by working simulated examples, but there is nothing inherently difficult in learning critical path methods.

Training in network techniques must be extended to other project participants, including all departmental managers if possible. It is at this state that most scepticism will be encountered and the support of the board must be given to ensure that key individuals will make their time available for training sessions. These sessions will not, however, occupy more than a few hours. In fact, after a brief description of the concept, the network analyst will do well to draw his first project network at the training session, involving all the participants.

This first network will probably contain errors in the logic. Errors can be expected both from inexperience in drawing networks and lack of experience in planning ahead in depth of detail. If an attempt were made to introduce networks to the computer too early, in all probability the money would be wasted because, according to the "garbage-in, garbage-out" principle, the computer must be fed with networks which are logically sound. Early networks, therefore, should probably be used as control documents for timescale only. They can be used as wall charts, events and activities, being checked off as they are achieved.

The remainder of the installation process should be a gradual progression. As more confidence is gained in the construction of logically correct networks, experience should also lead to duration estimates which become reliable. The computer can then be introduced, possibly for one project only. The services of an experienced computer bureau will be found invaluable at this stage. Finally, once a working schedule for the single project has been produced, other projects can be added until all projects are "on file" and true multi-project scheduling has been achieved.

## FURTHER READING

LOCK, D. L., *Industrial Scheduling Techniques* (Gower Press, 1971)

—— CHAPTER 25 ——

# Group Technology

*by* P K Digby

*General Manager, PERA Management Economics Division*

Few manufacturing companies can afford to ignore an opportunity of securing significant reductions in design time, machining costs, work-in-progress and capital expenditure. With its concept of families of parts and machine grouping, group technology provides the total approach that is necessary to ensure more effective use of total resources.

# 25 : GROUP TECHNOLOGY

By 1921, production control management had become recognisable in many manufacturing businesses. Its scope is the range of resources, used in manufacturing the product, to which the decision-making tasks of the work function of production control are applied. This range of resources comprises materials, work-in-progress parts and manufacturing facilities. Money is only a means of exchange and measurement and not a resource used in manufacture.

It is the aim of resource management to reduce, to a balanced minimum, the resources required to manufacture the requirements within an acceptable time cycle and level of profitability. This implies co-ordination of all the manufacturing and non-manufacturing functions and is a proper task of general management. It is not necessary for the directors of a company to take any current situation as inevitable. If means can be found and applied to reduce the direct resources required to produce a given commitment, then the direct costs of production and those management costs associated with production control and co-ordination will fall. One of the means available for doing this is group technology.

## GROUP TECHNOLOGY

Group technology is a technique for grouping parts into families in order to facilitate the use, where possible, of mass-production and flow-line principles in batch manufacture. It is based on the premise that small lots of different parts can be produced more economically if they are grouped and scheduled for production according to some common processing characteristics. Some of the developments during the last twenty-five years have been listed elsewhere[1,2] and although most of the examples to date have been related to machined components, there have also been applications to press-work, casting and non-metallic materials. This is not, however, intended to indicate that there are limitations to the use of the technique.

In production control, the technique is used to facilitate the planning and control of work. Jobs for which a similar set-up is required are grouped together and manufactured in sequence on a group of machines specially selected for the purpose. This reduces the setting time per unit produced, often the major cost in small-batch work. Depending on the scale involved, the flow-line principle can be used in laying out the group or groups of machines, typified in Figure 25:1.

Therefore, using group technology, some of the advantages of flow-line production, such as less handling, less work-in-progress, less storage space and greater certainty of delivery, can be secured under market conditions that demand small-batch production. Within the production control organisation, planning and procuring become relatively more critical than control, the systems for which may then be less sophisticated.

The scope of group technology ranges through the marketing and design functions of a firm as well as in manufacturing. The

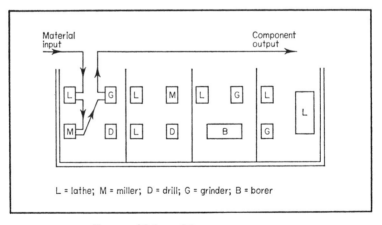

L = lathe; M = miller; D = drill; G = grinder; B = borer

FIGURE 25:1    MACHINE GROUPING

Group layouts use the flow-line principle for machining each family of parts identified by group technology. Machines can be used in any sequence within each group. These layouts contrast with rigid flow-line layout, and with the familiar pattern of machines grouped according to the machining operations which they perform, such as turning and milling

greatest benefits from an application will accrue when the "total approach", involving rationalisation of component design and reduction in variety of products offered, is reached. A total group approach extends beyond this, and aims at the use of similar, but not necessarily identical, components as well. This can save design time, reduce the number of drawings, help with standardisation of materials and facilitate the fundamental creation of families of parts.

# GROUPING OF PARTS

## Marketing policy

When a manager examines the particular function for which he is responsible, he will often overlook the total concepts within which the firm operates. Group technology is a technique, a means to an end, not a management task. When it is applied to design and production, pitfalls may be encountered if the market situation is not recognised.

The marketing policy may consist of making goods before they are sold, or selling goods before they are made. Sometimes it may be a combination of both these approaches. The policy decided influences design because, on the one hand, the designer may have some freedom of choice whereas on the other hand his choice is restricted. When the goods are sold before they are made, it is more difficult to apply group technology completely.

If a sound market research programme is undertaken, sales forecasting (and hence determination of the nature and extent of resources required in the future) can be more accurately assessed. As a result, the potential value of investment in design, design modification, production engineering facilities and more sophisticated planning and control can be judged with greater confidence.

The greater the predictability of the load, the more closely can the capacity be matched to it without prejudice to customer service. This reduces operating costs. The greater the frequency with which the product mix is changed, the more difficult it will be to arrange production in family groups, and the less likely that optimum grouping of machines and balance within a group will be achieved consistently. At some point, therefore, it may no longer be possible to implement group technology because the benefits normally expected cannot be obtained. An extreme case of this would be an obsolescent product, or one which is not going to catch on.

## Product rationalisation

It is often suggested that product rationalisation restricts both the freedom to create and the market to which the products can be sold. Nevertheless, the overall benefits that it can bring to company profitability are very great. In one known case, the inventory level was reduced by approximately £200 000 as a result of product variety reduction alone. This was achieved, as it may be in most cases, without affecting good relationships with customers.

Less spectacularly, perhaps, the use of common or similar components in the resulting smaller, but acceptable, product range can be even more beneficial to the company. Generally, there will be fewer different components to design, make, store, control and finance. To follow these principles in relation to new designs and gradually to amend old but current designs accordingly will mark a great step forward for any firm and open the way for application of the "total concept" of group technology.

From the foregoing, it is apparent that there is a need for sound design retrieval, and for classification and coding systems that give information about products, components and materials. These may be design-orientated, production-technology orientated or a compromise of the two. In a design-orientated code, the parameters often considered are shape, size and function and a number of different systems have already been devised.[3, 4, 5, 6] However, bespoke codes may be designed for a single application.

## Classification and coding

When the total approach method is used, a considerable amount of information must be collected about components, their features, and the technology used in their manufacture. The components are classified into families, and the machines classified into groups. The systems may be universal or bespoke, and within either of these categories the resulting codes may be design or production technology orientated. The total approach results in a combination of these features which is known as a *polycode*. This process is illustrated in Figure 25:2.

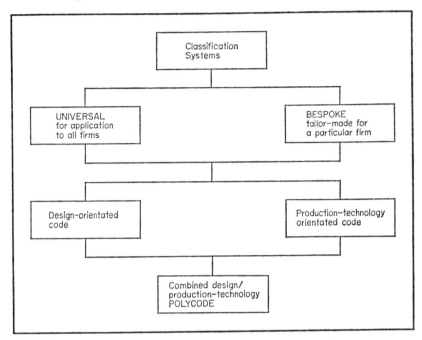

FIGURE 25:2    NATURE OF CLASSIFICATION AND CODING SYSTEMS
USED WHEN APPLYING GROUP TECHNOLOGY

Basically, a classification system may be suitable for universal applications of group technology in all firms. On the other hand, it could be designed specifically to take account of the needs of a particular firm.

There are four methods available for classification.

1    The elementary method achieves classification, to a degree, by observation. Some major families and groups will emerge but, generally, there will be a large residue of components which have not been identified adequately.

2    More formal classification by design features, such as shape or function, is very useful for variety reduction and component retrieval. This method is of limited assistance only in finding families and machine groups linked to production technology and a separate classification is usually needed for this purpose.

3    More significant for manufacture is classification based upon production features such as material, dimensions, processes and machines to be used and indications of quantities likely to be required. Each component is identified within its family and machine group according to one of many forms of code.

4    Some codes incorporate both design and production classifications (polycodes). These will cover all the usual requirements of a firm. Under these circumstances a computer is often necessary for undertaking the retrieval.

## GROUP TECHNOLOGY AS AN AID TO RESOURCE MANAGEMENT

### Production engineering

The resources used in production engineering can amount to a significant proportion of all those needed, particularly when the small-batch production situation is combined with a requirement for high quality and interchangeability. Group technology can facilitate the more effective use of production engineering resources.

A reduction in the number of different components to be produced means there is less process planning and estimating because fewer different operations are required and some of the machine setting is eliminated. The greater quantities of given components may make viable totally different manufacturing methods, (e.g. by the use of castings or forgings instead of machining from solid stock).

The amount of tool design and manufacture can be reduced significantly. Universal tools to suit complete families can be designed, thereby saving design, manufacture, operating and storage costs. Not the least important benefit to resource management is the vast reduction in cycle time from component design to production completion that is achievable. Advantage can then be taken of market changes.

Group technology can help to conserve expensive resources such as special-purpose or, perhaps, numerically controlled machine tools. Programming and tape punching demands will be less and, with increasing confidence, special-purpose machines can be introduced to a group and higher utilisation ensured.

The larger the quantity of a single component, or of similar components to be produced, the more can method study be applied without running into problems of diminishing returns. These benefits will also accrue, over a much wider range and make a cumulative contribution to economical resource management. Fewer studies, synthetics or work study engineers will be required to measure the resources needed for manufacture to a given degree of accuracy.

In an earlier part of this chapter reference has been made to layout. Group principles as described can reduce the materials handling and inter-operational storage space necessary. Standardisation permits lower inventories for a given level of customer service. Considerable savings in capital equipment are customary because chutes and simple conveyors can often replace trucks that otherwise would be required.

## Production control

When group technology is introduced less work is needed in production control itself, even though responsibility for planning the use of factory resources lies within this part of the organisation.

Particularly when a firm is undertaking piece-part manufacture and assembly in several stages of production on a batch basis, production control is concerned with the logistics of the whole situation; for all the resources used in making the product.[7] This includes the supply of materials, piece parts and subassemblies, each often being produced by different processes. Operators will be at different stages of the learning curve and batch size and cycle times will be variable. Often, different product lines compete for the same resources and successful co-ordination of the whole comprises a series of tasks of major importance.

Many of these tasks become easier when product variety is reduced and standardisation of components is undertaken. Fewer different records need be kept and less paperwork is required for procuring and controlling resources.

Greater flexibility is engendered if fewer different materials and parts are used throughout the product range and, when the batch size is increased, the probability of achieving target dates and quantities becomes higher. This arises because fewer "first offs" will be required with consequent reduction of scrap and wastage. This greater precision reduces the risks and offers the opportunity to plan and control more tightly and nearer to the optimum. This can lead to reduced work-in-progress, reduced waiting time and the most effective use of the fewer resources then required. Conversely, smaller batch quantities can become viable propositions.

The introduction of group technology, then, is seen as the key to obtaining these benefits through better total resource management. So far, the technique and its implications have been discussed but the impact which such changes may have on the organisation structure and responsibilities of different individuals must also be considered.

## IMPACT OF TOTAL RESOURCE MANAGEMENT ON THE ORGANISATION

Group technology demands a multi-product, centralised concept of organisation in production engineering and production control and specialists within these functions must consider the requirements of each other at all times. Barriers between those responsible for project groups must be removed.

When a product has to be made after it is sold, the installation and use of group technology and sound procedures can alleviate the short-term problems of production engineering and control. On the other hand, when goods are made before they are sold, batches are likely to be larger and more of the planning and investment decisions are "built in" at an earlier stage, based upon longer-term predictions and judgements. These decisions can have far-reaching repercussions with long-lasting effect. More thinking and co-ordination time is required by the senior personnel and the introduction of the additional level of assistant chief production engineer as shown in Figure 25:3 provides this. Installation of further procedures alone would not satisfy the requirements under these circumstances.

The organisation structure recommended for production control is shown in Figure 25:4. It provides unified responsibility "across the products" for all the planning, all the procuring and all the controlling separately. In nature it is horizontal rather than vertical. Both these structures facilitate optimisation in total resource management. Otherwise, there is a danger that the efficiency of one particular facility, or the use of one resource, may be sub-optimised to the detriment of the remainder of the overall objective.

In general and production management, centralisation enables the shop manager to concentrate on man management, quality and performance. A general increase in batch size and closer specification of work should automatically improve quality and reduce the supervision necessary. On the other hand, greater co-ordination between functional and line management is demanded if total resource management as achieved by group technology is to become fully effective.

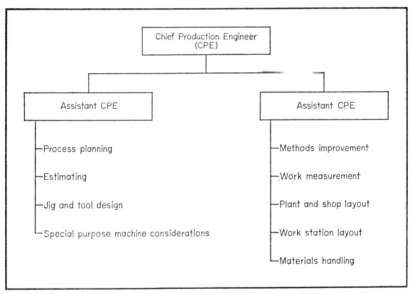

FIGURE 25:3    TYPICAL PRODUCTION ENGINEERING ORGANISATION
FOR GROUP TECHNOLOGY

The demands for centralisation and co-ordination of production engineering facilities require the introduction of another management level between the chief production engineer and his sectional heads. His span of control would otherwise be too great, causing unacceptable delays in decision-making.

## ECONOMICS OF GROUP TECHNOLOGY

In economic terms the advantages from applying group technology accrue for two reasons. Firstly because component designs are standardised, and secondly because components are classified and

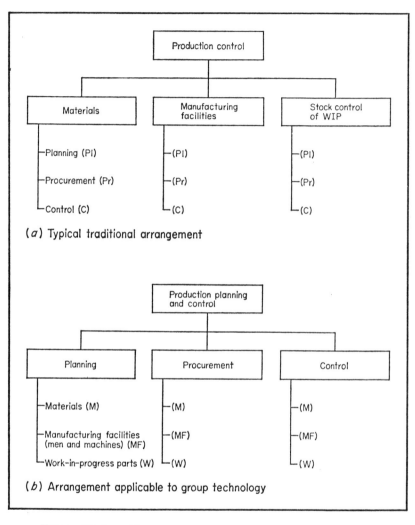

(a) Typical traditional arrangement

(b) Arrangement applicable to group technology

FIGURE 25:4    CHANGE OF ORGANISATION TO ALLOW OPTIMUM
APPLICATION OF GROUP TECHNOLOGY

Diagram (a) shows a traditional production control organisation which is based on individual resource management. In (b) the organisation has been reconstructed, so that each part of the production control organisation is related to a function. This arrangement ensures sound integration in the use of all resources used in manufacture.

manufactured in family groups according to the manufacturing operations required.

At the design stages, reduction of product and component variety can lead to substantial reductions of designers' time, drawing storage, work-in-progress, finished stocks and time cycle of production. Design quality can be higher because proportionally small increases in effort spread over fewer individual parts enable greater perfection in design at less cost. If the same sales are achieved from a smaller variety, marketing costs will be reduced and customer service improved.

Manufacturing costs comprise investment charges, pre-production costs and running costs. A case study of typical costs[8] shows that when group technology is introduced, fewer machines are required because of higher effective utilisation, hence capital costs may be reduced by 40 per cent. At the pre-production stage, planning costs tend to be higher but the remainder are reduced, resulting in an overall reduction of 40 per cent. The commensurate running and inventory costs are reduced by 50 per cent.

Costs of jigs and tools, tool maintenance, indirect labour and scrap may be halved. Costs of direct labour, work-in-progress, and work preparation may be reduced by 60 per cent; transportation costs may be cut by 80 per cent. Other economies can be secured in space, power and administrative paperwork.

It may be necessary to increase maintenance costs and introduce a planned maintenance scheme backed up by measurement of the work content for maintenance operations. This is to ensure that unplanned downtime of a machine due to breakdown does not disrupt utilisation of other machines in the group layout. The code numbering systems used for group technology may not be as meaningful in identifying parts for given products, but this appears to be a small price to pay for the other advantages. The classification systems of retrieval, for example, are much more effective than memory for determining whether suitable drawings already exist.

## IMPLEMENTATION

Group technology may be introduced either as an overall scheme or on a progressive basis.

Introduction of group technology on a progressive basis can be initiated by using a method called production flow analysis[9] from the process planning sheet. Families of components and groups of machines to manufacture them are identified from process planning sheets. The group layout needed can be introduced quickly to cover a large part of the range, without waiting for new tooling. This method does not directly involve the design feature of a component.

In practice an office is set up to allocate, against general sketches, code numbers for design and for the retrieval of any existing component drawings which may satisfy the new requirement. Drawings of parts which are nearly identical will gradually be eliminated in favour of a standard part, using statistical data to identify preferred items.

Tools and fixtures can be designed for manufacture of families of components on specific types of machine. Complete group layouts with a proper balance of all the operations to be performed in the group "cell" are then installed. Usually, the materials handling arrangements can be simpler. When balancing one must choose between high labour or high plant utilisation.

As would be expected, the time cycle necessary for application of the total concept is much longer than for the production flow analysis method. This is because it involves changes in the firm's philosophy, regarding layout, tooling, production control and organisational responsibilities. All of these need to be planned and "sold" throughout the various functions of the business, including marketing.

Persistence with a departmentalised organisation structure leads to "rough running" because application of group technology techniques forces consideration to be given to the optimum use of *all* resources.

These additional important management tasks of designing and implementing technical and managerial changes must often coincide with a normal, heavy, day-to-day management load. At present, only relatively few firms have personnel experienced in doing this work. It may be wise, therefore, when introducing group technology, to consider using consultants in order that the benefits may be reaped more quickly and with greater certainty.

# REFERENCES

1    LAWSON, H., and PUTNAM, A. O., "Group Technology: Challenge to a Job-Shop Management", *Metalworking Economics*, pp. 34–41, June 1971

2    DURIE, F. R. E., "A Survey of Group Technology and its Potential for User Application in the UK", *The Production Engineer*, volume 49, number 2, February 1970

3    "Engineering Outline 130 Group Technology", *Engineering*, 21 June 1968

4    EDWARDS, G. A. B., and FATHELDIN, A. T., "Component Statistics and Group Technology", *Works Management*, in two parts: pp. 21–4 June and pp. 16–17 September 1971

5    GALLAGHER, C. C., "Small Firms Benefit from Group Technology", *Metalworking Production*, pp. 55–7, 19 March 1969

6    HAWORTH, E. A., "Group Technology—Using the Opitz System", *The Production Engineer*, volume 47, number 1, January 1968

7    DIGBY, P. K., "The Logistics of Assembly", *Assembly and Fastener Engineering*, pp. 58–9, 1969

8    KNIGHT, W. A., "Economic Benefits of Group Technology", *Machinery and Production Engineering*, pp. 941–6, 23 June 1971

9    BURBIDGE, J. L., "The Production Flow Analysis." *The Production Engineer*, volume 50, number 4, April/May 1971

## FURTHER READING

BURBIDGE, J. L. *An Introduction to Group Technology*, Turin International Centre, 1969

CONNOLLY, R., and SABBERWAL, A. J. P., "Management Structure for the Implementation of Group Technology", *Annals of the CIRP*, volume XVII, pp. 159–69, 1971

GOMBINSKI, J., "Fundamental Aspects of Component Classification", *Annals of the CIRP*, Volume XVII, pp. 367–75, 1969

——"Group Technology—An Introduction", *The Production Engineer*, volume 46, number 9, September 1957

MITROFANOV, S. P., *Scientific Principles of Group Technology*, Translation. National Lending Library for Science and Technology, 1955

OPITZ, H., EVERSHEIM, W., and WIERDHAL, H. P., "Workpiece Classification and its Industrial Application", *Int. J. Mach. Tool Des. Res.*, volume 9, pp. 39–50, 1969

# CHAPTER 26

# Computers in Production Control

*by* D H Ralston

*IBM United Kingdom Limited*

The traditional way to improve productivity has been to install faster and more efficient machine tools, or to reorganise some of the shops along "flow line" principles. Mechanisation and reorganisation are only part of the solution. The major savings to be made are by better planning of shop and purchase orders resulting in on-time deliveries, reduced manufacturing lead times and fewer shortages; improved control of shop orders resulting in lower queues, reduced work-in-process and less idle time and bottlenecks; and monitoring and control of machine tools and production processes resulting in better utilisation and improved quality. It is in these areas that the computer can most profitably be used.

# 26 : COMPUTERS IN PRODUCTION CONTROL

It could be said that many companies remain successful in spite of their systems and not because of them. Their production planning and control systems are static in that they have not developed, expanded or refined even when the business environment changes and new problems arise. Systems should change with changing conditions if a company is to maintain its competitive position. Late deliveries, high costs and poor response to customer enquiries have to be things of the past. Today, a company is successful only in proportion to its ability to gather, transmit and interpret the information needed to make its products. Managers are too often trying to control more complex manufacturing activities with information that becomes increasingly incomplete and out-of-date. Many companies have turned to a computer as a solution to the problem.

## COMPUTERS IN THE MANUFACTURING COMPANY

A computer has the ability to handle, rapidly and accurately, large volumes of data. Figure 26:1 shows a typical medium-sized computer. It can hold central files (in computer jargon a *data base*) for all the company's information needs, and it allows rapid communication of this same information to any part of the company requiring it (Figure 26:2). It can perform more effectively and more economically most of the functions today done manually. The computer can replace neither the human factor nor the skills needed for decision-making, but it can provide management with an insight into the effect of decisions by simulating what the effect of those decisions would be. This is particularly useful, for example, in determining the level of inventory investment or in determining what the product mix should be in next year's master production schedule.

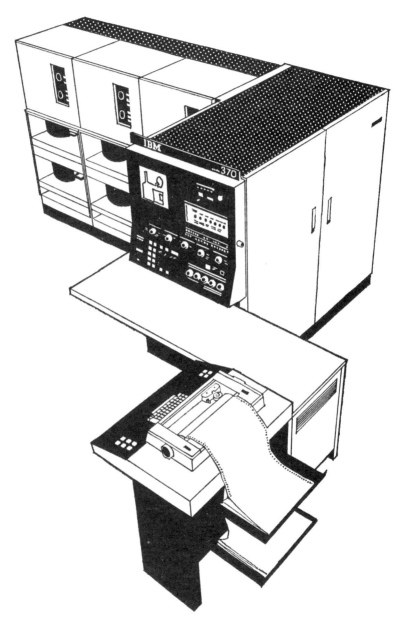

FIGURE 26:1     MEDIUM-SIZED COMPUTER SYSTEM
Disk drives, holding the data base can be seen to the left of the
central processing unit.

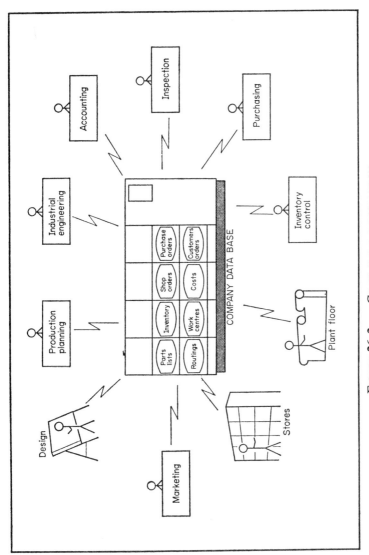

FIGURE 26:2   CENTRALISED INFORMATION

The computer holds the company data base which ensures that all departments work with the same information.

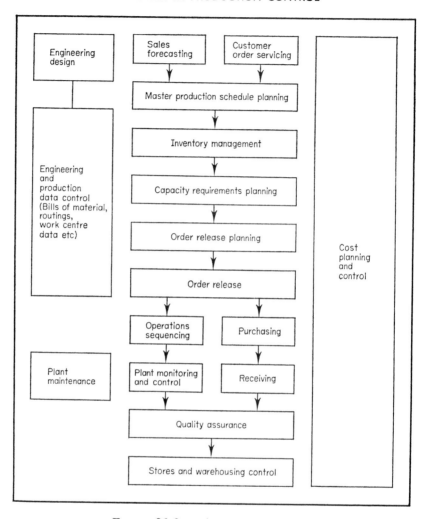

FIGURE 26:3    APPLICATION AREAS
Application areas in which computers are being applied in
manufacturing industries.

Computers have been used in just about every area of the business. Figure 26:3 illustrates some of the major application areas. Many of these applications involve the use of terminals linked to the computer. Figure 26:4, for example, illustrates a visual display terminal used in computer-aided design. However, this chapter will concentrate on three of the major areas where computers can be

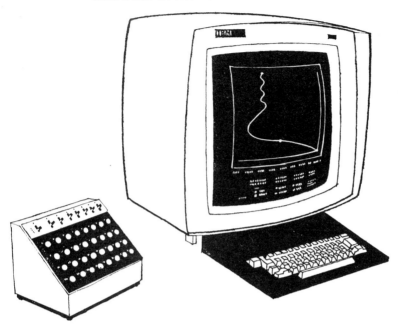

FIGURE 26:4    VISUAL DISPLAY TERMINAL

Stress calculations, circuit analyses and simulation of performance characteristics are examples of computer applications using visual display terminals to help the designer.

profitably applied in most types of manufacturing company:
—Inventory management
—Capacity planning and scheduling
—Plant monitoring and control

## INVENTORY MANAGEMENT

Inventory is one of the most significant investments in a manufacturing company. In many companies, management has little or no control over this level of investment. Inventories tend to grow until some form of crash action is taken to reduce them. Investment in inventory is not planned, it just happens.

Assuming an investment of £1M, an inventory reduction of 20 per cent would release £200 000 of working capital for invest-

357

ment in more profitable areas. It is quite common for the cost of carrying inventory to exceed 25 per cent of its average annual level. In this example a reduction of £200 000 would normally result in a direct annual saving of £50 000.

Excess stocks of some items usually result from a number of operating-level decisions by material control clerks. For instance, if one of them makes a decision that results in a severe shortage, he will not let it happen again. He will tend to stock more in future to avoid the recurrence of an embarrassing situation. He knows that shortages will hurt his relations with production, but that high inventories can be "explained" to top management.

Any attempt to cut down on inventories usually involves reducing order quantities, carrying less safety stock and scheduling purchase orders to arrive later. It often results, however, that the items that are really required are the ones that get cut back and the ones that are not required stay at the same level. Whatever happens, it always seems the parts that are needed have shortages and that there is plenty of stock of the others. This situation results from three basic factors:

1   The volume of parts to be handled runs into many thousands, making control difficult and resulting in "broad brush" inventory policies like "aim to keep two months' stock of all items" irrespective of the fact that some may need no safety stock at all and others may need much more than two months.

2   Inadequate control and recording procedures resulting in clerical errors and delays. Stocks are often "buffered" to allow for these discrepancies.

3   Use of the wrong inventory control techniques. This usually means the use of order point techniques on sub-assemblies, components and raw materials which makes the ordering of these items completely independent of the products they go into. This approach almost guarantees that parts will not be there when they are needed and plenty will be there when there is no demand. This is illustrated in Figure 26:5.

Use of order point techniques is fine when applied in the right place,

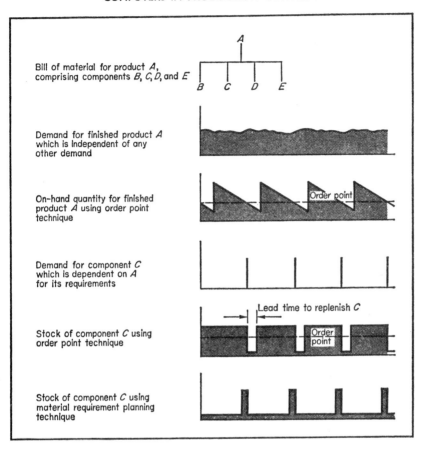

FIGURE 26:5    ORDER POINT VERSUS REQUIREMENTS PLANNING
Material requirements planning is preferable to order point techniques for components, subassemblies and materials.

usually to finished products and spare items. But it is not suitable for subassemblies and components because demand for these items is not constant but comes instead in large chunks to meet one month's or one week's assembly requirements.

One big advantage of a computer in inventory management is that it can apply specific management objectives to each individual item. For instance, it can determine the order quantities and safety stock necessary to give (say) a 95 per cent service on each finished product or spares item—not just an overall "two months" stock

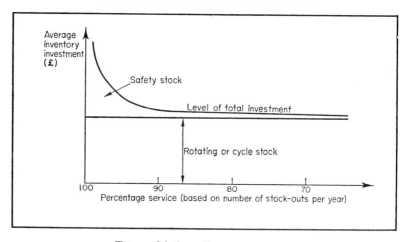

FIGURE 26:6    EXCHANGE CURVES

As the service level increases, inventory investment increases dramatically, 100 per cent service cannot be achieved when demand is forecast.

on every part which may result in one item being overstocked and another being able to service only 50 per cent of the demands. In fact, it can determine how much investment will be required in inventory to provide a given level of service. It can provide an "exchange curve" as shown in Figure 26:6, which will inform management of the effect of their decisions on the level of inventory or the level of customer service.

The computer can be used to plan for 100 per cent service on *dependent demand* items. These are subassemblies, components and materials which are dependent upon the end product requirements. The computer can determine how many to order and when to order. Planning the requirements of these items is called material requirements planning. It is based on "exploding" the end product and spares requirements established in the master production schedule by means of the bills of material (or parts listed) to get accurate requirements for the component items. Requirements are based on known demand and not forecast from what happened in the past. An example of a material requirements planning report is shown in Figure 26:7.

For a manufacturing company producing assembled products, material requirements planning is the only way to manage effectively

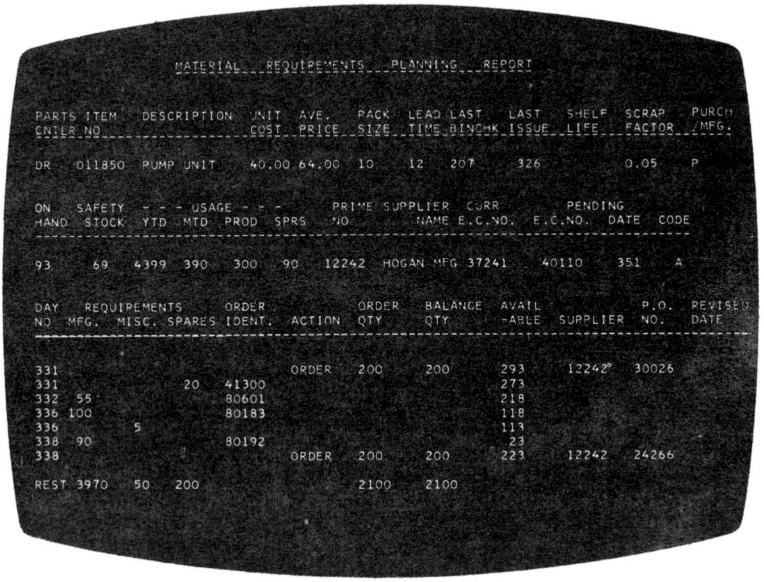

FIGURE 26:7    MATERIAL REQUIREMENTS PLANNING REPORT
This report is displayed for the material controller and shows
requirements and existing orders for one item.

the vast majority of its inventory. Benefits can be found in four
major areas:

1    Reduction of component inventory levels, due to better
     planning of requirements and orders
2    Improvement in customer service, because of tighter
     control over each individual item
3    Reduction in production cost, principally direct labour as
     reduced shortages mean less hold-ups in assembly
4    Reduction in inventory and production control personnel
     because of the reduced amount of recording and chasing
     necessary

In an APICS (American Production and Inventory Control Society) special report[1] a number of companies stated the benefits that they had gained from materials requirements planning by computer.

One decreased total inventory by 36 per cent. Another decreased component inventory by 33 per cent and achieved some improvement in customer service. A third reduced inventory by 22 per cent, improved customer service by 20 per cent, and reduced staff handling the ordering of components by 35 per cent. And a fourth company reduced component inventory by 33 per cent; the number of late orders was reduced by between 90 and 95 per cent and there were reductions of 7 per cent and 25 per cent in production costs and indirect labour, respectively.

## CAPACITY PLANNING AND SCHEDULING

Capacity planning and scheduling has been one of the most successful computer applications in Europe over the past few years. The substantial savings that firms have quoted for scheduling by a computer have, moreover, been achieved within a very short time of its introduction. Considering that, in most plants today, a job spends roughly 90 per cent of its time in queue or being moved around the plant, there is plenty of scope for improvement. Benefits, apart from higher machine utilisation, have included such factors as improved deliveries, reduced work-in-process, shorter lead times and a reduction in the number and duration of production meetings which executives and supervisors had to attend.

How is it done? Basically, by determining the level of capacity required to meet the production schedule, controlling the release of orders according to the level of capacity set by management, and sequencing the orders according to priority and conditions prevailing in each work centre (bottlenecks, idle time, etc).

Manual methods of scheduling cannot give a tight enough control over work-in-process in most factories simply because of the amount of detail to be correlated. The volume of data to be handled, the large number of combinations, and the frequent rescheduling necessary are at the whole root of the machine-shop scheduling problem in most plants.

[1] PLOSSL, G. W. and WIGHT, O. W. (editors), *Material Requirement Planning by Computer*, APICS special report number 2, American Production and Inventory Control Society, Washington, DC.

All too often the decision on which job to do next on the shop floor is left to the foreman. He usually does not have all the facts on which to make that decision.

Week numbering systems, use of different coloured job cards, coloured stickers and "urgent" stamps are nearly always out of line with actual priorities. Often the only priority system is based on shortage lists, with everybody chasing a different list—and this relies on parts already being late before the system will work. Instead of management by exception, this is *management by surprise*.

The computer tries to take the surprise out of controlling the shops, because it is able to correlate the priorities and sequence of *every* operation released to the factory. The priority rules it takes into account can include such factors as the number of days behind schedule, a priority number given to the batch, the value of work-in-process capital tied up in the batch, the length of queue at the

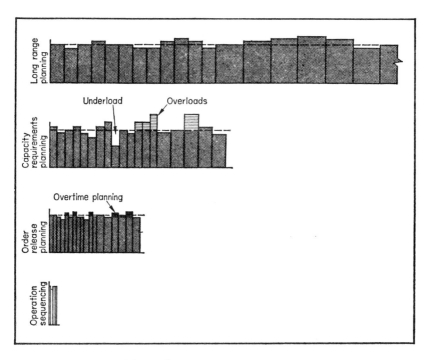

FIGURE 26:8    CAPACITY PLANNING AND SCHEDULING
Planning capacity requirements and scheduling orders on the factory is done in a number of stages.

next work centre, how many assembly orders require this part, and so on.

Most computer systems do the actual scheduling in a number of stages, as shown in Figure 26:8. Long-range planning can be done for several years ahead and provides executives with the information to make long-term decisions involving new plant, machinery and manpower.

Capacity requirements planning usually is done for several months ahead and involves analysing the overloads and underloads at each work centre to determine timing of new machine tool deliveries, arrangements for subcontract work or planning the transfer of labour. An example of this type of load report is shown in Figure 26:9. The capacity decisions made at this level are used in *order release planning* to level the load. This is done for several weeks ahead and involves adjusting the release dates of orders to minimise idle time and reduce bottlenecks. Overtime planning and specific subcontract orders can also be determined.

The final stage is done on a daily or by shift basis. This does the actual sequencing of operations at each work centre or individual machine and provides a work sequence list for the foreman of each work centre. Such lists highlight the preferred sequence of work and tell the foreman what work will be arriving in his department and when it should arrive. This is illustrated by the example in Figure 26:9.

The average time for installing such a capacity planning and scheduling system varies from four months to one year, depending on the amount and accuracy of the data available. One company with 15 000 shop orders installed a pilot scheme within four months and had 95 per cent of its total work-in-process on the system

---

FIGURE 26:9   CAPACITY PLANNING AND SCHEDULING REPORTS

1   *Order summary and schedule list.* Showing status of each shop order and operation. Any expected delay is shown in the last column.
2   *Work sequence list.* Showing suggested sequence of jobs at work centre 75205.
3   *Capacity requirements planning report.* Graphs show loads, idle time and un-avoidable overloads.
   —Indicates overload on this centre which can be off-loaded to another work centre.
   + indicates amount of idle time on this centre which can be filled by transferring work from other work centres.

ORDER SUMMARY AND SCHEDULE LIST

LOAD REPORT AND OPERATIONS LIST

IBM CAPACITY PLANNING AND OPERATION SEQUENCING SYSTEM (CAPOSS), VERSION 01 MOD 00, SS-2

CAPACITY REQUIREMENTS PLANNING REPORT FOR WORK CENTER 4002-847 VERTICAL MILL

within six months. This was done with only one extra clerk during the installation period.

Reductions of 10–30 per cent in the level of work-in-process are not uncommon with such a system. Fewer "tear downs", reduced overtime working, and early recognition of new plant and labour requirements are benefits which can be achieved in addition to the ones mentioned earlier.

## PLANT MONITORING AND CONTROL

Over recent years, the use of data processing techniques for inventory management, capacity planning and scheduling have received considerable attention. Attention is now being focused on to the shop floor to ensure that these plans are executed as efficiently as possible. In this area, the so-called "mini-computer" or plant-floor computer (Figure 26:10) has come to the fore—either as a stand-alone computer or linked to a larger central processor. It is used to support a shop-floor reporting system and directly to monitor and control production operations.

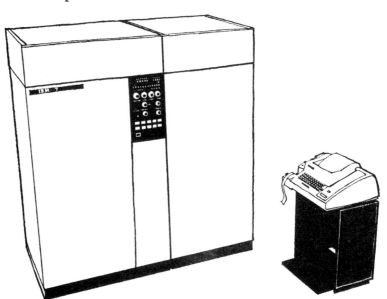

FIGURE 26:10     PLANT-FLOOR COMPUTER
This can be located in the production department to monitor and control production processes, handling and test equipment. Also used to collect feedback from shop-floor terminals.

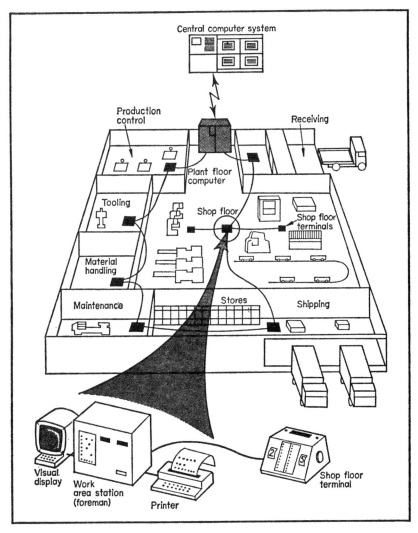

FIGURE 26:11    PLANT COMMUNICATION SYSTEM
Terminals located in all areas of the plant are used to assign new
work and to report job progress.

## Job reporting

Details of each machine or man (such as hours available and number of shifts) are held on a magnetic disk in the plant-floor computer. Work sequence lists for each work centre (determined in capacity planning and operation sequencing) are extracted daily from the central computer and transferred to the plant-floor computer. This is then updated with actual job progress throughout the day.

Job reporting is done via shop-floor terminals located at each work centre or by each machine. These terminals are linked to the computer via telephone lines (Figure 26:11). The terminals can include visual display devices, used by the foreman to display job status and assign work to his men. Printers notify the operator of his next task. An example of a shop-order status display is shown in Figure 26:12. Some companies use "audio response" terminals like telephone handsets which can give a spoken response from the computer system. The type of transactions which are reported at the shop-floor terminals include set-up start, job start, job interrupted and reason, job completion, end-of-shift count, etc. The terminals can also be used for attendance reporting.

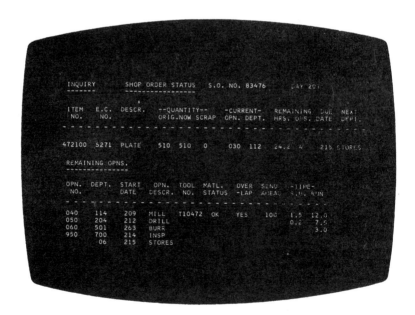

FIGURE 26:12    SHOP ORDER STATUS
This response from the computer shows the status of shop order number 83476.

## Production monitoring

The production operation—cutting the metal, forming the parts, assembling the components, etc.—is the primary event on the shop floor. All other activities support this event.

In order to increase machine utilisation and reduce the amount of scrap and off-standard parts, plant-floor computers are being used to monitor and control machines and processes directly. Figure 26:13 illustrates the types of equipment which can be handled by these computers—not only machines and processes but conveyor lines, stacker cranes and testing equipment.

Instrumentation on the machine tools, such as sensors, switches and counters, is used to record machine on/off status, feed rates, speeds, temperatures and pieces produced, etc. The information is transmitted directly to the computer system. The operator does not have to read or record production rates, machine stoppage, etc. and the foreman is relieved of time normally spent checking. As opposed to conventional methods which notify the foreman only when something has gone wrong, the system becomes "event responsive" in that it notices when things begin going wrong and reports accordingly.

All types of conventional and numerically controlled machines are candidates for production monitoring. Generally, with more complex equipment the need for production monitoring increases. The objective is to keep the machine as fully utilised as possible and thus improve productivity.

What sort of improvement can a company expect? A 1 per cent improvement for a company with a £10M turnover and a labour and machine content of 30 per cent could be

$$£10\,000\,000 \times 0.3 \times 0.01 = £30\,000 \text{ per annum}$$

Experience has shown that improvements in excess of 2 per cent are achievable, and several companies installing systems of this nature expect improvements of 5 per cent. Of course the improvement is heavily dependent upon the efficiency currently achieved in the plant. It is line management's responsibility to establish the target figures. Reductions in the indirect labour force can also be expected, particularly in the area of progress chasers, shop clerks and time-keepers.

25—GTMT  •

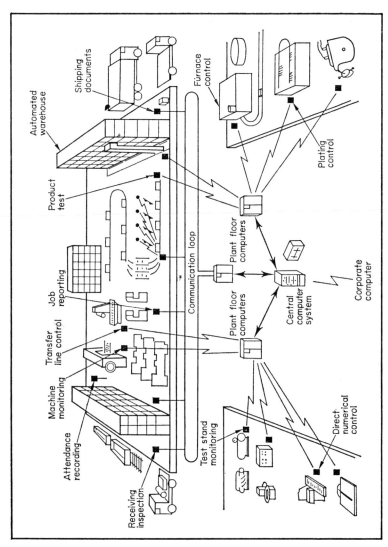

FIGURE 26:13    DIRECT MONITORING AND CONTROL
Computers can be used directly to monitor and control many processes in the plant.

## CRITERIA FOR SUCCESS

Much advice has been written on installing a computer system, a lot of it sound, some of it waffle. The bibliography includes one of the better books, particularly relating to production control systems. Here are a few of the more practical points.

*Get involved.* Management at all levels must be seen to be involved. Any production control system has to be run by the departments concerned and not by the data processing department. The systems design cannot therefore be left to data processing. The project leader responsible for installing a production control system must be the production controller and not a systems analyst.

*Set objectives.* Do not hope that because computer experts are on the job everything will be all right. They know the computer but they do not know the business as you do. Give them realistic objectives

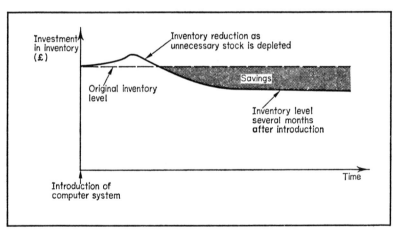

FIGURE 26:14    EFFECT OF INTRODUCING A NEW SYSTEM
Inventory increases immediately following the introduction of a new system before the improved techniques are able to take effect.

but do not expect miracles. Inventory does not come down overnight just because it is on a computer; it takes time to clean out the dead wood. Figure 26:14 illustrates this.

*Don't be too sophisticated.* Have an overall plan but install it in small stages. Many systems have been discredited, not because they were unsound but because the company tried to do too much too fast. People often prefer to live with problems they know than work with a system they cannot understand. Make sure they have time and the training to digest the new procedures.

*Use program packages.* Computer manufacturers provide production control packages based on experience with a lot of companies. Do not re-invent the wheel. The packages may not cover all your needs, but they work and save you a lot of money and time in installation, and ensure you use proven techniques.

*Get the basic data right.* Parts lists have to incorporate what actually goes into the product and not necessarily what the drawing says; the ins and outs from stores must be controlled by authorised personnel only. This means a lot more discipline, initial checking and locks on the stores, but any system will fail if the basic data is out of line with the actual situation. In any case there are not many companies who cannot benefit from tighter controls. To ensure data accuracy, a number of companies are using on-line terminals prior to installing new procedures.

## CONCLUSION

Computers have been around for a number of years. They have been used successfully to solve a wide variety of production planning and control problems. Inventory management, and capacity planning and scheduling are now relatively common. Program packages for these applications are available to help successful installation. The use of mini-computers for direct monitoring and control of production processes, conveyor lines, test equipment and automated warehouses allow significant improvement in the efficiency of these costly facilities. Terminals linked directly to a central computer reduce delays in communication and response, which significantly improves the competitiveness of any organisation.

The factors which contribute to a successful computer installation are many and varied. The key factor however is people. Whether the installation is successful or a failure can usually be attributed to the people involved and not to the computer itself.

## ACKNOWLEDGEMENT

The author wishes to thank IBM United Kingdom Ltd for permission to publish this chapter. The views expressed, however, are those of the author and not necessarily those of the IBM Company.

## FURTHER READING

ORLICKY, J., *The Successful Computer System,* McGraw-Hill

PLOSSL, G. W., and WIGHT, O. W., *Production and Inventory Control—Principles and Techniques,* Prentice-Hall

*The Production Information and Control System,* IBM Form No. GE20–0280

*Communications Oriented Production Information and Control System,* IBM Form No. GE320–1230

## CHAPTER 27

# Delivery Engineering

*by* H P A Moser

*Director, Moser Organisation*
*Consultancy and Purchasing Services*

*All directors would admit the importance of meeting quoted delivery dates but not all companies are adequately organised to achieve this objective. The concept of delivery engineering brings a new approach to this problem and the effective expediting of incoming supplies is seen as an essential prerequisite to maintenance of production schedules.*

# 27 : DELIVERY ENGINEERING

The task of meeting quoted deliveries is often difficult and complex. It can involve the co-ordination of most company departments and many external suppliers. The task can be simplified and made easier to perform if two important factors are recognised. These are:

1   The total responsibility for maintaining a company's deliveries is best organised as a central function.
2   Efficient expediting of supplies is the key to a company's ability to maintain its production schedules.

Delivery engineering is the task of ensuring that a company meets its delivery commitments. Its role in industry and its application within a company are described in this chapter, together with an effective and economical method of expediting supplies.

## ACTIVITIES OF DELIVERY ENGINEERING

Delivery engineering makes its impact on a company's performance through being organised as a central co-ordinating function whose overriding responsibility is the achievement of the company's delivery promises. It carries out its task through:

—quoting realistic delivery promises against sales enquiries
—controlling progress at suppliers and subcontractors
—controlling progress in the company's manufacturing and pre-production departments
—reporting suppliers' delivery performance through vendor rating or similar procedures
—initiating outwards subcontracting when manufacture falls behind schedule
—reporting to the chief executive on the company's delivery performance
—providing customer liaison facilities.

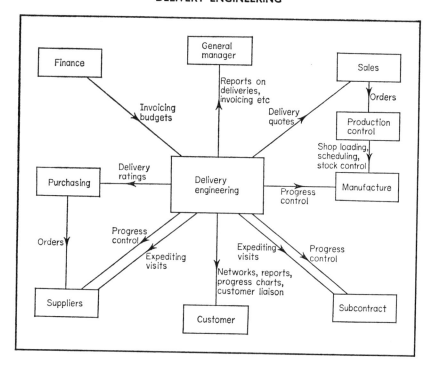

FIGURE 27:1    INTERDEPARTMENTAL PROCEDURES

Provision of a central delivery engineering department allows more
effective co-ordination of a company's production progressing
and gives a logical control point for customer liasion.

Most or all of these tasks are, of course, already established in
many companies. By centralising them, a department can be
equipped with the means necessary for ensuring that delivery
promises are met. Apart from the appointment of a delivery
engineering manager, little, if any, extra cost is involved in the
restructuring of the organisation.

The functional position of delivery engineering in relation to
other aspects of the organisation is illustrated in Figure 27:1 whilst
the interlocking relationship between delivery engineering carried
out by a company, its suppliers and its customers is illustrated in
Figure 27:2.

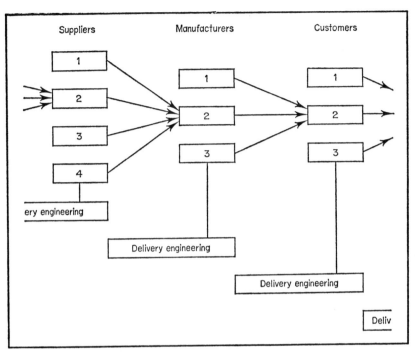

Deliv

FIGURE 27:2    SCOPE OF DELIVERY ENGINEERING

Delivery engineering includes both the expediting of incoming supplies and control of progress within the company; it is responsible for ensuring that the company's own delivery promises are met.

## Progress control and customer liaison

A key concept of delivery engineering is that progress control through suppliers' and the company's own preproduction and production departments is a continuous process. The former is normally termed expediting and involves special organisational and economic problems which are referred to later in this chapter Both, however, are concerned with the achievement of delivery promises and require similar administrative methods and managerial skills.

In a delivery engineering department, expediting and internal progress control are combined under the same departmental manager and delays at suppliers or in the company's own processes are highlighted and speedily corrected. This may involve cutting out inter-operational delays, allocating extra resources, subcontracting, changing priorities, arranging additional overtime working or other means. Some of these measures can be carried out by the department itself whilst others are initiated by it. In all cases, however, the delivery engineering department ensures that the necessary corrective action is taken.

This also makes the department particularly effective as a channel for customer liaison; it avoids the disadvantage of some customer liaison departments which are able to provide information but cannot directly influence progress either at suppliers or within the company. By combining customer liaison with progressing functions economies are also achieved in clerical tasks associated with the preparation of progress charts and records.

Figure 27:1 shows that whilst a delivery engineering department is responsible for progress control, the production control function includes overall shop loading and scheduling. Production control is thus seen as the equivalent of the buying department—it places work on the manufacturing unit whilst the latter places it on the suppliers. There are no intrinsic reasons why either department should also be responsible for the subsequent progress control; the advantages, on the other hand, of organising this as a separate function have been pointed out above.

## Delivery engineering in the company structure

Part of an organisation embodying a delivery engineering department is shown in Figure 27:3. The delivery engineering manager should be under the authority of the executive who is also responsible for the purchasing and production control functions. In many cases he will be the general manager and this term has accordingly been used in the chart.

This type of structure enables the delivery engineering department to carry out its responsibilities effectively and economically. It also emphasises to the company's employees, suppliers and customers that the company regards delivery commitments as of major importance. Moreover it enables any procedural matters which arise at the interfaces between buying, production and delivery engineering to be speedily resolved.

The delivery engineering manager must be a good organiser with a manufacturing background. The latter is needed since his principal work lies in the manufacturing departments of his own

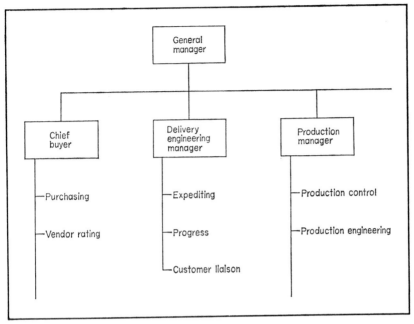

FIGURE 27:3    DELIVERY ENGINEERING IN THE COMPANY
STRUCTURE

In this company structure purchasing, delivery engineering and
production departments are responsible to the general manager.
(The chart is intended to illustrate lines of authority, not the
relative rankings of the positions shown.)

company and those of his suppliers; he must appreciate manufacturing problems in detail to organise corrective measures when
progress has fallen behind schedule. Good organisational skills
are necessary to carry out progressing, customer liaison and clerical
functions efficiently and at minimum cost. Personal qualities of a
high order are required—these must include enthusiasm and a
personality which is readily accepted at different levels of the company's, suppliers' and customers' organisations. He must be able to
attend closely to detailed information and yet have a sufficiently
broad view to identify potentially critical situations in the large
amount of information which he receives.

Lastly he must be highly profit and cost conscious since his activities and responsibilities bear closely on the company's invoicing
budgets on the one hand and on manufacturing, purchasing and
administrative expenses on the other.

# VENDOR AND COMPANY DELIVERY RATING

Suppliers will be aware that their delivery performance is recorded and summarised by the delivery engineering manager. This is most conveniently done as part of a formal vendor rating scheme; the scope of which is briefly reviewed below.

The technique of vendor rating is being used increasingly to assess and record a supplier's performance. The rating applies to factors other than price. It is normally based on an initial inspection and reviewed periodically thereafter. Typical factors considered are the supplier's quality performance, delivery performance, correct and prompt handling of paperwork, efficient response to telephoned and personal expediting, availability of good salesmen and sales literature and assistance with cost-reduction programmes such as value engineering. These factors are weighted to reflect their relative importance. Each company will attach its own scale of values to different aspects of its suppliers' performances. Commonly, quality and delivery will each carry up to one-third of the available points whilst other factors may together account for the remaining third.

Delivery rating can be based on the number of promised deliveries achieved as a proportion of the total; or on the relative extent of lateness in relation to quoted delivery times. The size or value of orders can be an additional factor taken into consideration in both cases.

The vendor rating assessment can be expressed numerically on a points scale or it may be converted into a notional addition to the quoted price. Thus a rating of 80 per cent may be translated into a supplier's quoted price being increased by, say, 5 per cent for purposes of comparison with other quotations. Suppliers should be told of their rating assessments so that they can endeavour to improve any weaknesses in their organisations.

The company's own delivery performance should be similarly measured and reported by the delivery engineering manager to the general manager. The rating should be widely publicised throughout the company and used as a target for effecting further improvements in the company's delivery performance.

## EXPEDITING

Reference was made earlier to special organisational and economic problems in controlling progress in suppliers' preproduction and production departments. These arise mainly because:

—for commercial and geographical reasons, monitoring of progress is more difficult and costly at suppliers than within the company

—when progress has fallen behind schedule, corrective action is more difficult to devise and enforce than in the company's own organisation.

Nevertheless the prompt receipt of incoming supplies is essential to efficient and profitable working. It is only when a company can rely on its supplies arriving on time that it can reduce buffer stocks to a minimum and organise production processes in such a way that deliveries are achieved, yet work-in-progress is kept to a minimum.

Several methods of expediting supplies are in use and experience has shown that personal visits to suppliers are the most effective. Telephone calls and written communications are often unreliable; penalty clauses in a contract merely penalise the supplier for being late but do not necessarily ensure that he will be on time. Any saving to the buyer who invokes a penalty clause may be greatly outweighed by the losses resulting from late delivery.

Personal expediting visits can be undertaken by a member of the company's technical or production staff. Or it might be possible to deploy a representative from a branch office. These methods can all result in relatively high expediting costs, both in terms of time taken in travelling, meetings and reporting, and through loss of the normal output of the individuals concerned. Moreover, the effectiveness often tends to be low. For repeated visits to vendors, and (where necessary) to their suppliers and subcontractors, use of experienced expediting engineers is essential.

Effective expediting in fact requires considerable skill and experience and, if used correctly, is a far cry from being a part-time occupation for an overworked member of a purchasing or production control department. An expediting specialist will be an engineer with a manufacturing background and keen attention to detail. He will consider the requirements of each order with great care and verify the information which he is given. He will record and report his findings accurately and impartially and take whatever steps are necessary to ensure that items which are in danger of falling behind are maintained on schedule.

## Organisation of expediting

To minimise travel, expediters should be located as near as possible to the suppliers concerned. It is sometimes possible for a company to appoint an expediter for an area in which several of their suppliers are located. However, care must be taken that this will not unduly restrict the future selection of suppliers to those within the areas visited by the company's expediters, to the exclusion of others who may be more suitable.

As a more effective alternative, the possibility of combining the company's own resources with the facilities provided by one of the firms of professional expediters should be considered. These will have experienced expediting engineers located near the main industrial areas and their organisation will be such that additional expediting can be accommodated economically and at short notice. Orders subjected to professional expediting assume greater importance in the eyes of vendors, and the purchaser is relieved of the administrative chores associated with expediting.

## Combined expediting

A successful way of combining outside professional and company expediters to best advantage is to entrust the more difficult suppliers and more important contracts to the former and all other expediting to the latter. The benefits of this combination of skills are illustrated in Figure 27:4.

In the upper part of Figure 27:4(a) suppliers $A$ to $K$ are arranged in decreasing order of the expediting which they require. In the lower part they are shown in decreasing order of their arrears. For the sake of simplicity it is assumed that the two rankings coincide, so that suppliers requiring most expediting are also those which are most heavily in arrears. Even if this is not the case, however, the following argument will remain valid.

The effect of introducing professional expediting help at the

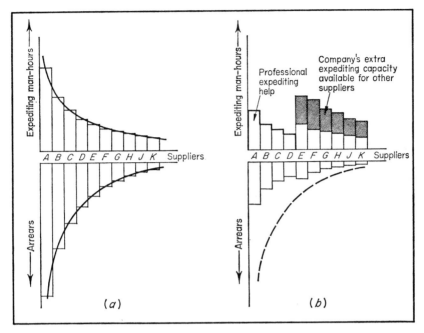

FIGURE 27:4    COMBINED EXPEDITING

In (*a*) ten companies *A* to *K* have been classified according to their delivery performance. At one extreme, company *A* is well behind with its deliveries, and must be subjected to a considerable amount of expediting time by its customer. At the other extreme, *K*, the customer can expect few arrears in deliveries, and needs to spend only a relatively small amount of time in their progress control.

At (*b*) the effect of combining internal and external expediting forces is shown. By concentrating specialised professional help into the real problem cases, internal expediting capacity can be released to deal with the less difficult suppliers, resulting in an overall reduction of arrears.

most difficult suppliers *A* to *D* is to reduce expediting time and arrears in deliveries from these suppliers. At the same time, some of the company's own expediting capacity will be released for reducing arrears at other suppliers, *E* to *K*. The resulting reductions in arrears are shown in Figure 27:4(*b*).

By balancing the use of the company's expediting forces and professional outside expediters, the purchaser has reduced his arrears of incoming supplies to an acceptable level. Of course, delivery performances of companies are never static, and in the event of a supplier's deliveries deteriorating, expediting drives must be repeated from time to time.

A guide to a cost comparison between company expediters and outside professional help is included in the following paragraphs.

## COSTS AND BENEFITS

The cost of improving a company's delivery performance, and the resultant benefits can be assessed. Companies differ so widely, however that generalisations based on such assessments would be virtually meaningless. The following paragraphs will, however, enable companies to consider the financial implications of this chapter in their particular case.

The extra cost of a centralised delivery engineering department is mainly that of its manager since its functions should already be carried out within other departments. By grouping them together, clerical economies will result and will partly offset the extra administrative cost. If the functions of the department are not already carried out elsewhere, their cost will, of course, be additional.

The employment of expediters on the company's staff involves the following costs:

—salary, possibly overtime payments, company and statutory pensions, insurance—these costs being incurred during holidays and other absences as well as when working
—recruitment, training and termination
—travelling and hotel expenses, possibly use of company car
—office expenses, including telephone, typing stationery, etc

The retention of professional expediting firms for some of the expediting will be on an hourly fee basis. Fees arise only when expediting is necessary and is carried out. Travelling times and expenses are low since expediters are based on the industrial areas concerned or are already visiting them for other clients. Coverage may also be available abroad and there may also be facilities for inspection, help in locating additional suppliers and the provision of vendor rating information.

The benefits to a company from prompt receipt of supplies and punctual delivery of its products depend on the nature of the business. For example, in the case of a manufacturer of capital goods who buys castings, forgings, etc., the benefits would include:

—increased customer goodwill, increased profitability, reduced penalty payments, improved plant utilisation, reduced work-in-progress; also lower costs of supervision, progress control and shop dislocation since there will be fewer delayed supplies which have to be rushed through to completion.

In the case of a company purchasing capital plant and associated supplies for a new process line or factory extension, the benefits would include:

—earlier profitability of new plant, safeguarding market for sales from the new plant, reduced site installation costs and reduced cost of interest on the project investment, including any marketing, training or other expenses.

In considering the delivery engineering function, and the expediting processes in particular, reference was necessarily limited to the manufacturing industries. Similar arguments apply, however, whenever goods are purchased or projects have to be completed on time. A company's delivery performance can generally be improved and the extra costs involved will be far outweighed by the resultant benefits.

## FURTHER READING

D'EATH and MOSER, *An Inspection and Expediting Service as an Essential Link in the Purchasing of Capital Equipment*, Paper presented at the British Engineering Week, Helsinki, October 1970, London Chamber of Commerce

BAILY, P., *Purchasing and Supply Management*, Chapman and Hall, 1969

# CHAPTER 28

# Evaluated Maintenance Programming

*by* J V Bosly

*Management Consultant*

The days when factory maintenance was done by one man, one boy and an oil can are long past. The servicing of modern plant and equipment is an operation which is both complex and costly. In some companies these costs can reach as much as £500 000. A saving of over 10 per cent on these costs is obviously worth while, and this kind of result can be achieved with a system of cost control called evaluated maintenance programming.

# 28 : EVALUATED MAINTENANCE PROGRAMMING

In order that production efficiency can be held at a level which ensures profitable manufacturing costs, a range of control techniques have to be applied. Among many other factors, it is essential that plant and machinery are maintained in reliable condition, and protected from premature depreciation. The cost of maintenance is itself an addition to manufacturing expenses, however, accounting in many firms for a significant proportion of the overhead. It follows that much is to be gained by extending control techniques to include the maintenance function. Evaluated maintenance programming (EMP) is the name given to a family of production techniques which have been adapted to the needs of maintenance.

## PROBLEMS OF MAINTENANCE BUDGETING

The difficulties of organising and exercising cost control over works engineering are considerable. Maintenance standards must be kept high, but plant continues to grow in complexity and specialisation. Established methods and practices, instilled over many years into skilled craftsmen, cannot be changed overnight.

The maintenance department may be called upon to deal with a wide variety of plant and equipment, demanding an equally wide range of technical skill and training. Cost accountants and work study engineers, accustomed to methods of control used in production, often find themselves unable to exercise similar methods in maintenance work because of the difficulties of setting standards.

Perhaps the most important difficulty associated with controlling maintenance costs is the attitude of many works engineers, which they have to adopt in order to save themselves from the consequences of naïvely conducted attempts at cost control.

This latter point deserves some elaboration, for we are not

seeking to blame maintenance engineers. For decades maintenance costs were small, even unimportant, by comparison with direct production costs. At the same time, any serious plant failure could cause large losses. In consequence maintenance budgets were virtually unrestricted. The budgets were often set by taking the figure from the previous year and adding a generous allowance to cover rising costs. If the control of these budgets was ever sufficiently loose to allow overspending, this sometimes led to an increased budget for following years.

In the midst of a world where the cost of every management decision had to be assessed for its probable profitability, maintenance engineers could concern themselves primarily with engineering problems. They were engineers first, and managers second. This is not to imply that works engineers have ever had an easy life. Anyone who has held down a maintenance appointment knows too well the difficulty of getting things done within time schedules which are usually too tight, and within budget limits—however generous these may appear to be.

# MAINTENANCE MANAGEMENT

In recent years the picture has been changing. Whereas maintenance costs used to form a relatively small proportion of the total, this proportion is now rising rapidly. Factors contributing to this increase include higher capitalisation, the shortage of skilled men and the continual claims from the craft unions for higher remuneration.

Formerly, there was sufficient scope in other areas for work study engineers, value engineers and others to exercise their skill in cost reduction programmes. As the normal spheres of production became subjected to routines of cost reduction which were more or less standard, attention has shifted to the comparatively virgin areas of maintenance, with the prospect of reducing the wastage there.

First attempts at reduction in maintenance costs often relied upon the use of techniques which were basically intended to cope with the essentially different problems of production. These methods included budgetary control, costing, incentive payment schemes, work study, and so on.

Any one of these advanced techniques, when applied by itself to the comparatively crudely organised activities of maintenance work can raise all sorts of obstacles. Advanced management techniques complement each other to form a coherent system. Employed by themselves they achieve nothing. Anyone who has tried to install one modern technique in an organisation which is basically unsound, for example, will be familiar with this fact of industrial life.

For these reasons, at least for a time, experiments along such lines gave way to those involving productivity bargaining of the Fawley type. [A FLANDERS, *On the Fawley Productivity Deal* second edition 1966, Faber.] Whether these succeed or not is beside the point. If craft unions can be bought or persuaded into giving up restrictive practices, so much the better. In the meantime, however, management continue to be uneasily aware of a need to put the maintenance house in order.


## RATIONALISATION PROJECTS

Just how much can be done immediately, and without bargaining with the unions, has been demonstrated by a number of rationalisation projects. These were conducted by cost investigation teams combining several different skills and using *ad hoc* methods as appropriate. From the findings of such projects, the conclusions emerge:

1   Maintenance engineering is too often attempted with the minimum of management accounting information.
2   When sufficient background information was compiled, truly enormous savings could be demonstrated in many directions and by the use of a variety of methods.

The immediate conclusion seems to call for bigger and better rationalisation projects; but here again we find difficulties.

The rationalisation project is a short-term, clumsy and unpredictable means of securing better works management. On the other hand, there is evidence that it is possible to base a routine activity on the best features of such isolated projects, so as to streamline their procedure and to get continuing long-term results.

## OBJECTIVES

EMP has two immediate objectives:

1   Routine compilation of basic information, similar to that which enabled the rationalisation project teams to direct cost investigations effectively.
2   Routine provision of answers to questions which can be expected to arise frequently during rationalisation studies.

Additionally, certain side benefits are claimed for EMP. These include scheduling of maintenance work by production control type methods, more accurate estimating and budgeting, and the direction of work study and other cost investigations into the most relevant areas. EMP can also lead to the simplification of these other routines.

The long-term objective underlying EMP is more important than these immediate objectives. The aim is that it should be developed into the basis of an effective management policy for maintenance, to complement the technical policy which is probably in existence.

The exponents of the method claim that it highlights areas of wastage and, by means of the information it affords, any responsible works engineer, willing to exercise not any particular technique but merely his own common sense, will make substantial savings.

## CLASSIFICATION OF COSTS

The procedure has been designed to assist the works engineer to overcome two of his immediate problems which, obvious as they are to him, are often unrecognised outside his profession.

The first concerns the varied nature of maintenance department responsibilities. It is too often assumed that these consist for the most part of having gangs of skilled men standing by ready to do repairs as and when occasion demands. In fact, the work can be broken down into three categories:

1   Routine or preventive maintenance including emergency provision and running repairs.
2   Special overhauls and modifications to plant/buildings not necessarily recurring annually.

3    New development work, installations and extensions of
     a capital nature including, of course, provision of jigs,
     tools and small equipment as required.

Careful planning is needed to synchronise these three categories of
work with the least waste of time.

## REALISTIC BUDGETING

The second circumstance which complicates maintenance management is that the rate of expenditure is not constant, and can show
appreciable fluctuation from one month to the next. A maintenance
budget may provide for the employment of a given number of
skilled men, but there are many other items which must be included.
These might include the payment of overtime, employment of outside subcontractors and technical consultants and the supply of
materials. These materials are often disproportionately expensive
and are required only spasmodically.

All this means that a monthly budget figure is not simply one-
twelfth of the annual figure; it may be nearer to half that amount
for nine months and three times that for the remainder. Budget
figures must be related to work programmes. If this sort of figure is
not available every month, there is no merit in comparing actual expenditure with the so-called budget provision; at least not until the
entire twelve-month period can be totalled and compared. By that
time it is too late for remedial action.

If works managers are not given budget figures which are relevant
during the operating period they can hardly be held responsible if
they exceed them. Works management using EMP adopts a procedure which avoids these difficulties, thus making possible both
the generation of information and the follow-up action of the type
used in modern production management. This procedure consists of
four stages:

1    Programming and budgeting
2    Cost reporting
3    Analysis, classification, investigation and feedback
4    Information and, where necessary, control action exer-
     cised by works management itself

## PROGRAMMING

Programming may have to start with no more than a handful of estimates for new capital work, with a vague all-in estimate for the remainder of the maintenance department. The programme is built up in stages: first, essential standby services for the period concerned, then new capital projects, then special overhauls, then routine maintenance tasks.

A maintenance task is the work to be done at one time on a specific item of plant, a group of similar pieces of small plant, or a factory area. Definition of these tasks is not difficult. It is developed either by analysis of the work in a previous period or by recording current work and continuing over a period long enough to disclose the recurring pattern which inevitably exists. The labour element in both projects and tasks must be broken down into the various craft skills involved.

This gives a three-part programme, with each part divided into a separate section for the various trades or craft skills to be employed. By making estimates of man-hours for each task, the total estimated usage can be found for every trade classification. To these totals, an allowance must be added, on a percentage basis, to cover lost time.

Once the load requirements have been established, they can be compared to known departmental capacities, on a week-by-week or day-by-day basis. After this, the dating of projects and special overhauls is comparatively simple, the aim being to avoid peak overloads in any department or trade whilst observing production priorities. Most probably, the resulting chart will demonstrate very uneven loads in some trades. It will be necessary to arrange some of the less important jobs into periods where spare capacity is forecast, to smooth out the work schedules.

Naturally, maintenance tasks have their own priority needs and they cannot be manipulated merely to satisfy the economics of the situation. In some cases, moreover, they will take priority over the scheduling of the other two types of work. It is inevitable, therefore, that a certain number of the hours of each craft will be impossible to schedule beforehand. It is essential that this proportion should be measured in relation to the whole and the success of the programming operation assessed in accordance with the trend of this percentage.

While the initial setting up of EMP on these lines is a substantial task, thereafter it involves less effort than the work of production control, in relation to a similar volume of output. As the year progresses, work scheduled under one or other of the three parts of the programme will be brought forward, delayed or prolonged beyond expectation. EMP programming then becomes a routine operation, continuing throughout the year so that a twelve-month forward plan is always available. This is, of course, similar to a production control scheduling operation.

## PROGRAMME EVALUATION

A budget figure is only meaningful if it is related to a specific work task or project. Rarely does the traditional budget recognise this principle—at least in connection with maintenance work—so as to reflect realistically a programme drawn up with due regard to priorities. Too often it is found merely to refer to the previous years' expenditure rather than experience. The monthly budget figure against which actual maintenance expenditure is compared is then often no more than one-twelfth of an overall annual total.

This is precisely the sort of loose procedure which EMP is designed to avoid. Since each item of maintenance work—project, task or standby—has already been broken down into trades concerned, proprietary materials, stores, outside contracts and other incidentals, the cost can be estimated with some degree of accuracy. Thus, the expense which will be incurred in any given month is the total of the items programmed for that month. Equally important, however, is the fact that the method lends itself to cross analysis by expense items, by projects and tasks, by departments, activities and, if necessary, by production cost centres.

Whenever the programme is changed in the course of the twelve-month period, the budget must be revised accordingly. If items are eliminated, the estimates for them will have to be deducted from the total maintenance allocation. These deductions may result in a need to increase the allowance for surplus labour, whilst the converse will be true if new tasks are added to the schedule and budget.

This feature is important when the next stage of cost comparison is considered.

## COST REPORTING

Stage two consists of organising the reporting of costs in such a way that they can be compared to corresponding estimates in the budget. This would entail the recording of costs for each part of the programme, and these might be further broken down by department, by machine and by the labour skills used. An analysis can then be made which classifies the cost variances. This leads to a summary report document, such as that shown in Figure 28:1

In the early stages of EMP implementation, and until estimates have achieved some degree of precision, it will be necessary to allow for inaccuracies. Percentage tolerances appropriate to each part of the programme may be adopted, with the object of restricting attention to the more important excess in each class. The items against which excesses have been reported are then listed.

The lists of variances may be annotated to show the reasons accounting for deviation from budget. Ideally, one seeks at this stage to indicate whether overspending was due to bad estimating or to bad performance. This process effectively deals with a number of deviations; the remainder are referred to the third stage: cost investigation.

## COST INVESTIGATION

The cost investigation for EMP should not be associated with the sporadic isolated studies occasionally undertaken by cost or work study groups. The differences between these two approaches are basic to the EMP method.

The analysis of cost variances, item by item, on a regular repetitive basis, serves to indicate important trends. Areas where cost investigation is likely to be most effective are shown up. More important, the information thus made available provides a structure around which the investigation itself can be conducted.

Any investigation started in this way has more material available at the outset than the usual type of study accumulates by the time it is half finished. The information provides a historical and current

## WORKS ENGINEERING REPORT    SUMMARY OF MONTHLY COST COMPARISON

Mechanical ⎫
Electrical ⎬ Section*
Building ⎭
Total

DATE.................

| | NUMBER OF ITEMS | BUDGET PROVISION | ACTUAL | | ANALYSIS | | | | |
|---|---|---|---|---|---|---|---|---|---|
| | | | SAVING | EXCESS | WAGES | OVER-TIME | MATERIALS | OTHER | TOTAL ACTUAL |
| Original budget provision | 100 | 50 000 | — | — | 20 000 | 2 000 | 23 000 | 5 000 | — |
| *Less:* Programme items not carried out | 2 | 2 000 | — | — | 1 000 | — | 1 000 | — | — |
| Budget provision for work completed | 98 | 48 000 | — | — | 19 000 | 2 000 | 22 000 | 5 000 | — |
| Actuals: | | | | | | | | | |
| Under 5 per cent of estimate | 25 | 12 000 | 5 000 | — | 2 000 | 400 | 4 100 | 500 | 7 000 |
| Over 5 per cent of estimate | 40 | 20 000 | — | 7 000 | 10 000 | 2 000 | 12 500 | 2 500 | 27 000 |
| Within ± 5 per cent of estimate | 33 | 16 000 | 1 000 | — | 7 000 | 600 | 4 900 | 2 500 | 15 000 |
| Total | 98 | 48 000 | 6 000 | 7 000 | 19 000 | 3 000 | 21 500 | 5 500 | 49 000 |

(* delete as necessary)

FIGURE 28:1    TYPICAL WORKS ENGINEERING REPORT

How excesses may be offset by savings so that they appear unimportant in total. In fact, the total figures conceal excess expenditure of 35 per cent for nearly half the tasks undertaken in the month.

picture, automatically dictating the lines along which the cost investigation should proceed. This is perhaps the greatest advantage of EMP, because the difficulty to which traditional cost studies are subject derives from the need to provide a precise programme for their conduct.

The formulation of terms of reference for studies, their direction and the actions arising from them have in the past demanded too much time from able managers. The routine nature of EMP, on the other hand, enables it to be entrusted to properly trained middle management. The subjects of study are automatically allocated to orders of priority, based on evaluation and magnitude of excess. Not least, EMP opens up maintenance work to the application of such techniques as value engineering and value analysis, which have proved so effective in production work.

Once again, findings will fall into two groups. Some variances will arise from poor estimates, whilst others can be attributed to bad performance or wasteful methods. Errors in estimating should be fed back, in order that future budgets can be made more accurate in the light of experience. Variances which indicate the need for corrective action are passed on to the next, and final, stage. Any studies or surveys which arise from one monthly report should be completed before the next monthly report is due.

## MAINTENANCE AND MANAGEMENT SERVICES

The last stage is concerned with action to be taken arising from the information derived from the evaluation programme. Both the monthly report and the outcome of studies undertaken as a result of the previous report can provide a call for corrective action. The relevant information is turned over to the works engineering department, which is expected to make effective and appropriate use of it. At the same time, every assistance must be provided to enable this to be done, particularly as regards communication.

Management appreciation courses may be conducted for the benefit of maintenance shop foremen, supervisors, and others, using the topical material available as case history. Progress bulletins can be issued which compare the results achieved by different sections of the maintenance department, so that a spirit of friendly competition is promoted. This is not unlike the practice of many large sales organisations, where competition between different groups is introduced to improve performance.

In general, the traditional atmosphere accompanying the conclusion of a survey is carefully avoided. There is no lengthy report to be prepared and circulated and there are no precisely formulated recommendations to be debated, subsequently modified and finally shelved. Instead, works managers are given the same sort of management service that their production colleagues expect. They receive a regular supply of information concerning the cost and progress of work under their control.

## COSTS AND ECONOMICS

At first sight, the cost of providing such a service might appear high. In answer to this objection two points are made:

1    EMP is to maintenance work as production control and costing methods are to production. It is equally necessary and much cheaper in relation to the savings which result.
2    Any technique which generates savings many times its own cost cannot be called expensive.

Since many plants these days have maintenance bills which exceed £500 000, these claims are likely to interest many industrialists.

# CHAPTER 29

# The Total Cost Approach to Distribution

*by* Gilbert R Cole

*Vice-President, Booz, Allen and Hamilton International*

Like the tip of an iceberg, only a small percentage of distribution-related costs are immediately identifiable in any firm. To discover the real cost of distribution, management needs to probe beneath the surface and track down a variety of seemingly unrelated factors, all of which can materially affect the final total cost. The technique, which has been developed in the United States, is known as the total cost approach to distribution, or TCD. The method has already been successfully applied to the operations of several large American companies, where it has led to bigger profits and wider margins. It is now being adopted by a number of leading British organisations using the services of Booz, Allen and Hamilton International.

# 29 :  THE TOTAL COST
## APPROACH TO DISTRIBUTION

The more management focuses the company's efforts on cutting distribution costs, the less successful it is likely to be in reducing the real cost of distribution. This apparent paradox is no abstract play on phrases. It explains why so many companies have diligently pruned distribution costs—in the warehouse, in stocks, in order processing and shipping—only to find that these hard earned savings have somehow been watered down or washed out altogether by increases in other costs scattered throughout the company.

These "other cost" increments seem to have nothing to do with distribution. They appear unpredicted and inexplicable at different times and anywhere and everywhere in the business—in purchasing, in production, in paper processing. But when traced back to their root cause, these gremlin-like costs are not as haphazard as they may seem. They are in fact all interrelated, and they do have one thing in common. They all result from the way the company distributes its products.

It is this aggregation of distribution-related costs—rather than the more commonly labelled distribution costs—that make up the *real* cost of distribution. It is these costs—rather than those usually attacked in distribution cost-cutting programmes—that represent the important and increasing drain of distribution on earnings.

The important difference between distribution costs and the real impact of distribution on the total costs and total profits of the business has now been measured and dealt with by a handful of hard-headed companies. Their managements have defined this cost complex and brought it under management control by applying the "total cost approach to distribution" (TCD).

Some very tangible results have been achieved. Here are three examples:

1    A major food manufacturer, after applying effectively an assortment of belt-tightening techniques, has found that TCD is enabling him to make additional profits of $3 800 000, enough to add 1.7 per cent to his margin of sales.

2    A major merchandiser, already enjoying the benefits of advanced distribution techniques, found that TCD was able to cut from its corporate costs an additional $7 500 000 — 2.8 per cent of the sales value of its products — while at the same time significantly improving service to customers.

3    At Du Pont, TCD programmes recently instituted are expected to cut $30M from the costs attributed to distribution — a 10 per cent reduction.

These success stories demonstrate why even companies which have tightened and tidied their distribution operations can still add substantially to their earnings by a frontal attack on the basic framework of their distribution decisions and practices. They have proved, too, that this broad and basic approach brings continuing returns. Once TCD has defined the most profitable pattern of distribution for the present operations of the business, management has a yardstick for measuring the impact on total profits of any proposed change.

The effectiveness of TCD is illustrated by the two following examples—each a different situation. The first traces the step-by-step process involved in the analysis of the factors that enter into a TCD analysis. The second shows how this information is exploited to provide management with the most profitable answers to some familiar distribution problems.

## TCD APPLIED TO A CHAIN OF RETAIL OUTLETS

Consider the first problem which faced the management of a large company whose business comprised a widely dispersed chain of retail shops, plus a few factories which produced some of the goods sold in the shops. The company distributed its products from one centrally located warehouse. The question arose: "Would there be any profit advantage in changing to a system of local warehouses, distributed across the country?"

When the company looked at the combined cost of warehousing and transport that would result from introducing local warehouses it found that the lowest cost system was one with five warehouses. But this would increase its distribution costs by $12 900 000. Thus, on the basis of conventional analysis, the central warehouse method seemed best.

However, when the question of how alternative distribution networks would affect other costs in the company was investigated, the answers were quite different. In the first place, the most efficient warehouse system turned out to be a network of six, rather than one or five, field warehouses. And this six-warehouse system would cut total costs dramatically.

When all distribution-related cost factors were considered for the six-warehouse system, increases in physical distribution costs amounted to $13 900 000 but there were substantial reductions in other costs amounting to $20 600 000. This total cost look at distribution demonstrated that the profits of the company could be increased by $6 700 000 a year.

What produced this increase which, incidentally, turned out to represent 22.4 per cent return on the investment required to design and install this field warehouse system? The answer is defined by tracing through the company the "other cost" implication of this distribution change.

It was necessary first to decide which interrelationships were economically significant. These will differ from industry to industry, and even from company to company. To illustrate this point, and to demonstrate how these interrelationships worked out in this instance, Figure 29:1 presents graphically the impact of a number of cost factors on the profits of the company.

The calculations are quite complex, and these graphs serve only to represent schematically the kind of impact that the addition of field warehouses would have on each cost factor. To do this, each point on this series of curves shows how an optimally designed system including from one to thirty field warehouses would add or subtract from corporate profits.

Graphs (a) and (b) show quite clearly how a consideration of warehousing and transportation costs alone would lead to the

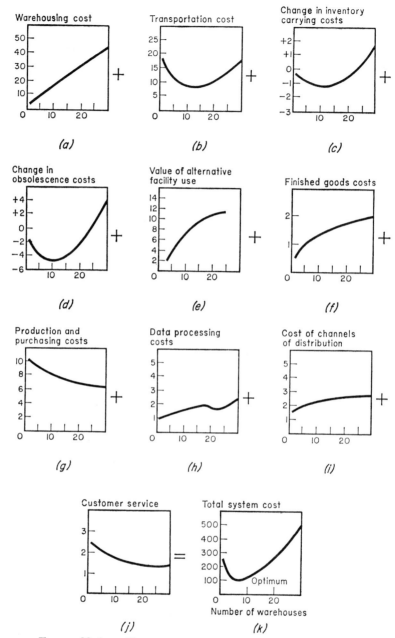

FIGURE 29:1    THE BUILD-UP OF TOTAL DISTRIBUTION COSTS

Each factor is considered in relation to the number of warehouses possible and a curve of the cost implications plotted. By adding all of these results together, a composite curve is obtained (k), which shows the total costs of distribution in relation to the possible warehouse arrangements.

answer this management was given when the conventional distribution cost analysis was made. It is the sum of these two graphs which leads to the conclusion that a five-warehouse system was the best alternative, although this would actually increase the costs of these two functions.

A further study of the company's operation showed that for each warehouse added there would be a different rate of inventory turnover, and therefore a change in inventory carrying costs. This is illustrated in graph (c). Including these charges in distribution evaluation is, of course, standard practice in many companies. But even the addition of this consideration would not have led management to the correct decision. A five-warehouse system would still appear to be the best alternative, even though economically unsound.

There are, however, other aspects of inventory which, in this case as in many others, prove to be more significant. These are shown in graphs (d), (e) and (f) of Figure 29 : 1 and they are :

1    Changes in the cost of obsolescence
2    The value of alternative use of facilities
3    Changes in the cost at which the company was able to
     buy finished goods

When these three cost factors were taken into account, it became clear that the original calculation had been invalid. A total cost curve that included these three factors would shift the decision to a six-warehouse system and begin to show the possibility of substantial profits from such a change.

The interaction between distribution, production and purchasing is traced in the relationships described in graph (g). The number and location of the field warehouses would directly affect the loading of the company's factories, which had a definable impact on the cost of raw materials and components and on production costs per unit.

The company's data processing costs would, of course, also be affected by decentralising its warehousing with the resulting need for the ability to exchange information between the field and headquarters. In this case, although there was substantial additional paper work, the cost was not great because it could all be put on the company's existing computer system. The projected results are shown in graph (h).

Finally, and most important, the impact of any proposed change in distribution has to be traced to its point of impact in the market place, for ultimately that is the measure of the effectiveness of the distribution system. Here the two critical elements are the channels through which a company elects to distribute its products, and the level of customer service it decides to maintain.

In this case, because the company distributed mostly through its own retail outlets, the channels seemed not to be an important consideration. There was, nevertheless, an important reason for following out the significance of distribution channels. As this company looked ahead, it could see the possibility that at some time in the future it might want to integrate backwards, and become more heavily involved in manufacturing. In that case, the channels of distribution factor become more important.

In this kind of analytical exercise it is essential to consider all possible directions that company growth can take. Otherwise, a new distribution system, however profitable it may be under present conditions, might freeze the company into a set of cost factors that would rule out an otherwise profitable growth opportunity.

Customer service is the other marketing decision that plays an important role in any total cost approach. In the last analysis, any distribution system is an effort to achieve at the lowest cost the level of service to customers which will afford the company the greatest opportunity for growth in the market place. The question is: how much does it cost to improve service to customers and how much can be gained in additional sales by that improvement? Graph (j) shows how warehousing would affect sales lost at the present level of customer service.

When all these factors are added up, they produce a single total cost curve that defines the best solution to this management problem. This is shown in graph (k) of Figure 29:1, which illustrates the fact that the six-warehouse system is the best alternative and one that would return a handsome profit to the company. The actual figures from this company's experience for the six-warehouse system are shown in Figure 29:2.

The graphs and figures demonstrate better than words the management meaning of the total cost approach. Study of the cost curves one at a time makes it apparent that the most profitable distribution network is somewhat different for each of these cost factors. This is what leads to distorted decisions when companies look at one, two or six of these variables and fail to consider the others. It shows the pitfalls of considering these various factors as single and static, instead of as interrelated and dynamic. Looking again at the first two graphs, it is apparent how the consideration of distribution costs alone—the cost of warehousing plus the cost of transportation—led to the conclusion that there was no change in distribution which could add to the profitability of the business. Only the final graph, summing up all the interacting factors involved, demonstrates unmistakably that a shift to the six-warehouse system would be a very profitable move for management.

| ITEM | GAIN OR LOSS ($M) | |
|---|---|---|
| WAREHOUSING | (14.4) | |
| TRANSPORT | 0.5 | |
| Total distribution costs | | (13.9) |
| STOCKS | | |
| Carrying costs | 1.4 | |
| Obsolescence costs | 4.3 | |
| Value of Alternative Use of Facilities | 7.8 | |
| | | 13.5 |
| PRODUCTION AND PURCHASING | | |
| Production and raw materials costs | 0.2 | |
| Reduced cost of purchased finished goods | 6.7 | |
| | | 6.9 |
| DATA PROCESSING | | (0.2) |
| MARKETING | | |
| Channels of distribution | 0.2 | |
| Customer service | 1.4 | |
| | | 1.6 |
| Total profit impact of distribution-related items | | 21.8 |
| PRE-TAX PROFIT INCREASE | | 7.9 |

FIGURE 29:2    PROFIT IMPACT OF DISTRIBUTION

Gains or losses projected by a TCD study, based on a changeover from an existing one-warehouse system to a six-warehouse system.

These graphs show, too, why major distribution problems could not be resolved at the operating levels of the company. In this case, a "no-go" decision would have been valid if a traffic or transport or warehouse executive had to make that decision on the basis of the cost data available. A reduction in warehouse transport and stock costs would lead to increases in other distribution-related costs, so that total costs would be increased and this significant profit opportunity missed. Only by increasing these distribution costs could total expenses be cut and total earnings increased in this company. It is by this kind of trade-off—robbing Peter to pay Paul—that the total cost approach brings a company closer to achieving its maximum potential profit.

The total cost approach does much more than offer a one-shot solution to a perennial problem. Every time management makes a decision of any magnitude, it ought to be in a position to get an answer to the question: "How will it affect distribution costs throughout the company?" The total cost approach enables a company to make continuing gains by applying a yardstick to any proposed corporate venture.

Every time manufacturing management designs a new plant or develops a new production process, the pattern of distribution costs will be changed throughout the business. Similar far-flung changes will take place whenever marketing management adds a new product or a promising new group of customers. The total cost approach enables boards to define how these changes will interact with distribution to affect the total costs of the company and its total profits. It tells boards what distribution decisions need to be made to avoid the loss of potential profits, or to add to them.

## TCD ANALYSIS OF A LARGE MANUFACTURING ORGANISATION

How this is done can be seen quite readily in a case in which the TCD approach was used by a division of a large American manufacturing company. This division does an annual business of about $45M, with over 300 customers located in every state in the US. It manufactures and warehouses at five points across the country, shipping to customers via both rail and road.

412

Some of the profit questions this management posed have a familiar ring:

1   Without any major investment, can we increase our profits by changing our distribution system?
2   Can total cost be reduced by shifting some of our equipment from one factory to another?
3   Can we further reduce costs and increase profits by changing our marketing approach?

Then there were some longer-range questions to be resolved:

1   Is there any profit advantage in changing the capacity of one or more of our present plants, or perhaps building a new facility at another location?
2   Could we further improve profitability by changing our warehouse capacities or locations?

An analysis of this company's business shows quite readily what factors and interactions determined the total profit of the product delivered to the customer. Every distribution study has to start with a definition of where the customers are and the requirements they impose on their suppliers. In this case, it was vital to differentiate between the customers that had to be served by rail, and those that had to be served by road.

What was done, therefore, was to determine for each sales district what proportion of sales came into the district by rail, and how much was shipped in by road. And for each sales district data on f.o.b. as against delivery pricing was obtained.

The next step was to determine from which of the five plants and warehouses each sales district should be supplied. This involves an in-depth analysis of the production and warehousing costs per unit in each of the plants and warehouses. This analysis had to be carried out for various volume levels.

The total plant cost is built up by analysing the cost for varying production volume, inbound freight, direct labour and plant overheads. All of these cost elements will, of course, differ at each plant, even within the same company. These plant and warehouse cost calculations were made for each of the company's five facilities.

Figure 29:3 shows these total cost curves for all of the plants and warehouses. These costs are, of course, different for each facility at each level of volume. Not only does each curve start at a different point—reflecting different overhead costs—but the rate of increase is also different, reflecting different variable cost factors at increasing volumes for each of these installations.

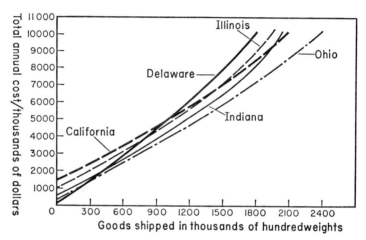

FIGURE 29:3     TOTAL PLANT AND WAREHOUSING COSTS AT FIVE
PLANTS

Differing fixed and variable costs of installations at five different locations for a large manufacturing organisation in the USA.

With some further analyses it became possible to determine, for every unit of production and for all individual customers, the profit contribution under all possible combinations of production and distribution. The problem that remained was to put all these possibilities together into a single solution that would maximise the company's total earnings.

Conceivably this could have been done by a series of pencil-and-paper calculations in which each combination of factors could be worked out and the profitability of each pattern determined. The enormous and costly chore which that would represent is, of course, the reason why the total cost concept has not found its way into management thinking until recently. What was needed, of course, was the computer to process the data.

To introduce this data into the computer called for a mathematical technique (known as non-linear programming). The technical aspects of this are not important for its managerial implications. What is significant is that the technique does exist, that it does work, and that once the program has been written, this kind of distribution problem can be solved in minutes.

Returning now to the questions confronting the management of this company, TCD was able to provide a very precise answer to each of them:

**1** By rearranging the company's distribution pattern and making appropriate shifts in production and warehousing loads, it was possible without any change in facilities to increase this company's profit by $492 000 a year.

The largest ingredient in this change would come from reduced materials cost at $200 000, with warehouse savings contributing $183 000. Direct labour savings in the plants would add a further $57 000. What is particularly interesting is that transportation, so often over-stressed in distribution decisions, turned out to contribute only $54 000 to this total profit improvement package.

**2** Additional savings of $180 000 could be effected by shifting equipment from one plant to another.

To determine this, it was necessary to develop new production cost curves for alternative arrangements of equipment and run these through the computer, comparing them with the most profitable way of using the equipment as presently located.

**3** Additional savings of $447 000 a year would result if about half of the customers could be persuaded to shift from road to rail delivery.

These reduced costs could be added to earnings or passed on to the customer, thus giving the company a competitively significant price advantage.

**4** It was determined that there was no way to increase profitability by any change in production facilities.

Although building a new plant in Michigan would result in lower production and warehousing costs amounting to $225 000, when the impact of this change on total costs was seen, this turned out to be one of those instances in which the "other costs" which have been discussed more than offset any possible gains, so that this investment would not be a wise one.

**5**   On the other hand, an addition to the capacity of the warehouse at their Delaware plant would add $75 000 a year to profits and represent a sound investment.

Again, this was determined by setting up new warehousing cost schedules and running them through the computer alongside the costs under existing conditions. The comparison showed that the investment in the added Delaware warehouse capacity would return almost 25 per cent a year.

The total addition to profits adds up to almost $750 000 a year.

The point that needs to be underscored is that these profits could not have been generated by decisions based on the insight or the experience of even the most competent executive. Only the total cost approach could have established, for example, that the earnings of this business could be increased by supplying its customers in the Dakotas from a plant in Ohio rather than from a much nearer facility in Illinois. Yet when total profits were calculated, this turned out to be an element in the most profitable use of the existing facilities of this company.

Similarly, only a total-cost calculation provided the background for estimating the return on investment that could be expected from building a new facility in Michigan. It is this ability to put precise price and profit tags on each pattern of alternatives that makes the total cost approach such an effective management tool. In a few years TCD in the larger company may well become as routine as budgetary control or standard costing.

*Section Six*

# EDP and Management Services

# CHAPTER 30

# Controlling Indirect Personnel Costs With Group Capacity Assessment

*by* Kenneth Rackham

*Partner, Arthur Young & Company*

Failure to control the activities of indirect personnel is costing the economy £1500M each year. This is the price the nation pays for not recognising the practical implications of the present deployment of staff in the clerical, administrative, service and other indirect support functions. One method for obtaining the necessary control is group capacity assessment, developed originally within the US and later introduced into Britain.

# 30 : CONTROLLING INDIRECT PERSONNEL COSTS WITH GROUP CAPACITY ASSESSMENT

Most managements exercise some form of control over direct productive labour on the shop floor; far too few, however, have examined the possibility of cutting back overheads in the form of indirect staff costs. If substantial improvements in productivity are to be made, attention must now be turned to the personnel engaged in support activities or in the service sector of the economy, who form the major part of the total national labour force.

The consequences of inadequate planning and control of time expenditure on service and support activities are evident in nearly every organisation in the country. Companies who rightly pride themselves on their management controls still accept standard costs that show figures such as:

| | | | | | | | | |
|---|---|---|---|---|---|---|---|---|
| Material | – | – | – | – | – | – | – | £9 |
| Direct labour | – | – | – | – | – | – | £8 |
| Overheads (350 per cent direct labour) | – | | – | £28 |

A works manager or production director can control over-expenditures of a few pounds on materials or direct labour, but is frequently left groping in thin air when he tries to attack the amorphous figure for overheads, much of which is attributable to the cost of the indirect labour force.

In the service sector of the economy the problem of costing is acute and little work has yet been done on costing the individual transactions carried out. Here most of the cost is again clerical and administrative.

In recent years there has been a considerable advance in techniques for obtaining the control that is obviously needed. Group capacity assessment programmes have been developed in the United States during the last fifteen years and have been operated in Britain for over five years. By now over 200 000 personnel are being controlled by this advanced system. In application it has been found that from 60 to 70 per cent of all personnel in manufacturing industries can be included in effective manpower planning and control schemes.

By planning and control, reductions of between 15 and 25 per cent have been obtained in indirect labour forces. An equally important result is that managements have been provided with improved means of planning personnel requirements and thus controlling the cost of future operations.

| TYPE OF CLIENT | FIRST YEAR SAVINGS | SAVINGS-COST RATIO |
|---|---|---|
| Electro-mechanical manufacturing | £59 000 | 3:1 |
| Insurance | £116 000 | 8:1 |
| Municipal Government | £21 000 | 4:1 |
| Aircraft manufacturing | £2 452 000 | 5:1 |
| Petroleum production and marketing | £282 000 | 5:2 |
| Air transportation | £125 000 | 2:1 |
| Book publishing | £45 000 | 3:1 |
| Light engineering | £13 000 | 3:1 |

FIGURE 30:1    TYPICAL RESULTS OF GCA

Typical results achieved by management using GCA programmes showing annual payroll savings and the ratio of these recurring savings to the one-time programme installation costs.

The programme has been installed in organisations ranging in size from those employing only a hundred or so to those employing tens of thousands. The economic impact of the scheme is illustrated in Figure 30:1 and the types of area which have been covered in Figure 30:2. From this it can be seen that the ratio of the return from first-year savings to initial costs has ranged from 2 to 1 to 10 to 1, and typically a 4 or 5 to 1 ratio can be expected. Once the scheme is in operation the ratio of continued savings to the cost of operating it is of the order of 20 to 1.

These returns are higher than for many other projects and they do not require a big initial investment. Savings begin within four or five months of starting the programme. In organisations which are expanding these savings may be absorbed by increasing the work load without increasing the staff. Not only does this save the cost of

| | | |
|---|---|---|
| Accounts payable | Machine accounting | Property accounting |
| Accounts receivable | Mailing | Purchase invoicing |
| Branch banking | Maintenance engineering | Purchasing |
| Calculating | Marketing | Quality control |
| Contracts department | Material control | Sales and service |
| Cost accounting | Office services | Sales invoicing |
| Data processing | Payroll and salaries | Secretarial services |
| Draughting | Pensions and welfare | Security |
| Engineering services | Photographic and | Shipping |
| Estimating | reproduction | Spares provisioning |
| Foundry planning | Policy writing | Stores |
| General accounting | Production control | Technical publications |
| Inspection | Production scheduling | Transport |
| Insurance department | Project costing | |

FIGURE 30:2    AREAS COVERED BY GCA

Examples of the wide range of functions which have been successfully covered by the GCA programme.

additional space, furniture and equipment, but also in many high employment areas the internal transfer of surplus staff to new projects is the only solution to the increasingly difficult recruitment problem.

## CHANGING ATTITUDE TOWARDS CONTROL METHODS

The basic techniques of group capacity assessment are derived from work measurement practices which have been in use for many years on the shop floor. There has been a reluctance in the past to use such techniques in service and support areas and it is relevant to discuss why.

It is an unfortunate and widely held fallacy that the only purpose of work measurement should be to determine financial rewards, often by giving direct incentives to individual workers. If this were in fact so, work measurement would be inappropriate in indirect areas. In group capacity assessment programmes measurement is used as a tool to study and evaluate in quantitative terms the working patterns of groups of people. It is not used to provide "bonuses" or individual targets of performance.

Another answer lies deep-rooted in the very history of industry. The first mill in Britain was equipped with a bell to regulate the comings and goings of the eighteenth-century factory worker. From that day to this he has worked by the clock and been controlled by the clock. The administrative and technical worker has come into being due to the division of management skills and originally inherited both the right to live free from the clock and the associated disadvantage of working all hours for no extra pay. Although these attitudes and conditions have gradually changed, the lack of time-consciousness still persists outside the works areas.

Finally, and most significantly, many executives believe that supervisors should be left to control their staff as best they can. Results from GCA programmes highlight how inadequate such subjective controls usually are. This is not of necessity an indictment of supervisors. The supervisor usually lacks the means to perform the task of planning and control set him. If he chooses to rely on visual checks that his staff are working he must be with them most of the time. In fact, most supervisors spend most of their day dealing with other group leaders, away from their own groups. In addition, they usually have enough work of their own to do without spending much time consciously looking around.

Very few people make a habit of being idle in an obvious way, and casual visual control is completely inadequate. The better supervisor will make some effort, usually erratically and as time permits, to rough check how long jobs have taken. In doing this he must rely on his own experience or his estimating ability to decide if the time taken is acceptable. Unfortunately, jobs change and estimates can be notoriously unreliable, even when prepared by skilled estimators.

Many supervisors suffer from a further major difficulty. Service departments, ranging from the messengers to the design drawing office, are judged mainly on their ability to meet any demand made of them, often at short notice, and discounting the economy of their operation. As a result, from the bottom of the ladder to the top, the commonest method of adjusting staff requirements is to give way slowly and to allocate additional staff according to the volume and forcefulness of the requests submitted.

Radical changes are, however, taking place in company thinking. Measurement and control are becoming increasingly important in determining company strategy. Engineering firms are continually concerned with standards and specifications, insurance companies will not move without actuarial advice, the merchant bank has its investment analyst. It is not surprising then that these same managements are coming to believe that manpower planning can only be achieved through quantitative information. This demands some form of measurement.

## UNAMBIGUOUS UNITS OF OUTPUT

The basis of any manpower planning and control scheme rests on the ability to equate time requirements with work outputs. The necessary units of output can be identified for most human activities; for instance; even the girl at the enquiry desk has a readily identifiable output: queries answered.

In many clerical, administrative and technical jobs, the output is intangible. Experience shows, however, that careful analysis almost always reveals suitable units of output, although it would be unwise to link payments with performance in such cases, and incentive schemes are in general inappropriate in indirect areas.

## RELATIONSHIP BETWEEN OUTPUT AND TIME REQUIRED

It is under this heading that techniques of measurement must be considered. Management of support and service departments are usually unfamiliar with such techniques and can become confused over their use. While they should assure themselves that the basic methods are valid, there is a danger of a preoccupation with methods of measurement obscuring the main objective which is the production of an overall planning and control scheme.

All techniques have a common output, a standard time in which some defined operation or series of operations should normally be performed. The available techniques, all of which have been used in GCA programmes, are shown in Figure 30:3. The important practical point is to suit the technique to the situation, and the general range of applicability of each technique is also shown in Figure 30:3.

Although estimation is a valid planning technique provided there is adequate feedback to help the estimator adjust his future figures,

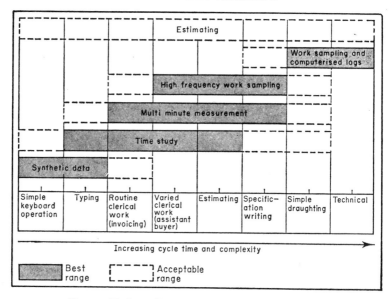

FIGURE 30:3    RANGE OF APPLICABILITY FOR GCA
Measurement techniques which have been used in GCA programmes and an indication of their range of applicability shown
against a job spectrum.

it is really to be used only as a last resort where planning figures are
highly desirable and would not otherwise be obtainable.

To avoid setting unrealistically high or low standards, observed
times are adjusted to normal by rating each element of work as it is
done. Measurement staff are trained in this skill which is used only
as a safeguard against accepting extreme values. It is not practical
to "rate" thinking which may occupy up to two-thirds of all time
spent in a technical area. For example, the clerk may have to think
before he writes any item on a shortage list. A series of observations
of a number of operators will usually yield a pattern, and that shown
in Figure 30:4 is a typical example.

Results such as these can be analysed statistically. It can be shown
for the pattern illustrated that the mean value is 3.22 minutes and
that this calculation is not in error by more than 6 per cent. This
mean element time evaluated under controlled conditions can then
be used in building up a standard time for the job. This same analysis
can be applied to jobs taking any range of times. The practical

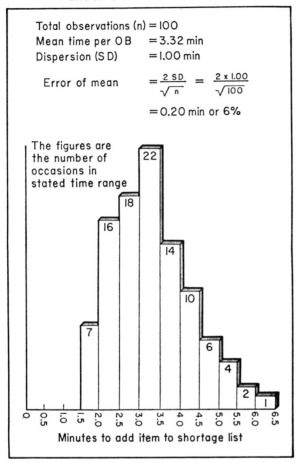

Total observations (n) = 100
Mean time per O B  = 3.32 min
Dispersion (S D)  = 1.00 min

$$\text{Error of mean} = \frac{2\,SD}{\sqrt{n}} = \frac{2 \times 1.00}{\sqrt{100}}$$

$$= 0.20 \text{ min or } 6\%$$

The figures are the number of occasions in stated time range

22
18
16
14
10
7
6
4
2
1

Minutes to add item to shortage list

FIGURE 30:4    CALCULATION OF TIME FOR A THINKING ELEMENT
Typical pattern of observed times for an element of work involving "thinking". Statistical analysis reveals a mean time of 3.22 minutes and this calculation is not in error by more than 6 per cent.

limitation is the time required to collect enough data to reduce the margin of error to acceptable limits.

In complex areas there is one difficulty that must be overcome if a viable scheme is to be produced. Jobs are frequently not only lengthy but may also vary in length from one occasion to the next. Measurement cannot stop such variation, it can only put a dimension to it. To illustrate the problem, suppose an operator works on one type of job only and that this job has been found from a large

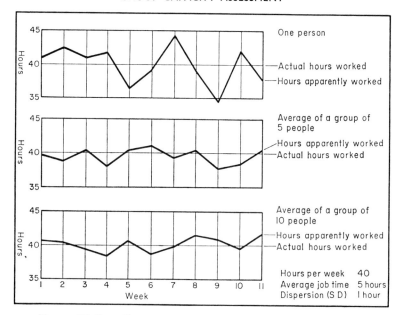

FIGURE 30:5    SMOOTHING OF RESULTS USING GROUP REPORTING

In many indirect activities job times are frequently highly variable as well as lengthy. Group reporting will reduce the effect of this variability and may be not only desirable but technically necessary.

number of readings to average six hours per occasion with a variation of one to eleven hours. Figure 30:5 illustrates the number of hours which an operator, who is in fact working consistently for forty hours each week, would appear to have worked in successive weeks if the job time was counted as a standard six hours per occasion. Similar figures are shown in the diagram for groups of five and ten people.

It is apparent that the larger the group the more consistent the results. Thus in such areas a group scheme is not only desirable but is also technically necessary. In cases of more routine work, it is, however, possible to use the standard times to plan work in detail and the supervisor can be assisted to improve the work scheduling system. Measured groups vary in size from three to twenty people. In practice reports on group performance have been found to provide an excellent supervisory tool and it is not necessary to move to individual reporting systems.

Allowances must be made for activities not covered by the jobs measured such as time to receive instructions, answering queries etc. Where possible these times should be related to the volume of work handled by the department, and a considerable amount of effort may be required to obtain a satisfactory treatment of such allowances. Allowance must also be made for a legitimate amount of personal time. In this latter case, nearly all measurement programmes are the same, treating such allowances as a policy matter based on broad guiding principles as to their overall level.

## MAINTENANCE OF SAFETY, SERVICE AND QUALITY STANDARDS

Safety standards are not usually a problem, but obviously wherever hazards are present time standards are double checked to ensure that adequate time is available for safe operation.

Quality standards are usually protected by involving the supervisor thoroughly in each step of the installation. However, more advanced organisations are beginning to move towards quality control in non-manufacturing areas, such schemes having many advantages over and above those directly relevant to a measurement situation.

As many departments covered by the programme are service departments the protection of service standards is a key factor. In practice the first problem encountered is that the level of service is not known and supervisors adjust their staffing on the criteria of who complains and how often. Measurement can be used to assess the cost of a service against the level achieved. The service level can be consciously set and reviewed, improving the situation rather than causing it to deteriorate.

A similar type of problem exists in considering peak loads (or their mirror image, peak absences). From the start the measurement team must be aware of any cycles or patterns of work which influence the operation of the department.

Provision of quantitative data will not in itself solve such problems but will enable better solutions to be reached. Obviously a major factor in such situations is a close co-operation with supervision at all stages.

# ECONOMIC OPERATION OF THE PROGRAMME

Economy is obtainable in two ways, firstly by minimising the cost of installation of a scheme and secondly by ensuring that results are used to obtain the optimum effect.

Installation costs can be minimised by planning each phase of the scheme and by ensuring that those implementing it adhere to agreed time targets. Group capacity assessment programmes employ comprehensive planning techniques to ensure that costs are predictable and are met. A typical installation plan is shown in Figure 30:6.

| Activity | Time span | | | | | | | | | | | Hours of work required by measurement analyst |
|---|---|---|---|---|---|---|---|---|---|---|---|---|
| | Week ending | | | | | | | | | | | |
| | 1 May | 8 May | 15 May | 22 May | 29 May | 5 June | 12 June | 19 June | 26 June | 3 July | 10 July | 17 July | |
| Analysis of work | ▨ | ▨ | ▨ | | | | | | | | | | 40 |
| Study | | ▨ | ▨ | ▨ | ▨ | ▨ | ▨ | ▨ | ▨ | | | | 115 |
| Review time standards | | | | ▨ | ▨ | ▨ | ▨ | ▨ | ▨ | | | | 20 |
| Install reporting system | | | | | | | | | ▨ | ▨ | ▨ | ▨ | 45 |
| Prepare budgets | | | | | | | | | | | ▨ | ▨ | 50 |
| | | | | | | | | | | | Total | | 270 |

FIGURE 30:6    EXAMPLE OF INSTALLATON CYCLE AND TIME REQUIREMENTS

Diagrammatic representation of the installation cycle and time requirements of a GCA programme applied to a typical department of twenty staff.

To ensure that results are used to the best advantage controls must be provided to the immediate supervisor of the group, to financial management, and to general management. Many schemes have failed in the past owing to the absence of such controls.

Group capacity assessment programmes include the following steps:

1    Provision of weekly data to line supervision showing a performance index which can be compared with a target figure of 100 per cent, this figure indicating that work force and work load are in balance.

2     Preparation of initial departmental budgets showing the staff required to reach 100 per cent performance. At this stage a combined effort is made by both measurement specialists and management to allow for any anticipated changes in work load.

3     Quarterly revision of budget figures.

4     Submission to the financial control function of all budgets, with supporting data for comment and approval.

5     Notification of any change in staff level to the personnel department.

6     Regular reports to the organisation's executives of the department's current status with respect to performance and budgeted and actual staff.

The actual format of reports must be adapted to the needs and structure of each organisation using the programme. Senior management need only monitor minimum information on overall staff trends and performance levels, and can quickly detect and call for information on any deviations from normal. The line supervisor will be in a position to run his section or department according to an agreed plan and will be free from unwanted pressures over his staff levels as long as he achieves his targets.

In addition to direct benefits from the programme, the provision of information on times for jobs enables them to be accurately costed. This in turn gives a basis for proper direction of organisation and methods appraisals to areas with the maximum scope for financial return. In the course of analysing a department's work, there will often be opportunities for immediate elimination or simplification of some jobs, and this again will be reflected in financial benefit.

## ACCEPTABILITY OF THE PROGRAMME

Supervisors are faced with the problem of implementing the results of any work measurement programme, be it on the shop floor or in indirect areas. A common failing is for the measurement staff to carry out their exercise without fully gaining the supervisor's confidence or properly explaining their work to him.

The enlightened approach is to involve the supervisor in the programme from the start. In installing group capacity assessment programmes, the supervisor is regarded as part of the measurement team. He participates in analysis, is kept informed of the progress of measurement, and reviews and approves every time standard produced in his area of supervision.

To ensure that this is done thoroughly, the supervisor signs each standard before it may be used. All reports on work done by his group are checked and approved by him, and he signs all budget papers. Thus, the supervisor makes a vital contribution to the programme and his involvement should guarantee that he will be fully informed by measurement staff.

Provision must be made to service or update any scheme as changes occur and supervisors will expect prompt attention to their maintenance requests.

Two further vital points are:

1    Support for the scheme and interest in it must be present at the highest level of the organisation.
2    Authorised budget changes must be implemented as quickly as possible by the personnel department.

Under these conditions the scheme is accepted as a valuable control instrument by most supervisors. Where difficulties are encountered the measurement team must resolve the supervisor's doubts and problems before an installation can be considered to be complete.

As far as the employee is concerned, he must be assured that the policy is a good day's pay for a good day's work. This implies that with a successful manpower planning system an organisation can afford improvements of pay, or, in the case of a larger concern, it can offer fringe payments through job evaluation, merit rating or similar schemes. A further point of much interest to employees in many industries is that effective planning and control of manpower is their best protection against redundancy.

It should be noted that a time of steady or rising activity is the time to introduce measurement programmes. Staff surpluses can then be dealt with either by absorption in increased work load, or, at the worst, by slowing down recruitment to allow wastage to reduce staff levels without redundancy.

Most employees will feel entitled to an assurance that measurement will not mean redundancy, nor a loss of pay. These assurances should be given.

In medium or large companies without job evaluation or merit schemes these should be considered in conjunction with the introduction of group capacity assessment. In this respect information on jobs arising from measurement can be used directly to write the major part of the job description necessary for job evaluation.

It can be seen that applying the programme is a complex undertaking requiring staff of a high calibre. Quality is more important than work measurement experience. Young men, with obvious management potential, and education to at least GCE "A" level, are most suitable. They bring to the programme the necessary enthusiasm and intellectual ability to make it a success and they take from the programme invaluable experience of management problems.

—————— CHAPTER 31 ——————

# Systems Analysis and Management

*by* Alan Daniels

*Managing Director, Metra Consulting Group*

Systems analysis is a process devoted to the study of business management problems where a data processing solution is indicated. The managers served by this process may not understand the jargon and approach demanded by these new techniques with the result that management control information will not be effective. If data processing is to serve management well and provide a decision-making tool, then managers must recognise the need to direct the function of systems analysis in order that their specific needs are met.

# 31 : SYSTEMS ANALYSIS AND MANAGEMENT

During the last ten years, the computer, which was originally regarded as a scientific tool, has burst into industry with dramatic effect. Its movement into the field of commerce has presented a large number of difficulties at all levels. It has been viewed as a large complicated device, causing psychological problems at senior management and staff levels. At each level the individual wonders whether he will be able to cope with this new technological development. It has been viewed as a threat in many ways but chiefly as a device that will bring about redundancy at all levels of personnel.

All directors who have gone through the painful experience of introducing computers into their organisations will recognise that redundancy is the last thing that actually occurs. They have yet to experience the reduction of overheads that were promised by the computer salesman. In many cases overheads have doubled owing to an increase of expensive personnel such as systems analysts and programmers together with the time spent in systems design, programming and testing.

Although this is a drastic statement to make to a businessman, it does not indicate that the computer installation is a failure. It merely points out that it is extremely difficult to quantify the benefits of the computer to an organisation.

In many cases an initial investment in data processing by organisations can be traced to an ill-defined problem which could have been solved by an experienced systems analyst.

## ROLE OF THE SYSTEMS ANALYST

The description "systems analyst" means many things to many people. Therefore it will be more meaningful to acknowledge that there is a systems function within which there are many stages which merge. One of these stages will be considered as a job specification and for the remainder of this chapter the systems analyst will be referred to in this context.

The development of systems analysis within a company has been discussed fully in many reports. It is clear from the points already made that deep understanding of the problems of management is essential, but entry to the field of systems analysis can be either from commercial management or from computer programming.

The systems analyst must have a strong commercial background so that he can appreciate all the company business systems, including accounting, stock control, production control, etc. He must be able to recognise their interrelationship so as to achieve the company objectives. The total business runs on the basis of a movement of information throughout the company. This information has to be available in various departments at certain times for decision-making. The systems analyst's experience will allow him to examine the efficiency of each system and the efficiency of the interrelationship so as to recognise a data processing problem.

The systems analyst must have an up-to-date understanding of all data processing equipment and the problems of programming. This point is made quite strongly because if the systems analyst is carrying out a preliminary survey for top management prior to the purchase of a machine, he may well be able to suggest various methods for solving the data processing problems. Solutions could include punched-card equipment or bureau time. The use of a bureau, for example, could prove much cheaper than the leasing or outright purchase of data processing equipment.

If after the survey the systems analyst recommends a computer, he will be able to give top management a specification of the machine they need. This specification would then be put out to tender to the computer manufacturers. This is probably the best method of approach for any new installation.

In many cases the systems analyst is faced with an entirely different problem. Suppose that a computer has already been purchased with a range of package computer programs (available free from the manufacturer). These might have been intended to solve the major part of his systems problem. But he may be given the specific task, for example, of putting the stock control system on the computer. He then finds that although he has planned the information flow efficiently, certain facilities that he thought were included in the computer programs are not available. The total package which is designed to suit all situations is so large and cumbersome that it becomes extremely inefficient.

The analyst is now faced with the task of designing a system tailored to the requirements of his own company and specifying a whole new set of programs for the chief programmer to develop. This is where the expenses of the system begin to soar and directors wonder what is happening to their carefully planned budget.

The McKinsey Report on successful computer installation found it very difficult to quantify the success of a computer in an organisation. One major factor of their report was that, in the installation which they did regard as successful, there had been a history of close communication between line management and the systems analyst.

## RESPONSIBILITY OF MANAGEMENT TOWARDS THE SYSTEMS ANALYST

In the past, top management has left a great deal of decision-making to the data processing manager and his systems analyst. From what has been said, top management would be unwise to ignore the advice of this department but it is only fair to point out the problems arising from off-loading too many decisions on to this department.

Management often withdraws from decision-making in data processing systems, either because they are against the installation from the very beginning or because they believe they do not have the technical computer knowledge to become closely involved in the system design. The system is a reflection of the requirements of management. A manager must know what information he needs for decision-making and how often he requires it. When faced by the various figures that the systems analyst is able to provide, instead of the manager evaluating the business system and specifying the exact requirements, it is left to the systems analyst to choose the range of data reported. He invariably plays safe and provides as much as he can. Much of this information is never used and very expensive. Printouts often go straight into the waste paper basket.

Another important feature of a system is that it is only as good as the basic data fed into it. Managers tend to be cynical about the efforts to design an extremely complicated and expensive computer system when they know by experience that the basic data the systems analyst is planning to use is unreliable. In many cases this is not pointed out. If it were, the systems analyst would concentrate his efforts on specific areas in order to improve accuracy, or even stop the system design because it was not promising to be cost effective.

These are just a few points to show where the line manager can give positive directives towards influencing the cost effectiveness of the systems analyst's work to the company. A good systems analyst will anticipate these problems and use his skill in communication to overcome them, so getting the manager's active participation.

However, quite naturally, a manager will concentrate on work which directly affects the performance on which he will be judged. If the computer department is a service spread in total company over-heads, it receives second priority. Some companies have found that greater control can be achieved by charging managers for the computer services they require. Another approach would be to organise the education and training of managers ahead of the systems analyst.

Many managers have found that the systems analyst's visit has stimulated their interest but at the time they had very little background information and did not really know how to discuss the system. They immediately arrange a course for themselves, typically lasting about three months. After the course they are now aware of many more points that they wish to discuss with the systems analyst but it is too late. The system design is already well advanced. If this training had been built into the plans for the system installation and given well in advance, the meeting between the line manager and the systems analyst would have been much more effective.

## ORGANISATION

There are various methods of organising a data processing department. These range from the very simple structure of the data processing manager carrying out both systems and programming to a clearly defined function of data processing management where the emphasis is on management ability as well as technical efficiency.

Figure 31:1(a) shows the type of organisation commonly found in small companies. Larger firms are able to afford a structure like that shown in Figure 31:1(b). The latter arrangement gives the advantage of flexibility, so that complete project teams can be

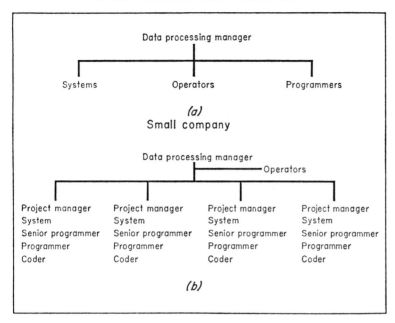

FIGURE 31:1    DATA PROCESSING DEPARTMENTAL ORGANISATION
The organisation structure shown at (a) would be relevant to a
small company, whilst the data processing department of a larger
organisation might be organised along the lines of (b). Obviously
the larger organisation allows more flexibility in assigning staff to
the study of problems.

moved from one systems problem to another. In a larger department,
the systems analyst is provided with a career development path,
which can be assisted by selected methods of "sandwich" training.

It is possible that during the next ten years there will be a definite
change in the way in which organisations use computers. There
seems to be a move towards centralised computer power with multi-
access. That is a large organisation could reduce the number of
small computers it uses, install a large central computer and use local
computer terminals to give access to the computer for the processing
of information and the design and testing of programs. The
terminal is small, efficient and could be positioned many miles away
from the central computer. Good commercial examples are the
various ticket reservation systems and large bureaux.

This type of computer organisation will require a different
approach from the function of systems analysis. There will have to

be a closer relationship between systems and programming. The term "systems programmer" is growing in popularity and adding yet another piece of jargon to the field of computer terminology. Certainly the job specification varies considerably from that of the systems analyst.

The art of computer systems analysis in business is the use of the computer in a business system. The emphasis is on a business system where a series of subsystems is contributing information to management information. Unless the term "management information" is to become academic the manager must take an effective interest in the work of the systems analyst and direct his efforts rather than follow them.

―――――――― CHAPTER 32 ――――――――

# Decision-Making with Industrial Models

*by* P A B Hughes

*Managing Director, Logica Limited*

Increasingly, board rooms must use science rather than intuition in business decisions. Science depends on experimentation, but in business such experiments would be difficult and risky to conduct. One answer is "model building". Dynamic models can be set up which allow experimental testing of new ideas or policies before a company is committed to the actual implementation in the real business world. The aim is to help directors understand complex situations and give them pointers to possible courses of action without committing real resources.

# 32 : DECISION-MAKING WITH INDUSTRIAL MODELS

Rational management decisions are made by a process of sorting out the factors relevant to the problem in hand, trying to visualise their implications, and from this deriving some policy which will get the right results. As organisations become increasingly complex, however, the number of factors which have to be taken into account increases, and the results of the decisions are more vital.

This places a heavy burden of responsibility on the manager. In addition, the high rate of change of many aspects of business means that he can no longer rely solely on "experience" or intuition. There must be some means of getting to grips with the fundamental and underlying principles of the operation involved.

More and more it is realised that some scientific approach is needed to the problem of decision-making. Scientific method, however, is based on controlled experimentation, and this is hardly applicable to most business or industrial situations. For one thing, experimentation is generally expensive and in some cases just impossible. Another problem is that control of the environment in which a business finds itself is not entirely in the hands of the management. Manipulation of many factors for experimental purposes cannot be achieved, for they are controlled by external influences.

One answer to these problems is to adopt a more indirect method of approach and construct a model of the system under investigation. A model in this sense is something which represents in some way part of the real world and can be used for experimentation without disturbing the "real" situation.

## TYPES OF INDUSTRIAL MODELS

Model building and testing have been going on a long time in the physical sciences, but more recently it has been realised that the

445

same principles can be applied to complex situations involving the management of men, money, machines and other resources. There are several ways of representing parts of the real world in model form. These can be classified basically into three groups, iconic, analogue and symbolic. The function of all three is to provide information on the likely performance of the "real world" simply, and without excessive risk.

An *iconic* model looks like what it represents. Examples of iconic models are the scaled-down aircraft used in wind-tunnel experiments on design and performance characteristics. Pilot chemical plants are also iconic models. The main feature of these models is that they are usually on a different scale from the "real-life" things which they represent. They are therefore easier to work on and cheaper to construct or modify.

An *analogue* model is one in which the features of the real world are represented by analogous features in some other medium. A map is a simple example of such a model, being a graphical representation analogous to the relationship of things in the real world. Electric circuits are also used to model other physical phenomena in an analogue fashion in analogue computers. Here it is the simplicity of measurement and use which are the main criteria.

In a *symbolic* model, situations in the real world are represented by symbols, usually mathematical in nature. An example of this type of model is a company's accounts, which represent in a series of numbers, a model of financial transactions of that company. The formula for working out the area of a rectangle, $A = l \times b$ could also be regarded as a symbolic model because it represents the relationship of area to length and breadth in the form of mathematical symbols.

## MATHEMATICAL MODELS

While there are many examples of iconic and analogue models in use in industry, by far the greatest use has been made of symbolic or mathematical models. There are two reasons for this. One is that the symbolic model is easier to adapt to different circumstances than the others. The other reason is that by constructing the model in mathematical form, all the power of mathematics can be used to operate on and manipulate the model to produce the results required.

The basic requirement of a mathematical model is obviously that it should be realistic. There must be a correspondence between the elements of the model and elements of the real world. There must also be correspondence between changes in the real world and changes in the model. This does not necessarily mean that a model must be very complex. Quite the reverse in fact. One of the basic reasons for using models at all is to gain understanding. If the model is as complex as the real world then such understanding is unlikely to result.

A model may therefore be *incomplete*, in the sense that some real-life conditions are omitted; it may be *approximate* because complicated relationships are simplified; it may be aggregative because a number of detailed relationships are given in a summarised form. Provided that it has been carefully worked out, however, simplification in these senses is not a bad thing if increased understanding of the situation results. The importance of adopting the modelling approach is that it provides a concise and consistent basis on which to develop inferences and decisions. Refinement and extension are then possible as more knowledge is gained.

There is a wide area of application for the techniques of mathematical modelling in business, industry and government. They can be used in fact in any situation where the interaction of factors is too complex to visualise as a whole, but where information on the separate functions is known, or can be deduced. The form of model used in any given situation depends on the purpose for which it is to be used, and whether uncertainty is the core of the problem.

Uncertainty is a common feature of many situations. This must be taken into account in the model if it is an important factor in the area concerned. For instance in calculating the total time taken to complete some multi-stage manufacturing process, it may be necessary to take account of variable factors which make this figure subject to uncertainty. To neglect this variability could lead to incorrect decisions being made. It must therefore be brought into the calculations, possibly by adopting a statistical approach.

Apart from the considerations of simplicity already mentioned, the level of complexity of a model is determined by the area being studied, the available data and the degree of experience achieved.

It is convenient to consider the development of company models in three stages of refinement:

1    Simple statement of the major factors
2    Improvement of functional relationships
3    Optimisation and refinement

The following is a simple representation of the profits made by a one-product company in a particular year:

$$R = M \times S \times P - F - M \times S \times C$$

where  $R =$ the profit
       $M =$ total market size
       $S =$ company's share of market
       $P =$ average selling price of product
       $F =$ fixed costs incurred
       $C =$ variable cost per unit

The level of each of these variables could in turn be defined by equations or sets of equations relating to a more detailed breakdown of the cost structure. The whole system of resulting equations would be essentially the company's accounts expressed in algebra.

Even such a simple model is not to be despised. As far as reporting past achievement it would do no more than the accounts, but because it represents the basis of financial operations in mathematical terms it can be manipulated and experimented on in a limited way. It can be used for instance to show the sensitivity of company profit to a particular variable, and it can be used for planning ahead and testing alternative management strategies.

While the simple accounting model may prove of use, it is possible to add to it further features which are not necessarily included in the traditional reporting role of accounting, and which make it a very valuable management tool. One such feature is to include some account of the effects of trends over a time period. This is important if the model is to be used for forecasting. Trends in market prices, escalation of salaries, etc., must all be included if the model is to represent future situations realistically.

It is also possible to include relationships, to indicate the situations where a change in one factor causes changes in other conditions not directly related to it by the explicit relationships. Another improvement which can be added at this stage is that of improving the methods of comparisons and evaluation by, for instance, the use of techniques such as discounted cash flow. These can help to give a more realistic index by which to compare alternative strategies.

In some circumstances it is possible to use the model to determine the optimum method of allocating resources in a given situation. For instance, if there exists a choice, say in product mix, or in investment timing, it may be possible to include in the model an optimising process such as linear programming, which can show the best strategy taking into account the commercial, technical and policy restrictions which must apply.

Refinement can also cover at this stage the inclusion of the uncertainty factors into the model. At the lower levels of refinement uncertainty may have been taken into account by the tedious process of trying different values of the uncertain variables. There are, however, means available whereby, in some circumstances, this uncertainty can be included in the model. When all this is done, the model represents a very much more powerful management aid.

## USE OF COMPUTERS

It is clear that, for any but the simplest mathematical models, the amount of calculation involved necessitates the use of computers. A mathematical model is thus usually in the form of a set of computer programs which carry out the specified operations on the supplied data.

Very often "standard" programs can be incorporated. The most notable example is an optimisation model, which will almost invariably involve the use of a standard mathematical programming code. In such a case the programming associated with implementing the model is confined to producing special-purpose input and output routines.

The development and use of mathematical models has gone hand in hand with the development and increased availability of computers. The need to use computers to carry out the calculations involved is only part of their importance in this field. The other, and most necessary part, is in the handling and preparation of the data involved.

In many situations it is not the formulation of the model which presents the difficulty, but the collection of the data. Although many organisations generate a great mass of data about their operations for administrative purposes, it is quite commonly found that the information needed for a model is not immediately available. This means that a certain amount of extraction of data may be called for, or some system devised for getting the required information.

This business of information gathering may seem a fairly mundane aspect of the work, but it is a vital one if the model is to be successful. Fortunately, it is a subject which is being studied in a much more scientific way. The increasing application of computers in business and industry in general is leading to the availability of comprehensive, consistent data bases which are the essential pre-requisite for the really effective implementation of mathematical models.

There has been a rapid growth in the use of computers via remote terminals, each of which gives access to a computer in an interactive way with the demands of other terminals connected to the same computer. Time sharing, as this development is known, has given great impetus to the use of computer-based models. Model "testing" is more rapid by this process because the actual user is able to communicate directly with the computer from his own office. The intermediate human operator and the wait for computer time are virtually eliminated.

## EXAMPLES AND CASE STUDIES

The use of models is best shown by example. A number of case studies are now given in summary form. Each of these examples outlines models that have been developed and used to assist the process of decision-making.

### Tube works simulation

A simulation model of the operations in the finishing area of a large tube works has been developed. The problems here are caused by variability in the process times and in the processing requirements of different batches of materials (Figure 32:1). By using the model to test various alternative operating strategies, the management have got a valuable insight into how the available resources can be more efficiently used, and production increased. The model can also be used to determine what expansion of production capacity will be required to achieve any specific level output.

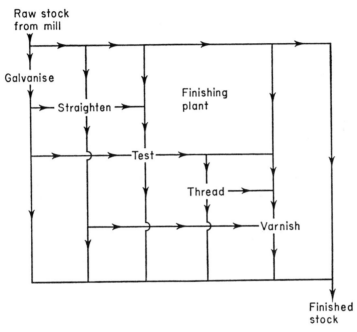

FIGURE 32:1    FLOW OF STOCK IN A TUBE WORKS
Various possible routes which might be taken through a works during final operations.

## Materials mixing

A mathematical model of a mix process was established to determine, from figures relating to cost and amount of materials used, the actual total cost of the mixed product compared with its standard cost. The model was in the form of a computer program and was based very closely on the standard cost system.

From weekly usage figures and costs the model can produce the actual total cost variance of each mix from its standard cost. In addition to the calculation of these *actual* cost figures, the adoption of the model approach has made it possible to feed in details of *proposed* mixes and investigate their profitability in a matter of minutes, using a small computer.

Although this is an example of a simple model, it provided a level of service to management which had not been previously available through the normal accounting function.

## Total company model

A model of the operations of a medium-sized plastics company has been formulated, in order to calculate its profit in a given time period, or set of time periods. These periods can be extended for several years into the future.

The financial data used in the model follow closely those in the company's accounts, with some simplification of the very detailed sections. The model includes formulae to escalate future labour costs and certain other factors. Uncertainty in, for instance, sales prices and market share is dealt with by using several values for each variable and re-running the program. It is planned to include optimising routines to help with the selection of the product mix and with the timing of investment.

## Ore-buying model

In order to guide its ore-buying policy, a steel company devised a model which describes the interaction between materials fed into a blast furnace. The purpose of the model is to minimise the sum of the raw material and operating costs whilst meeting predetermined target outputs of pig iron.

It has been in operation for a number of years and is estimated to have directly led to cost savings of at least 1 per cent—it has also been used as a tool in assessing various possible development plans.

## Optimisation of container ship turn-round

To derive full benefit from the use of a fleet of specially built container ships, it is necessary to keep time in port to a minimum. This means that dockside handling arrangements for loading and unloading must be made as smooth, and rapid, as possible.

From a technical point of view berth operations are regarded as two cycles of events linked by a queue. Each of these cycles has built-in delays to include events such as hatch removal and replacement, etc. There are three phases of operation (see Figure 32:2):

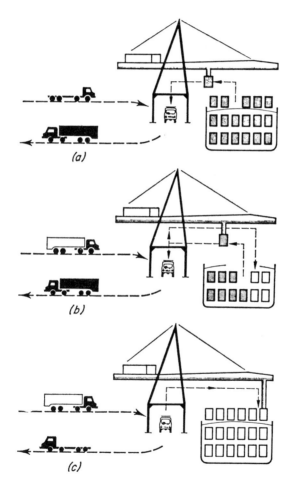

FIGURE 32:2    SHIP CARGO HANDLING

Three phases involved in container ship loading and unloading. In (a) imported containers are being unloaded from the deck; at (b) the hold is being unloaded, and at the same time reloaded with containers for export; (c) is the final phase, with export containers fully loaded.

1    Unloading import containers from deck to berth

2    Unloading import containers from hold to berth, at the same time as loading export containers into the hold

3    Loading export containers to deck

In order to determine the most suitable arrangement for any particular port installation different types of handling equipment and different berth layouts must be assessed. Short of expensive field trials, the only method of producing the information needed for planning of facilities is by simulating the container ship turn-round operations by computer.

In this way a complete turn-round that would take many hours in real life can be simulated in a matter of minutes. Much operating experience can be obtained in a very short time.

There are many other examples which could be given. Models have already been profitably developed to assist in solving many problems in a wide range of industrial activities. Undoubtedly this range will spread, as will the number of companies who will adopt the modelling approach.

Generally, the limiting factor in the use of industrial models is not in the technique, but in the lack of appreciation on the part of the management of what can be gained. Ignorance of this type frequently takes one of two forms. One is the thought that there are so many factors having influence over most business situations that it is impossible to define them, let alone quantify them. The other is the fear that too much reliance might be placed on the results obtained from a necessarily simplified model, with misleading results.

Both show a basic misconception of the aims and use of the modelling approach, which are to enable complex situations to be *understood* more readily and to give *pointers* to possible courses of action. Neither of these relieves the manager of his responsibility to ensure that the model is realistically formulated and to use its results for decision-making. With these in mind it is possible to adopt a policy which can benefit fully from the advantages offered by industrial models.

# Part 2

## GLOSSARY OF

## Management Terms

*Figures in parentheses refer to chapters in Part 1*
*Terms in italics are defined elsewhere in the glossary*

# GLOSSARY OF MANAGEMENT TERMS

**Absorption costing** is a method for calculating costs (and prices) appropriate for a jobbing organisation where a variety of products are made using common facilities, and short-term fluctuations in demand are inevitable. Indirect costs, which often outweigh direct costs, are distributed over common units of production (usually man-hours) assuming a *normal volume* of output. When summing direct costs, the indirect costs are thus automatically absorbed. (21)

**Accounting models** simulate a business situation in an elementary form as an aid in *decision-making*. (32)

**Acquisitions** are one of the most popular methods for implementing long-range corporate plans. The term usually refers to the outright purchase for cash or equity of a business as a going concern by another business. (7, 9)

**Amortisation**—see *depreciation*.

**Analogue models** simulate a situation in a different medium from the prototype. Electrical, pneumatic or hydraulic analogues are employed. Often used in training, but not suitable for *decision-making* owing to the slow response, high cost of construction, and difficulty of changing the model fundamentally. (32)

**Analytic job evaluation** is one of three common *job evaluation* plans in which common features of jobs are compared one by one. The methods employed are *factor comparison* and *points rating*. Other plans are *integral* and *dominant element* job evaluation. (14)

**Annual value** is an alternative expression for the results of *financial* *analysis* (and the converse of *present value*) in which the normalised yield of investments is used as a basis of comparison. (9)

**Apprentice training**—see *training plan.*

**Attitude surveys** are *image studies* conducted within an organisation to determine staff attitude and to suggest areas requiring intervention and areas offering scope for improvement. Surveys are conducted through interviews or questionnaires, and the interviews may be structured (directive) or unstructured (non-directive). (15)

**Back-selling** is promotion directed at the customer's markets. It is common practice among household durable manufacturers and producers of semi-finished products. An example is the promotion of a brand-name fibre in mass media to stimulate demand among consumers; then in turn the retail trade, the garment industry, the textile finishers, and the weavers, up and up the channels of trade and all the way to the bank. (20)

**Booster training** is aimed at narrowing the *spread of productivity* within groups of workers by helping the least productive to acquire the necessary skills. (17)

**Break-even point** in project assessment is the point in time when the cumulative value of *cash flow* equals zero, that is when all money invested in the project has been recovered. It is one measure of the attractiveness of an investment project and is the basis for the *equivalent mean investment period* system of project assessment. (9)

**Budget** has two distinct, though related, meanings in management terminology. In *planning* it represents the final distillation of information and decisions at a point in time. It is in this sense that the word is applied to the business of governing a nation as well as a commercial enterprise, and generally refers to a document. Budget also refers to provisions of quantities (money, manpower, resources, space) or targets (sales, production) arising from a plan, and usually embodied in a budget document. (10, 11, 13, 17, 28)

**Capacity planning and scheduling** aims, through the use of computer techniques, to improve the effectiveness of production by determining the level of capacity required to meet schedules and controlling the release and sequencing of orders according to priority and conditions prevailing at each work centre. (24, 25, 26)

**Capital expenditure** is the part of a company's negative *cash flow* which an accountant can convert into tax free income through the device of *depreciation*. *Discounted cash flow* calculations make no distinction between capital expenditure and operating *expense*. (9)

**Capital investment** is the commitment of capital to a business risk. (9)

**Cash flow in financial analysis** is the movement of cash (or cash equivalent of goods and services) across an imaginary boundary drawn around a project. In cash-flow techniques of assessment, a project is regarded as a "black box" (its boundaries serving to define the project, which may be a company, or any part of it, or any investment proposal) and only genuine movements of cash are considered in the assessment. Thus depreciation and transfers to tax or other reserves are ignored, but tax is included on the date payment is due. (9)

**Checklists**—see *weighted factors and checklists*.

**Communication** in personnel administration—see *attitude survey*.

**Communication grid** is a display of information used in *strategic space planning* and provides an analysis of the frequency of communication between departments of an organisation. (5)

**Computer simulation**—see *symbolic models*.

**Contribution** in *marginal costing* is the difference between selling price and marginal (or direct) cost. (21)

**Controllable costs** are assessed during the course of *responsibility accounting*, and represent those elements of costs incurred in an organisation which are subject to management control. (10)

**Cost**—See *total cost approach to distribution*.

**Cost-plus pricing** is a somewhat naïve, and potentially suicidal method of calculating *prices* by adding a percentage to the estimate of *cost*. In modified form it is used by most jobbing companies for want of a better alternative, and by far too many manufacturers for want of knowledge. (21)

**Critical path planning** is a technique for project planning in which the steps necessary for its completion are displayed to show their dependence on the completion of other steps, the time required for each step is estimated, and the sequence of steps requiring the longest elapsed time (critical path) determined. Application of the technique permits (*a*) implementation of changes in methods designed to shorten the critical path; (*b*) focusing attention on the important steps; (*c*) better allocation of resources; (*d*) greater reliability in completion. (24)

**Customer cost analysis** aims to establish an information base needed by management in making a variety of decisions in pricing, product development, investment, and contract negotiations. It is recognised that the contribution of a product to profits varies with the buyer. This is the consequence of the uneven distribution of purchasing power among the buyers. Under these circumstances, it is impossible to arrive at rational management decisions without a detailed analysis of the costs and margins involved in servicing the requirements of each major customer. (22)

**Customer service** is a function of a *marketing* department concerned with maintaining the goodwill of customers through the provision of free technical assistance connected with the use of the company's products. The concept originated with oligopolistic manufacturers of standard or quasi-standard products (industrial gases, washing machines) as an effective means of non-price competition, recognising that all buyers of the product are past, present or future customers. (29)

**Data processing** embraces the collection of raw data, its physical processing, and the generation of the required output in the form of payroll, invoices, etc. or financial statements. The cost of data processing is a significant element in optimising administrative systems (see also the *total cost approach to distribution*). (31)

**Day rate** is the simplest time-related *payment scheme*. It may be coupled with monetary or non-monetary incentive schemes in *measured day work systems*. (16)

**DCF**—see *discounted cash flow*.

**Decision band** in *dominant element job evaluation* is a measure of responsibility attached to a job based on the type and importance of decisions required. It is used for the indirect comparison of their worth. (14)

**Decision-making with industrial models** is the technique of simulating a dynamic business situation in order to explore the consequences of various decisions and events under laboratory conditions. The simulation may involve an *iconic*, *analytic*, or *symbolic* model of the situation. Symbolic simulation using a computer model is the most convenient and is almost invariably used. (32)

**Demand** is a want backed by purchasing power; want being an awareness of a need. (A man exerting himself needs energy but will not want food unless hungry and contribute to demand only if solvent.) (20, 21)

**Depreciation** is an artifice of accounting, now firmly embedded in the rituals of corporation tax. In theory, depreciation is the amount by which the *value* of capital equipment diminishes through use (or disuse) over a period of time. In practice, it represents an arbitrary deduction from the taxable surplus of a company. While firmly wedded to the concept, businessmen happily operate fully depreciated machinery (that has no value in theory) and replace undepreciated machinery if the accounting fails to keep pace with the rate of obsolescence. Since depreciation is an accounting, not a cash transaction, it is ignored in the calculation of *cash flow*. (8)

**Direct costing**—see *marginal costing*.

**Direct productive labour** is the payroll cost component of manufacturing attributable, in accounting terms, to material transformation performed on products manufactured for sale. (30)

**Directive interviews** in attitude surveys record answers to a prepared list of questions. (15)

**Discount rate** is a measure of the time-value of money, and is one form of expressing the results of a *discounted cash flow calculation*: it is the time rate (expressed as a percentage), that will reduce the algebraic sum of negative and positive cash flows of a project to zero. (9)

**Discounted cash flow** is a technique for comparing the *return* on investment in projects of similar risk but dissimilar *cash flow*. Cognizance is taken of the fact embodied in the definition of *return* that the value of cash depends on the time of accrual: money now is preferred to money in the future. In DCF analysis future *cash flow* is (*a*) discounted at arbitrarily chosen rates to arrive at a *present value*; or (*b*) discounted by arbitrary methods to arrive at the discount rate. Either rate or value can be compared for different projects but a choice on this basis alone implies the judgement that equal *risks* are involved in both (or all) projects. (9)

**Discounting** in *financial analysis* is the converse of compounding (that.is the calculation of compound interest with a negative rate), and reflects the fact that less value is attached to a sum accruing at a future date than to the same amount available immediately. (9)

**Distribution** as a business policy is the process of apportioning goods to resellers. In a narrower sense it is the process of moving goods to the points of sale, and involves management decisions concerning stockholding, warehousing, methods of transportation, data processing and a number of secondary effects in terms of the use of facilities and the channels of distribution. See also *total cost approach to distribution*. (29)

**Dominant element job evaluation** is one of three common *job evaluation* plans in which only the most important element in a job is used for comparison with others. The method is indirect, and the dominant element is commonly the *time span of discretion* or the *decision band.* (14)

**Dummy activity** in a *critical path network* is a device to represent the interdependence of events not connected by one activity. Usually shown as dotted arrows on the diagram, they indicate that the event at the tail of the arrow must be completed before the event at its head. The device is essential to correct completion of a network diagram. (24)

**Earnings** in business is the cash surplus remaining when *costs* are subtracted from revenue. In the more usual usage, earnings attributable to a unit of common stock are used as a measure of the *value* of the stock in relation to its price, as in the price to earnings ratio. (8)

**Economic effect** is a measure of *economic sense,* and is the basis of *financial analysis* applied to non-profit making investments such as hospitals and roads. In the absence of a measurable economic effect, financial analysis cannot be employed in decision-making. (9)

**Economic sense** is a concept of *financial analysis* analogous to profitability, but applied to non-profit making (social) investment. Thus investment in hospital care or public roads is judged on the basis of their economic sense expressed in terms of their *economic effect.* (9)

**EMIP**—see *equivalent mean investment period.*

**EMP**—see *evaluated maintenance programming.*

**Equivalent mean investment period** (EMIP) is a method of project assessment, and a refinement on *discounted cash flow.* It is particularly useful for comparing high-risk projects with radically different patterns of cash flow, since net expenditure (cash flow) up to the *break-even point* is converted to a common (normalised) base using the maximum cumulative value forecast for each project as unit. The technique has the advantage (among others) that revenue need not be forecast beyond the break-even point. EMIP should not be used to compare development projects involving short-life cycle products (novelties) with long-life cycle products (staples) because in the absence of risk analysis there is a built-in bias favouring the former. (9)

**Estimating techniques** in *work measurement* are the substitution of estimates of *time/output relationships* made by trained observers, for the rigorous measurements of *work sampling*. (30)

**Evaluated maintenance programming** (EMP) is the application of production planning techniques to maintenance. It relies for effectiveness on maintaining comprehensive performance and cost records, and establishing procedures to deal with recurring phenomena. (28)

**Expense,** or operating expense, is the part of a company's negative *cash flow* which no accountant can convert into tax-free income through the device of *depreciation*. (9)

**Factor comparison** in *analytic job evaluation* is the assignment of money value to common job factors, and the establishment of job worth through the direct summation of value. (14)

**Factory maintenance** costs can be controlled and reduced through *evaluated maintenance programming*, that is the application of production planning techniques to maintenance. (29)

**Final demand** is for a product's function. *Indirect demand* is for a product as a constituent. (A car is bought by a consumer for its function; the fan-belt is bought by the car manufacturer as a constituent. But the car manufacturer also buys lubricants and machine tools. These he buys for their function, and hence the *demand* is final.) (20)

**Financial analysis** is the process of converting financial and other information about an enterprise into a judgement of its prospects. Originally the skill of institutional investors such as insurance companies, it is now the stock-in-trade of brokers, merchant banks, acquisition-minded companies, and professional managers. (9)

**Float** in *critical path analysis* is the difference between the time available for completing an activity as determined by the time required for the critical path, and the estimated time required for the activity. (24)

**Function** is the complex of tasks, responsibilities and relationships assigned to a position, and ultimately a person, in an *organisation*. (2)

**Graded measured daywork** (GMDW) is a *payment scheme* with monetary incentive designed to stabilise earnings and at the same time to maintain productivity at consistently high levels. This is achieved through the creation of performance bands and corresponding wage rates. To qualify for a higher rate, improved productivity must be maintained for long periods of time. (16)

**Grading** in *integral job evaluation* is the comparison of jobs with examples placed along a salary curve. (14)

**Group capacity assessment** is a technique for the planning and control of *indirect payroll* costs based on the application of *work measurement* principles developed for use on the shop floor to office personnel. Owing to the interacting nature of the tasks, group capacity assessment is concerned with evaluating in quantitative terms the working pattern of groups of people, rather than the *performance* of individuals. Hence the technique does not aim at providing information for payment systems, as in *job evaluation*. (30)

**Group technology** is a method of improving the effectiveness of batch operations in industry. A recurring problem of production planning is to arrange operations in a way that makes the best use of available facilities in minimising the costs of production. Economies can be attained if batch quantities of component parts are grouped for the purposes of production according to characteristics to which the production process is cost sensitive. The same technique could be used in design and development tasks. In order to operate a group technology scheme effectively, it is necessary to apply a method of classification that permits retrieval on the basis of the features significant to good scheduling. (25)

**Group training** is designed to provide practical experience to managers in handling people under synthetic, laboratory conditions. The laboratory is provided by the participants in the group: the participants learn by observing their own reactions and the reactions of others under circumstances favourable to learning. If successful, the participants become more sensitive to the reactions and behaviour of individuals working in a group, and become more skilled in collaborating with them. (18)

**High day rate** system of payment consists of paying employees a high fixed day rate with little or no other financial incentive. It is best introduced after an incentive scheme has been in operation for several years and the work force is fully accustomed to working at a high rate of output. (16)

**High-frequency work sampling** is a technique of *work measurement* in which time/output relationships are established on the basis of records of work and other activities of a whole group, kept by the operators and spot observations by measurement staff over a period of days. For the purposes of *group capacity assessment* in clerical staff work measurement this is an effective and relatively cheap technique, making the fullest use of the subject's own clerical abilities to provide time/output records. (30)

**Iconic models** are laboratory copies of a real-life situation. Often used in engineering (ship or aircraft model tests, pilot plants), iconic simulation of a business situation is a rarity. Examples are business or decision games where individuals represent buyers and competitors. (32)

**Image study** is a systematic examination of attitudes to a company or its products among the buying public. (15)

**Incentive schemes** are methods of improving productivity through the application of a wages policy. The schemes are based on the realisation that a marginal gain in production is worth more to the company than the rate established for the anticipated average, and that part of the gain can be turned into an incentive for the operator. (16)

**Indirect demand**—see *final demand.*

**Industrial Training Act,** passed in 1964, aims to increase the availability of trained manpower, to improve the standard of training, and to distribute the costs fairly through a system of levies and grants. While supporting its aims, the Act has been criticised by the Confederation of British Industry on important points of detail, notably the danger of indulging in training for training's sake, the escalation of costs without improvement in productivity, and the detrimental effect of levies on small businesses. (14, 17)

**Information** is a word of highly elastic meaning now being stretched to the breaking point. Originally denoting communications between individuals, the word now serves a spectrum of meaning. It may be a polite name for commercial intelligence, or a group noun for raw data in *data processing.* In data processing system design information tends to be applied to facts varying in kind and quantity; reserving the word *data* for facts varying in quantity only. (31)

**Input–output tables** are a statistical model of an economy, showing (in the usual case) the contribution of one industry's products (input) to output by other industries. The tables provide a most useful display of statistical information, though the time lag between output in one industry and input in another is ignored. This results in stocking–destocking cycles, which vary in amplitude and periodicity from industry to industry, and are not reflected in the tables. (20)

**Integral job evaluation** is one of three common *job evaluation* plans in which jobs are compared as a whole. The methods employed are *ranking* and *grading.* Other plans are termed *analytic* and *dominant element* job evaluation. (14)

**Intrinsic value** is a concept of dubious merit born from imprecise thought. Some suggest that precious materials (in jewellery for instance) have an intrinsic value, as opposed to the added value of design and craftsmanship. In this case intrinsic value is merely an unwelcome synonym for material cost. Others suggest that intrinsic value is the price a consumer will pay for a class of products, while the *objective value* is the marginal price over (or presumably below) the intrinsic price the consumer will pay for a particular brand of the product. Examination of a few examples can show that the distinction lacks precision to the point of uselessness. (21)

**Inventory** as a concept of management and financial accounting, represents an estimate (obtained in accordance with agreed procedures) of the cost of materials processing in a business at a given moment in time, and includes raw materials, work-in-progress, and finished parts and products; or, in the retail trade, *merchandise* on offer. (29)

**Inventory management** is the discipline of harmonising the levels of inventory with corporate objectives in order to balance the advantages in terms of access, against the costs incurred. (26)

**Inventory turnover** is a useful measure of performance, particularly when assessing the performance in an enterprise over time, or comparing the performance of similar enterprises. Defined as the ratio of *turnover* to *inventory*, it is a measure of the effectiveness of (*a*) business housekeeping, (*b*) *distribution*, and (*c*) financial control. (8, 26, 29)

**Investment criteria** are rules of thumb for making investment decisions, derived from past experience and expressed as a minimum acceptable *discount rate* in DCF calculations. (9)

**Job evaluation** is not a technique but an approach to personnel management and salary/wage administration. It uses a variety of techniques to compare the worth of jobs in one organisation with the aim of creating a rational salary structure that can be administered with minimum cost and friction. The techniques of comparison may be direct (job to job), or indirect (job to scale), and may involve *ranking, grading, factor comparison, points rating* or evaluation of the *time span of decision* or decision band. It may be applied to the whole job (*integral*); to common features (*analytic*); or to the *dominant element*. (14)

**Job time** in *work measurement* is the sum of times required to perform all *elements* or *motions* involved in a job. In clerical *work measurement*, and particularly in *group capacity assessment*, a job may involve the co-operation of several individuals, and may require repetitive elements, as the retrieval of files, calculations of quantities, etc. (30)

**Linear programming** produces a *symbolic model* in which all relationships are expressed as linear equations. It is sometimes stretched to cover situations that cannot be adequately represented by linear equations. (32)

**Long-range corporate planning** was the management fashion of the middle sixties, producing a healthy crop of staff executives with long-range titles. In essence it is an examination of the context in which a corporation operates (say heavy engineering), and its comparison with other contexts (say the leisure industry), leading to decisions on possible reorientation over a long period of time. The conglomerate mania of the late sixties took some of the enthusiasm out of long-range planning by claiming that a corporation, unlike Gamow's bird, could be in all places at once. That fad is also about to pass, hopefully to be replaced by the realisation that a company should do what it does best. This may be long-range planning or even conglomerate management, but could be any number of other things. (3)

**Maintenance**—see *evaluated maintenance programming*.

**Management control units**—see *organisation*.

**Management development programmes** are designed to provide a systematic framework for re-stimulating the executive ability of managers. The learning curve of management functions is initially steep, but flattens out remarkably quickly. Soon after acquiring a position of responsibility, a manager's opportunity for learning diminishes, often to the vanishing point. This is the result in some cases of the individual's limited capacity for surprise, in others of the demand made on the individual's limited capacity for surprise, in others of the demand made on the individual's time by matters (such as administrative routine) that do not expose him to novel problems or facts. Thus there is a danger that any manager, after a period of time, ceases to improve his performance. Ultimately, he may cease to be an executive and devote his time to a sterile form of administration. Management development programmes are designed to counter this danger. Elements of the programme include job rotation, formal training, responsibility accounting, performance appraisal, and career planning. (18)

**Management techniques,** though often complex, are only rules of thumb, and no more or less useful. Any technique is a condensation of thought and experience. It permits transmission in short-hand form, and application with convenience. But used without understanding its principles can be as dangerous as driving at night without lights.

**Manpower budget** is the provision made in a corporate plan for future manpower requirements, in terms of recruitment and training. (13, 17)

**Market exploration** is a brief but penetrating assessment of the commercial environment of a business or proposition, performed to provide an information base for decision-making. It is particularly relevant to new ventures or acquisitions, and should review the economic situation, source of demand, the structure of the industry, the state of technology, competition, marketing methods employed, and other factors affecting the market. (3)

**Margin** is the amount left over; whether as free space on the edge of a piece of paper, or a strength in an aircraft wing when fully loaded. In business it may denote an operating margin, or profit margin, or margin for error, and there is never enough of it. (21)

**Marginal costing** is a method of calculating costs, and hence prices. It is appropriate for a manufacturing organisation mass producing commodities (or products with a market-established price). Also known as direct costing, in this system only costs directly attributable to a product are charged against the product. The difference between costs thus calculated and the selling price is the product's *contribution* to overheads and profits. The system is called marginal because direct cost can be defined as the cost of making one more of a given product. (21)

**Market followers** are new competitors to established products, embodying only a weak element of innovation. Pioneer products are new products with a strong innovative content. (21)

**Market penetration** is the share held by a product or company of demand within a market. (3)

**Market place,** a vivid and apposite re-issue of an archaic word, represents collectively the balance of *marketing* influences controlling *demand* for a product or service, including the prosperity and mood of potential buyers, the effect of promotional activities (including those of competitors), the kind and number of buying opportunities offered by sellers, and the effect of substitute products or services on demand. (29)

**Marketing** is a concept of many definitions, including: "marketing is a management function which organises and directs all those business activities involved in assessing and converting customer purchasing power into effective demand for a specific product or service and in moving the product or service to the final consumer or user so as to achieve the profit target or other objective set by a company" (Institute of Marketing); or the more succinct "creation and exploitation of a monopoly" (Abe Schuchman); and "market oriented planning" (E Peter Ward). It has been the focus of a profound revolution in management thinking. Having succeeded overwhelmingly, it is likely to disappear as an area of concern, leaving behind a legacy of words in search of new meaning. (3, 19, 20, 21)

**Marketing research** is the creation of an information base for *marketing* decisions. Its scope includes research on the behaviour of consumers, the activities of competitors, the influence of economic developments, or the effect of substitute products or satisfaction. (20, 21)

**Mathematical programming**—see *symbolic models.*

**Measured day work** is the application of *incentives* to *day rate* systems. (16)

**Measured day work system of payment** is based on fixed rates of payment related to output by setting of time standards which are regularly reviewed. Time standards are set by normal work measurement methods and regular checks are made to ascertain how actual performance compares with standard. (16)

**Measured day work value** is the time allowed for the completion of a job in payment systems based on measured day work. (16)

**Merchandise** is the collective name of goods made or offered for sale in the consumer product industry. (29)

**Model building**—see *decision making with industrial models.*

**Multi-minute measurement** in *work sampling* is the collective of a series of measurements of time/output relationships taken continuously (at few-minute intervals) over a long period of time to obtain a representative value. (30)

**Network** in *critical path planning* is a diagram showing the inter-relationship of all activities required for the completion of a task. The network comprises arrows (representing activities and elapsed time) joining nodes (representing events and points in time). The direction of the arrows defines precedence between two nodes. (24)

**Non-directive interviews** in attitude surveys allow a free exchange of ideas and information. (15)

**Non-monetary incentive systems** provide stimulus to increased productivity through competitions, participation in group management, free-time awards etc. (16)

**Normal volume** is the basis of calculating the distribution of overheads in *absorption costing*. If the basis of costing is direct labour, normal volume is the budgeted level of productive man-hours. (21)

**Normalised cash flow** is the basis of *project assessment* by means of the *equivalent mean investment period* method. *Cash flow* for a project up to the *break-even point* is reduced to a common basis by dividing the cumulative cash flow figures by the arithmetic value of the maximum cumulative cash flow reached between the start of the project and the attainment of the break-even point. The normalised figures are plotted and examined for significant features, and form the basis for comparing dissimilar investment projects. (9)

**Objective probability** is the likelihood of the outcome of future events governed by cyclic physical phenomena, as the height of floods in a river basin, or the frequency with which a tossed coin will land on one side. (9)

**Optimisation** is the search for a combination of values for independent variables in a system which will provide the best value for the dependent variable. In decision-making common pitfalls of optimisation are (1) the mistaken choice of dependent variable (e.g. maximising short-term book profit when cash flow is needed); (2) optimising a subsystem to the detriment of the whole (e.g. producing a highly efficient delivery service that antagonises the customers by ignoring their needs); (3) errors in estimating interactions (e.g. price elasticity); (4) omitting important variables. (32)

**Organisation** is (a) the formal relationship between people co-operating and (b) a group of people acting in concert on divided tasks. Since the division of labour (among people, or, in a one-man band, over time) is one of the foundations of modern industry, effective business implies effective organisation. (2)

**Objective value**—see *intrinsic value.*

**Organisation and methods study** is the planning of administrative and clerical work for maximum effectiveness. Standards of effectiveness must be separately established to suit the needs of an enterprise, and will represent a compromise between cost, speed, error rate, reliability, level of service etc. Since administrative work involves the processing of information, O & M studies rely on tracing its flow, analysing the action required in processing it, evaluating the time involved, and devising flow pattern, staffing, physical disposition, equipment and business forms to suit the purpose. Judgement of the *information* requirements of an enterprise are outside the scope of O & M. (31)

**Pace** denotes variations in the rate at which repetitive work is performed under varying conditions. Allowance must be made in *work measurement* for pace by making a statistically significant number of observations and deriving from them a "normal" *time/ output relationship*. (30)

**Payment by results** is the application of an *incentive scheme* to a *payment system*. (16)

**Payment systems** are the means for administering a payment-of-wages policy. Common systems are *day rate, piecework*, and *measured daywork*, with *graded measured daywork* a more recent refinement. (16)

**Peak absence** in *work measurement* is the converse of *peak load*. (30)

**Peak loads** in *work measurement* are cyclic (hourly, daily, weekly etc.) accumulations of work load. In *group capacity assessment*, particularly where several groups are engaged in complementary tasks, careful attention to the cycles can reveal opportunities for improving effectiveness where peaks (and absences) are unavoidable, provision can be made by the judicious scheduling of disposable personal time and the setting of *allowances*. (30)

**Performance** is the degree to which an enterprise, project, product or individual meets expectations. (8)

**Piecework** is the simplest output-related *payment system*. It may be coupled with an *incentive or bonus scheme*. (16)

**Pilot production** is a stage in the development of new processes and the launching of new products. In process development it is an intermediate between laboratory-bench experiments and full-scale production and serves to refine the design of the equipment and to provide operating experience. In a product launch, pilot production serves to resolve marketing uncertainties by producing a quantity sufficient for *test marketing*. (21)

**Pioneer products** (i.e. genuinely new products), require a different approach to *pricing* than market followers (i.e. new competitors). The alternatives are skimming (maximising profit margins, offering the product at a high price and lowering the price stepwise to saturate the market from top down) and penetration pricing (maximising market share by offering the product at a low price) and the choice depends on how quickly *market followers* are expected to appear. (21)

**Planning** is defined by Wassily Leontief of the Harvard Business School as "the organised application of systematic reasoning to the solution of specific practical problems". Since this definition includes problem solving in forms that would not be regarded as planning (i.e. solving a puzzle), the following modification is proposed: "planning is the ordering of activities to solve specific practical prolems". (20)

**Plant monitoring and control** describes the introduction of computer techniques to the control of activities in a jobbing shop and comprises a communication system for reporting information and disseminating instructions. (26)

**Points rating** in *analytic job evaluation* is the comparison of all job factors with sets of definitions to determine a point value for each. Total points are converted into pay rates through a rating curve. (14)

**Present value** is one form of expressing the results of a *discounted cash flow* calculation in *financial analysis*: it is the sum of forecast cash revenue discounted at an arbitrary rate considered appropriate to the level of *risk* involved. (9)

**Price** is the amount asked for in an intended transaction, while *value* is the amount someone is willing to pay. (21)

**Pricing policy** can be merely an approved method of calculating *prices*; it can be a set of principles for maximising profits; or it can be a powerful tool in *marketing*. Pricing policy as a concept of marketing is concerned with the relationship of *price, value, elasticity* and cost, and the pursuit of corporate objectives. (21)

**Probability** is the likelihood of an outcome, and its assessment is the basis of *risk analysis* applied to decision-making. (9)

**Probability belief** is the estimate of probability concerning the outcome of a future event governed by extremely complex and/or essentially unpredictable phenomena typical of the business environment. The mathematical treatment of probability beliefs is identical to that of *objective probabilities.* (9)

**Product analysis pricing** is an attempt to relate *value* and cost to the *price* at which a product is offered on the market. It is a difficult method to apply since *value* is in the eyes of the buyer, and thus varies not only from buyer to buyer, but also with time. It is nevertheless a worth-while discipline which, if nothing else, will show up the inadequacies of *cost plus pricing.* (21)

**Productivity** is a measure of *performance* in terms of physical output per unit of (labour, capital etc) input. (4, 17)

**Productivity standards** are indices of performance expected from operatives. Through *training*, these can be raised significantly, thus affecting the *manpower budget.* (17)

**Profit target** may be the starting point or end point in planning or budgeting, depending on whether the plan is indicative or normative. The mechanism of marginal costing relates profit targets to *volume targets.* (21)

**Project assessment** is the application of *financial analysis* in one of its many forms (*DCF, EMIP*) to individual projects such as the development of a new product, or the building of a plant. (9)

**Ranking** in *integral job evaluation* is direct job-to-job comparison through successive pairing. (14)

**Rate** is simply a multiplier, as in tax rate (too high) or growth rate (too low).

**Resource allocation** is a problem in decision making involving the allocation of scarce resources (cash in the usual case) to competing needs. *Computer simulation* may be employed in homogeneous cases with great effect and at little cost. (24)

**Resource appraisal** is a method of self-examination through checklists designed to highlight weaknesses in an organisation. (1)

**Responsibility accounting** is a tool of higher personnel management. The aim is to identify the controllable variables affecting performance throughout the organisation, and to build up a hierarchy of such variables reflecting the performance of the whole. Realistic expectations of improvement are then established and agreed, and responsibility for managing each variable is assigned to individual managers in accordance with their functions within the company. The system then permits the establishment of quantifiable performance targets and provides a continuing monitor of performance. (10)

**Retraining**—see *training plan.*

**Return** on investment is (a) the reward for foregoing alternative uses of resources; and (b) the payoff for committing resources to *risk*; usually in combination. (8, 9, 14)

**Risk** is the possibility that an expectation may remain unfulfilled. It is the essence of enterprise, and is inherent in all business decisions. Shrewd assessment of risk is the stock-in-trade of the businessman, whatever his field of endeavour. (9)

**Risk analysis** is a refinement in the groundwork for decision-making and may consist of (a) evaluating the elements of uncertainty involved in a forecast, assigning or determining the distribution of probability for each, and summing the results; or (b) estimating reasonable limits for the uncertainty of each element, assuming that each limit is equally probable, and assessing the implications. The former approach appears appropriate to decisions that can be made repetitively (as in institutional investment in common stock), while the latter is relevant to important once-for-all corporate decisions, where for instance an unfavourable outcome might force the sale of assets or precipitate involuntary liquidation. (9)

**Sales forecast** is a simple or sophisticated extrapolation of past experience to produce a quantitative assessment of sales expectation. In its simplest and most dangerous form it involves an extension of past trend lines into the future. More sophisticated techniques derive a forecast indirectly by extrapolating underlying phenomena (such as economic conditions). No matter how sophisticated, a forecast is always an extrapolation and should be treated as such. (20)

**Satisfaction** in a job—see *attitude survey*.

**Share-of-production plan** is an *incentive payment scheme* relating the incentive to company performance rather than the performance of the wage earner. (16)

**Spread of productivity** is the difference between the *performance* of the least productive and the most productive workers in a group. (17)

**Support activities** are essential or inessential services performed by indirect staff in an enterprise (including administration, supervision, marketing, promotion, planning, development etc.). The management control of some costs connected with support activities may involve *group capacity assessment* and other techniques. (30)

**Symbolic models** simulate a situation by expressing its behaviour in symbolic, that is mathematical, form. In the form of computer programs, symbolic models can be conveniently used to simulate a dynamic business situation as an aid to its understanding and decision-making. (32)

**TCD**—see *total cost approach to distribution*.

**Test marketing** is a stage in launching a new product designed to minimise the risk in full-scale marketing. Ideally the product is offered to a representative sample of the population under conditions simulating those of a national market and the product's *performance* is carefully observed. In practice, the sample is never completely representative and the simulation of conditions is poor. The test may be confined to a small geographical area (unrepresentative sample) exposed to heavy local promotion (reasonable simulation of national promotion); or it is based on a random selection of outlets (good sample) without promotion or accompanied only by promotion at the point of sale (poor simulation). The closer a test marketing programme to the ideal, the greater the expense (approaching that of a national launch). Decision-making connected with the launching of new products is a fruitful area for applied intelligence and presents some intriguing problems of trade-off between *risk* and *return*. (21)

**Time analysis** in *critical path planning* is the process of estimating elapsed time required for the completion of a project by estimating the time required for the individual activities, finding the longest chain of interdependent activities and events (the critical path), and summing the total. The procedure also provides an estimate of the *float* available for activities that are not on the critical path. (24)

**Time/output relationship** is the measure of *productivity* in terms of *work units* and time units, and is the immediate object of *work measurement*. (30)

**Time span of discretion** in *dominant element job evaluation* is the time taken to detect bad decisions in a particular job, and is used as a measure of responsibility for indirect comparison of job worth. (14)

**Time study** in *work measurement* is the collection of *time/output relationships* by direct observations of the work performed and usually the isolation of *elements* or *motions* and their timing. (30)

**Total company model** is a simulation, usually using a computer, of all important internal and a few external relationships characterising a business as an aid in decision-making. The word "total" is not a claim for completeness but merely serves to distinguish it from models of parts of the business (such as the distribution system). (32)

**Total cost approach to distribution** is a technique for optimising a system of *distribution* which avoids the pitfalls of suboptimising only variables directly identifiable as affecting the cost of distribution. In addition to the costs of warehousing and transportation, variables such as changes in inventory costs, obsolescence costs, finished goods cost, production and purchasing costs, data processing costs and customer service costs as well as the value of alternative uses for facilities and the costs of maintaining the channels of distribution are included to derive the optimum system. Suboptimisation relying on only some of these variables may in fact increase the cost of distribution. Careful attention to details may yield remarkable cost reductions and rigorous application of the principles is essential when appraising investment proposals affecting the company's distribution system. (29)

**Trainee turnover** is an index of effectiveness in training and has a strong influence on establishment of an appropriate training plan. (17)

**Training**—see *booster training, analytical training* and *retraining.*

**Training boards** are industrially based boards established to implement provisions of the *Industrial Training Act.* Employers, employees, and professional educators are represented on each board. (17)

**Training plan** aims to relate a company's *productivity standards, training times* and *trainee turnover* indices in a manner satisfying the *manpower budget.* (17)

**Training time** is the time required for trainees to reach the desired productivity standards. (17)

**Turnover** is a normalised measure of performance widely used in *financial analysis, cost analysis,* and management *control,* relating one or more measured variables to a time-span, usually the business year. Thus the word turnover by itself is usually applied to the value of sales per annum, but compound variables such as *inventory turnover* (annual sales divided by inventory at a given time or averaged over a period of time) are also frequently employed. (8, 9, 29)

**Uncertainty**—see *risk*.

**Unit of output** in clerical *work measurement* is the smallest repetitive element that can be readily identified and counted, such as numbers of calls handled by a switchboard, or numbers of estimates completed by an estimator. (30)

**Value** is the amount someone will pay (or the sacrifice someone will make). It is a variable independent of *price* or *cost*, though profoundly influencing both. (12, 21)

**Value analysis** is the systematic examination of a product's design and the methods of production in relation to intended functions with a view to enhancing *value* or *performance;* or reducing costs; or achieving a combination of these objectives. (12)

**Value concept** or value assessment concept is the realisation that systematic and continuing attention to detail in the design of (mainly mass or repetitively produced mechanical) products can yield large benefits stemming from lower costs per unit *value*. The benefit can be realised in a variety of ways (higher margins, lower prices, more promotion, greater productivity or lower *inventory* costs). Application of the value concept involves *value analysis* and *value engineering*. (12)

**Value engineering** is the consistent application of *value analysis* to all products introduced by an enterprise at a sufficiently early stage in design and development to ensure the attainment of a desired combination of *value*; *performance*; and cost. (12)

**Volume target** is the volume of production in a budget. It can be related to the *profit targets* of the budget through a *break-even* calculation based on the concept of marginal costing. (21)

**Weighted factors and checklists** are used in numerous instances where a choice has to be made between possibilities that meet the requirements only imperfectly, and to widely differing degrees. The problem is encountered when selecting candidates for a post, products for development, or sites for a new plant. A variety of techniques using checklists of factors and weightings have been described in the literature for handling the associated problems of information processing. The intellectual content of the techniques is trivial and they can be invented or re-invented at will. The principle is invariably to list all factors relevant to the decision; to apply a weighting to the factors from an arbitrary scale to reflect their relative importance to the decision; and then to assign a number, again from an arbitrary scale, to reflect the degree to which a particular choice would meet the requirements. A simple summation of the valuations multiplied by the weighting will provide a ranking of candidates. (19)

**Work measurement** is the systematic breakdown of manual/ intellectual tasks involved in work into elements and the measurement of the time required for the task for various purposes such as *manpower planning* and *budgeting*, production planning and the establishment and administration of *payment schemes*. (30)

**Work sampling** in *work measurement* is the collection of a truly random series of measurements of *time/output relationships* aimed at obtaining a statistically correct "normal time". (30)